155.5
C 88o

68584

OUR TEEN-AGE BOYS AND GIRLS

Our Teen-Age Boys and Girls · · *Suggestions for Parents, Teachers, and Other Youth Leaders*

by Lester D. Crow *and* Alice Crow

Essay Index Reprint Series

BOOKS FOR LIBRARIES PRESS
FREEPORT, NEW YORK

155.5
C 880
68 584
January, 1970

STANDARD BOOK NUMBER:
8369-1030-3

LIBRARY OF CONGRESS CATALOG CARD NUMBER:
68-58783

PRINTED IN THE UNITED STATES OF AMERICA

PREFACE

At this time, as probably never before, there is apparent among all adults an appreciation of the seriousness and extent of adolescent problems of adjustment, and of the need of constructive and careful guidance. Parents and other adult leaders of youth are recognizing the degree to which wholesome adult living is an outgrowth of the kinds of environmental influence to which an individual has been exposed during his earlier years. Out of this recognition has come a sincere desire to achieve an understanding of the complexity of youthful development and a knowledge of practical suggestions that may effect better relationships between adolescents and adults as the latter attempt to set the stage on which the drama of adolescent development may unfold.

For many years young people and their parents and adult friends have come to the authors for help in solving adolescent problems. Through the teaching of young people and the participation with them in varied adolescent activities, they have been able to win the confidence not only of teen-age boys and girls themselves but also of their adult associates. Consequently, it has been possible to become acquainted at first hand with the many inherent and environmental factors that are productive of adolescent adjustment and maladjustment.

The authors have been privileged, in many instances, to guide adolescents and adults toward a better understanding of their respective rights and responsibilities. They also have known what it means to encounter situations that make desirable adolescent adjustment very difficult, if not impossible, without a definite improvement in society's fundamental attitudes and practices of which young people are the victims.

"Our Teen-age Boys and Girls" is the result of these many years of working with young people and of studying intimately all the influences that so potently affect the growing-up process. It is the authors' belief that their experiences with teen agers, both individually and in groups, might with profit be shared with parents, teachers, social workers, club leaders, religious workers, and other adults who are interested in the welfare of all young people.

All adolescents need guidance. In this book, which is functional throughout, mental-hygiene principles have been applied in the form of suggestions to all youth leaders as they live with, work with, and guide young people from day to day. The authors have been careful to use a style of expression which, they hope, will arouse the reader's interest. At the same time, any overemphasis or appeal to sentimentalism has been sedulously avoided.

Some of the most pertinent and often asked questions of young people themselves are included in this book. By way of illustration and emphasis there also have been presented many brief stories of adolescent struggle for an adjustment that has or has not been satisfactorily achieved. Where satisfactory outcomes have resulted, the reader is led to recognize the factors of guidance or changed environmental conditions that have made them possible. In those individual cases in which the outcomes were less satisfactory or well-nigh hopeless, the basic causes of such failure have been analyzed and recommendations have been offered for the mitigation of undesirable conditions.

The authors are especially indebted to the Atlas Powder Company, Ravenna, Ohio; to the *Brooklyn Eagle;* and to local and national leaders who have permitted the use of quotations from their writings. The authors also appreciate the helpful suggestions given by those who critically read the manuscript.

BROOKLYN, N.Y.,   LESTER D. CROW,
October, 1945.   ALICE CROW.

CONTENTS

Section V

SOCIAL ADJUSTMENT OF YOUNG PEOPLE

Section VI

JUVENILE DELINQUENCY

Section VII

CONCLUSION

STORIES OF TEEN-AGE BOYS AND GIRLS

INTRODUCTION

Chapter 1

American Youth on Parade

Young America is on parade, ten million strong— the energy of the present, the hope of the future. What are they like? Some are tall and some are short. Some are stout and some are slender. Some are graceful and some are awkward. Some are well dressed and well groomed, and some are slovenly and unattractive in appearance. Some are strong and healthy, and some are weak and puny. Some seem to be mature beyond their age, and others are still children.

There are those among them who swing along in the full glory of adolescent strength and beauty, with chins up and dreams of conquest in their eyes. Others, with timid feet and bowed heads, appear to have difficulty in keeping up with the procession. A few others lag behind, as if hesitant to join the procession, as if bewildered and fearful of what is ahead.

These young people represent all degrees of economic security or insecurity. They are the products of many national, cultural, and religious backgrounds. As they move along, we realize that they have already experienced varying degrees of success or failure. They possess great potentialities for good or for evil. Unless their ardor has been dampened by unfortunate childhood experiences, they are equipped with boundless energy and enthusiasm and are looking to us for help in achieving the ideals and ambitions toward which they are striving.

1

These are our sons and daughters—Americans all. The extent to which they, as adults, shall be fitted to meet their responsibilities of American citizenship depends in part upon the kind of guidance that we give them now and the examples that we set for them. The future is theirs. What they will make of that future is our responsibility as well as theirs.

Youth is a time of conflict. The more disturbed the environmental conditions in which the adolescent finds himself as he is struggling for self-realization, the greater will be the possibility of inadequate or undesirable development. The individual must progress successfully from dependence upon adult protection toward personal decision making and freedom of behavior. This transition, if it is to be effective, must be gradual, since the adolescent at one and the same time needs both a feeling of security and an opportunity for self-expression and self-determinism. Too much and too suddenly gained liberty finds the adolescent unprepared to meet it; then he may become a prey to undesirable influences. Adult overprotectiveness or domination of the teen-age boy or girl during this period may lead to resentment, confusion, or arrested development.

Fortunately, many American parents, with the assistance of other adults, can and do help young people to achieve a desirable balance of security and individual freedom. This is no accident. Perhaps never in history have adults evidenced a greater interest in adolescent psychology and mental hygiene than is now apparent. However, there is danger in the fact that with this increased concern for the welfare of young people there may develop an undue emphasis upon failure rather than upon success in achieving adolescent adjustment.

"What is wrong with our boys and girls?" "Young people have no respect for authority." "I have no control over my child; he will not listen to anything I say." "Juvenile delinquency is increasing daily." These and similar criticisms of the young people of America have become the theme of newspaper and magazine articles and are a popular subject for general conversation. Many groups have been organized for the purpose of solving the great national problem of teen-age adjustment in a maladjusted society. At first, these groups limited their discussion to a survey of the known delinquencies. They admitted the existence of a youth problem but found it difficult to discover the causes and to agree upon the treatment of specific individuals. Gradually, however, they have been able to analyze some of the more potent factors of teen-age disturbance and are beginning to set up certain basic principles for the guidance of adolescent boys and girls toward desirable behavior controls.

It is probably true that the great majority of the young people of America are making an excellent adjustment to the abnormal requirements of disturbed world conditions and are developing powers that will enable them to become virile and forceful leaders. However, the fact that a minority of teen-age boys and girls seem unable to make a socially desirable adjustment to present conditions should not be ignored.

If a chain is as strong as its weakest link, it is similarly true that a society's progress is retarded by its unadjusted members. The planning of social reorganization and the maintaining of a stable world society require the intelligent and enthusiastic cooperation of every one of its members. If the average American is unable or unwilling to do his share in the building of a wholesome and strong world democracy having a nice balance of rights and responsibilities, the task will fail of ultimate fulfillment.

The history of the development of civilization has been the story of conflict between constructive and destructive influences. Every chapter of history presents a story of rights to be fought for and responsibilities to be met. Nonconformists have often been forced at the point of a sword to an acceptance of behavior controls deemed desirable by right-thinking leaders.

The present chapter of world history is no exception. A great battle is still being fought for the attainment of justice for all people. At the same time, since human beings—no matter how high their ideals—are the prey of their own inherent urges and desires, it is natural that we find among us many examples of adult striving for the satisfaction of personal interests, in spite of a fundamental idealism.

Young people do not live in a world apart. They are encouraged to study and to gain an understanding of human motives and behavior and of apparent inconsistencies among these. They have been taught, for example, the value of rationing as a means of fair distribution of life necessities, yet they have seen reputedly honest people (members of their own family, perhaps) attempt to obtain more than their just allotment of a necessary commodity. They are told that everyone should give generously of his time, money, and service for the general good of humanity. However, they often see their friends and relatives requesting excessively high wages for their work, and spending the money thus earned for immediate self-indulgence.

The great need of personal sacrifice at the present so that greater benefits may be possible in the future is stressed on all sides, yet there are those who live their lives with little thought of the welfare of others. Although this apparent inconsistency between ideals and actual behavior is not common to the majority of the American people, there is enough of it to cause confusion in the thinking of our maturing young people.

Americans, in general, are sincere and honest in their efforts to do all in their power toward the setting up of a more equitable world order. Sacrifice of life, loved ones, money, personal ambitions and interests is common. Such stories, unfortunately, do not make exciting copy. Examples of failure to live up to idealism make more thrilling headlines and more interesting subjects for magazine articles. Hence, an easily influenced adolescent, unless he is fortunate enough to be surrounded by people in his own immediate environment who practice high ideals, is constantly stimulated by exciting accounts of adult malpractices.

Since the years between twelve and twenty represent a period in an individual's life of finding himself as a person, there is bound to be a constant struggle within the growing person as he attempts to determine his rights and responsibilities in his relations with others. He is relatively unformed, and he has strong natural impulses toward self-expression. He views himself as an adult. He is encouraged to do so by the present educational emphasis upon the importance of an adolescent's need to develop maturity of judgment and self-direction.

To what directing influence does an adolescent respond? Does he respond to precept or example? Can we require a young person to do as we say, or must we expect that he will do as we do? Have we the right to set up one code of ethics for our children, because this code will be of value to them and to society in the future, and at the same time direct our own behavior in terms of individual satisfactions and interests rather than according to group ideals? If we as adults wish to prevent adolescent maladjustment or delinquency, we must be certain that our own behavior is above suspicion.

During normal world conditions, the period of development from childhood dependence upon adult authority toward personal self-control is difficult. There are always some young people who are unable to make the transition adequately or without great suffering to others or to themselves. At a time like the present, when even normally stable adults are experiencing severe conflicts between the desirable and the desired, the stresses and strains of growing up are terrific.

Parents, teachers, employers, and social leaders should feel gratified that so many of our young people seem to be making wholesome and healthful adjustments. At the same time, as was suggested before, it is proper for us to be deeply concerned about the welfare of those adolescents who seem to find it impossible or difficult to make desirable adjustments. There is needed an intelligent analysis of all the factors that are inherent in youthful maladjustment. We must become thoroughly acquainted with the specific forms of existing maladjustment and delinquency. We must give serious thought to the possible ways of rehabilitating the delinquents and of preventing maladjustment among those adolescents who have not yet shown overt signs of undesirable behavior.

This emphasis upon the achievement and maintenance of mental health is in accord with the mental-hygiene point of view. Briefly, mental-hygiene principles emphasize the value of preventing the development of unwholesome attitudes and behavior, and of preserving desirable habit patterns, as well as of curing observable evidence of inner conflict and maladjustment. Prevention of mental disorder and preservation of emotional stability are socially and economically satisfying both to the individual and to the group. However, even though they are more costly and difficult, therapeutic procedures must be continued for the rehabilitation of those who have been allowed, through society's indifference or neglect, to become maladjusted or nonconforming members of the group.[1]

The majority of young people are confronted by more or less serious problems connected with their home life, their school experiences, their work activities, and their social relationships. The factors most commonly cited as those which are likely to predispose toward adolescent maladjustment include the following: economic instability, parental discord, inadequacy of school offerings, lack of understanding of adolescent psychology on the part of parents and school

[1] Crow, L. D., and Alice Crow, "Mental Hygiene in School and Home Life," Chaps. I–VI, McGraw-Hill Book Company, Inc., New York, 1942.

Sherman, Mandel, "Basic Problems of Behavior," Chaps. I, II, VI–VIII, Longmans, Green and Company, New York, 1941.

faculties, unwholesome neighborhood or community conditions, inadequate recreational facilities, unpreparedness for vocational activities, or unintelligent job placement.

A study of many cases of individual maladjustment indicates that no one of these factors, in and of itself, is necessarily a cause of delinquency. Sometimes the difficulty must be sought in a subtle blending of causes or in the interrelation that exists between the inherent nature of the individual and the external factors. To one young person an economically underprivileged home may offer a challenge, which will encourage him to develop within himself the power to improve these conditions. Another adolescent in a similar situation may become so discouraged by the apparent lack of opportunity to improve himself or his conditions that he will allow himself to be influenced toward undesirable ways of satisfying his natural longing for those comforts of life which are enjoyed by other young people.

Those of us whose function it is to help young people achieve a respected and useful place in adult society cannot be satisfied with the acceptance of certain glittering generalities concerning the adjustment process of all young people. Our task must be much more painstaking and individualized. Although good groundwork can be laid by working with individuals in a group, our real guidance must be directed specifically toward each individual and his own personal problems.

We must study and understand each young person with whom we are working. We must become thoroughly acquainted with his inherent nature—his mental ability, his state of health, his degree of emotional stability, his interests, and his habitual attitudes. Moreover, we must know and evaluate his home, his school or his job, his community environments, and the interrelations that exist among them. We must be able to probe beneath the overt behavior of the individual and thereby gain as much knowledge as we can of the underlying causes of such behavior. We must be trained to recognize the extent to which mental and physical health act as cause or effect of apparent disturbance.

Finally, we cannot lay down general rules or regulations or therapies as applicable in any or all situations. In one case, emotional instability points the way toward desirable adjustment in a hospital for the mentally ill. For another disturbed adolescent, emotional stability can best be achieved in guided group living. There are no straight and wide-open roads leading toward the goal of wholesome adolescent adjustment. The way is often twisted and obstructed. A sound basic knowledge of human nature, a wide acquaintance with the many subtle environmental influences by which young people are stimulated, and infinite patience and sympathetic understanding are prerequisites for the task of guiding the teen-age boy or girl toward effective and happy adult living.

An analysis of an individual's personal characteristics and of the multitudinous stimuli to which he responds more or less desirably is basic to any program designed for the prevention of delinquency. Any study of an adolescent's behavior should begin with a consideration of all the factors within and outside himself that may cause maladjusted behavior.

Such factors include a young person's mental alertness and emotional stability as these are affected by his home life, his school experiences, his vocational life planning and vocational success, and his social adjustment. The effect of any or all of these factors upon an individual's behavior must be considered in whatever attempts are made toward the solution of adolescent problems.

Chapter 2

The Teen Ager Lives and Grows

As we attempt to analyze the behavior of maturing American youth, emphasis is given to the fact that the majority of young people make a desirable adjustment to their home, school, social, and vocational experiences. When serious problems arise, these usually can be traced to maladjusting factors within a young person's experiences. Although all children and adolescents encounter problems as they meet their day-by-day responsibilities, most boys and girls can solve these problems satisfactorily. The stories of actual young people who have experienced or are now experiencing difficult problems of adjustment indicate that their difficulties often can be traced to a lack of understanding on the part of adults of the psychology of childhood and adolescence.

The developmental pattern of childhood is relatively uniform for most boys and girls. Variations may occur in terms of national background, economic status, geographical location of the home, educational and social status of the parents, number of children in the family, kind of school attended, and the number and kind of associates of the same age. However, such factors do not have too much effect upon the fundamental experiences of the growing child, if conditions during his early years are relatively normal.

The average American infant benefits today from the advancement that has been made in the scientific study of child care. During his early childhood he contracts and recovers from various childhood diseases. He is trained in the habits of talking, walking, eating, and otherwise behaving himself according to accepted standards of the group.

There are certain unpleasant experiences that are common to most children. The ordinary child encounters tumbles, cut fingers, bumped heads, denial of desired privileges, quarrels with brothers and sisters or playmates, and competition with schoolmates. He has his bright days and his dark days.

Sickness or death in the family or changed economic status may occur; but, unless it is a parent who is lost, or unless the economic change is too great, the child is not much affected. He is resilient. He is interested in himself and his own life and, hence, is not too deeply affected by extraneous matters. The great majority of American children develop normally through the first twelve years and bring to their teens healthy bodies, wholesome attitudes, and fundamental behavior patterns that make it possible for them to meet the problems of adolescence with confidence, enthusiasm, and success.

Even though individual differences may show themselves during childhood, it is usually desirable during this stage of an individual's life to stress similarity of behavior, so that the child may adjust easily to group living. With the approach of adolescence, the emphasis should be placed upon differentiation rather than upon uniformity of development and experience. Individual differences should be recognized and guided into desirable channels, so that the individual not only practices those forms of conduct which make him like everyone else, but also prepares himself to make his own special contribution to the welfare of the group.

Teen agers differ in their urges, interests, and potentialities. There are also differences between boys and girls in their developmental patterns. Consequently, there is no such person as a "completely normal" adolescent. Rather, there is a normal development of many different types of adolescents having a wide range of experiences to be met and solved. The term "normal," if it is to be used in a general meaning, implies the fact that the adolescent, whatever his own personality characteristics and his interest or experiences during the teen age, reaches adulthood well adjusted and prepared to meet adult experiences successfully.

Interpreting the term in this way, the "normal" adolescent suffers no great conflicts as he makes satisfactory adjustment to the following:

1. *In the home.* Daily routines, chores, parental rules and regulations, sister-brother relations, extent of personal freedom, presence of other relatives, financial status of the family, recreational activities, and the like.

2. *In the school.* School routine, subjects of study, extra-classroom activities, vocational choice and preparation, competition for grades or place on a team or such other activities as school play and debate team, relationship with teachers and fellow schoolmates, and the like.

3. *In social life.* Participation in organized and unorganized activities, service to the community, relationship with members of the same or the opposite sex, attitudes upon large social and political matters, religious affiliations, and the like.

4. *In vocational life.* Placement in job, job requirements, job responsibilities, adjustment to supervisors, relationship with fellow workers, and the like.

In any one of these areas there are many varying adjustments to be made by adolescents. These follow different patterns for different individuals. As the problems are met and solved successfully, gain rather than loss results from the experiences. In effect, the average adolescent boy or girl must meet disappointments, overcome difficulties, or submit to denial of individual interests and urges. It is through struggle that strength and power are gained. Although every adolescent needs careful guidance and sympathetic assistance in making his adjustments, these aids can be indirect for the majority of American youth, and teen agers can be allowed to fight their own battles and to achieve their own successes.

A Well-adjusted American Family

Meet John, who at nineteen is a healthy, active, and successful sophomore at a good American college. He excels in science and, although he has not yet definitely planned his career, he believes that it will be in the scientific field. He is, therefore, electing courses that will prepare him for his later specialization. His sister Anne, at eighteen, because of her special interest in commercial art, decided against a college education. She is at present employed by a well-known advertising company, where she is enjoying her work of writing advertising copy, training for which she started during her high-school course and continued in a specialized school.

John and Anne are proud of their parents, who are "tops," and of their stimulating younger brother and sister. Robert, a fifteen-year-old high-school sophomore, is a regular fellow, who sees himself as a future Babe Ruth. Dignified Enid, a high-school freshman of thirteen, has already informed her friends and relatives that teaching will be her career.

Although John and Anne are bound to the family by strong ties of love and companionship, they do not exclude other young people from their lives. John is beginning to appreciate the growing charm of his sister's pal Ruth, and vies with other young men of their acquaintance to be her escort to parties and dances. Anne allows herself to become a little starry-eyed as she admires the modest but satisfying ring on the third finger of her left hand and dreams of the future when she will be the mistress of Arthur's home, the mother of his children, and the partner of his daily work; for Arthur is a fellow worker with her and has already embarked upon a promising career in advertising.

Here is an example of a well-adjusted American family. Father and Mother, with a background of good health, average education, and modest means, started out some twenty years ago to build up a home and a family. The going has not always been easy. Setbacks included a temporary period of unemployment for the father, severe illness for the mother, the death of a baby girl, and the common childhood diseases and accidents for the four living children. Minor school troubles and disappointments, which were made the common concern of the entire family, have been experienced by all the young people.

There have been happy days and sad days, laughter and tears. Mother has not always completely understood her children's attitude. Occasionally, tired father has been a little impatient of youthful boisterousness. The children have experienced moments of resentfulness toward parental intolerance of childish whims.

John and Anne have known what it means to want this or that little luxury for which there was not enough money. They are glad that Robert and Enid can enjoy certain liberties that were denied to them; but they are careful not to spoil the "youngsters," who in turn thoroughly approve of their handsome and brilliant older brother and attractive and talented sister.

The entire family is active in community affairs; and the home, which is far from pretentious but neat and attractively furnished, is often the center of community group projects. Each one of the young people of this family has his or her own social group, the members of which are always welcome visitors at the home. Sometimes the meeting dates of the groups conflict, and mother or father is called upon to be a modern Solomon and guide the decision as to what can be done about it in terms of justice to all.

Regular church attendance with cooperation in church activities is as much a part of the family program as are attendance at motion pictures, the theater, and concerts; hikes and picnics; and participation in sports, games, and parties. Theirs is a rich and full life.

As can be expected, home chores are sometimes neglected and school assignments are carelessly completed by Robert and Enid. John has an occasional urge to drop out of college and get a job, especially since Anne is earning money and he can do no more than pay part of his college expenses through part-time employment. Even placid and good-natured Anne is at times moved by some act of Robert or Enid to wonder what the younger generation is coming to.

These four teen-age people are normal, healthy adolescents, striving to express their respective stages of adolescent emotional development. In so doing, they are bound now and again to attempt to impose their will upon others. They make mistakes, as we expect all adolescents to do in their struggle for attention and a place for themselves in society as self-directing individuals. However, intelligent parental guidance throughout their formative years and favorable home and social environments have combined to develop in them basically sound behavior patterns by which these adolescents are enabled to meet their day-by-day problems adequately and thus maintain a generally wholesome and happy attitude.

Their parents, too, have made mistakes. They realize that their judgment in dealing with their children's problems has sometimes been wrong. Nevertheless, they have always been sincere in their efforts to guide rather than to direct the behavior of these young people. They have recognized the wisdom of cooperation with one another as they attempted to encourage the development of fine character in their children. Theirs has been a practical mental-hygiene approach to their parental responsibilities. Their own attitudes and behavior have exemplified the practical utilization of the old maxim— "an ounce of prevention is worth a pound of cure."

Misfortune, sickness, disappointments, unexpected change of plans, and other unpleasant experiences may enter the lives of this well-adjusted family, but the years of practiced self-control and satisfactory adjustment which, to the present, they have enjoyed will help them to meet, with a minimum of friction, whatever difficulties they may encounter. One cannot predict what the future will hold for any one individual, yet it may be concluded that, when family attitudes are wholesome, the adolescents who are stimulated by them are likely to become resourceful and well-adjusted adult members of society.

Unfortunately, not all American teen agers have been helped to achieve a similar wholesomeness of personality. The application of mental-hygiene principles toward the formation of desirable behavior patterns is too often absent in the economically underprivileged or broken home, or in the indifferent or unfavorable neighborhood. Even when conditions are favorable, many parents and other adult leaders who are sincere in their desire to help adolescents toward desirable adjustment are bewildered by the attitudes that may be exhibited by young people, the questions asked by them, and their actual behavior.

The story of John and his family presents a brief picture of good adolescent adjustment as teen agers live and grow. However, for a variety of reasons, not all young people make similar satisfactory adjustments. You will find interspersed throughout the book many examples of individuals who exhibit behavior ranging from that which is slightly maladjusted and easily corrected to that which shows extreme maladjustment and delinquency. As you read the stories of these young people you may wish to evaluate the factors that have prevented their achieving the wholesome attitudes and behavior that characterize the members of John's family.

HOME ADJUSTMENT OF
YOUNG PEOPLE

Chapter 3

Teen-age Problems in Home Life

IT IS a common saying that home is where the heart is. It is probably also true that the heart is molded in the home. Psychologists tell us that the first six years of an individual's life are the most important. This is the period during which fundamental attitudes and habits are developed. Since the child usually receives his first guidance in the home environment, it can be concluded that the family is primarily responsible for the kind of person a child ultimately will become.

By the time an individual reaches adolescence, he should have been trained in the practice of desirable health habits, such as eating, sleeping, and protecting himself from possible infection or accident. He has achieved a greater or less degree of emotional control, and he has acquired from his parents and other members of his family certain religious, political, social, or family attitudes.

With adolescence comes an enlarging of the horizon. The individual often finds that the attitudes held by the larger social group differ from those that he had learned in his family group. The extent to which a young person has grown up in a family environment in which desirable social ideals are accepted and practiced will largely determine how difficult it will be for him to make wholesome adjustments in his relationship with persons and groups outside his family circle.

17

In instances where the family group displays ideals and attitudes toward society in general and toward the child in particular that are too different from those accepted by the majority of American people or by his particular group, the teen-age boy or girl may be faced with serious problems of adjustment. Conflicts may arise between the adolescent and his family that may be difficult to solve if neither is willing or able to compromise.

As was suggested earlier, a normal American youth is an energetic, ambitious, and sometimes visionary individual. He is beginning to feel the urge toward adulthood and, rightly or wrongly, believes that he possesses within himself the power to make his own decisions and to direct his own behavior in the light of those ideals which he considers right and just.

The conflicts that may arise between an adolescent and his parents do not always limit themselves to differences of opinion on large issues. There is often constant, daily argument concerning matters that may seem relatively unimportant to the parent although they loom large in the mind of the developing adolescent. The wise parent is able to compromise in small matters so that he may earn the loyalty and confidence of his adolescent child and thus be enabled to guide the young person in the making of decisions that are of major importance.

Differences of opinion between experienced parents and their experiencing son or daughter may lead to inner conflicts on the part of the young person. The parents may neither know about nor understand these conflicts. Other resentments may have their roots in brother and sister relationships, relationships with other relatives, relationships between parents, financial matters, home responsibilities, and adolescent social activities.

"Intolerant" parents and "intolerant" boys and girls often come to grips concerning such matters as home chores, spending money, apparent favoritism of one child over another, dates, selection of friends, vocational choice, parental rejection or overprotectiveness, youthful impatience with parental opinion, and the like.

Brothers and sisters, in spite of their fundamental love for and loyalty to one another, sometimes do get on one another's nerves. Adolescents, in their struggle for independence, cannot tolerate family interference or domination on the part of grandparents, uncles, aunts, and cousins. A word, a look, or a gesture is often sufficient to set off the spark of youthful antagonism. It takes all the tact and understanding that stable parents possess to handle their young firebrands. If the resentment is kept smoldering within the young person and not brought to the surface in a mild or violent eruption, the task of the parents is even more difficult.

The writers have obtained from thousands of young people between the ages of twelve and twenty their questions concerning problems connected with home and family life. Certain disturbing home situations are referred to over and over again by these adolescents. Some of their most common questions are presented here.

1. Should parents treat us as if we were children?

2. How much of my experiences should I tell my parents?

3. Why do my parents laugh at me when I confide in them and tell them my dreams?

4. Should parents open their children's mail?

5. Should a girl have the right to choose her own wardrobe?

6. Are parents always right?

7. Must a boy agree with his family's political views?

8. Why is it that when a girl of thirteen asks her mother a question pertaining to life the mother often puts it off and never answers?

9. When and how should a teen-age boy or girl be punished?

10. Should my parents make all my decision for me?

11. If my mother approves of my doing something, my father is sure to disapprove. This leads to arguments. What can I do about it?

12. Should parents have arguments in the presence of their children?

13. What can an adolescent do about a broken home?

14. What should be the relationship between a boy or a girl and a stepparent?

15. I have a stepfather who is grand but I do not feel that I can call him Father. What can I call him?

16. How can quarrels be avoided among brothers and sisters?

17. Should my brother, although he is younger than the rest of us, be loved more than anyone else by my parents?

18. Why is it that younger brothers and sisters refuse to take our advice but tell us to mind our own business?

19. Who should have the use of the radio?

20. Should brothers and sisters borrow one another's possessions without permission?

21. Should an adolescent be compelled to take care of a younger brother or sister?

22. Should a younger brother or sister insist on staying around when a girl has a guest?

23. Should boys be made to help with the housework?

24. How should a girl or a boy treat grandparents or other older relatives in the home?

25. Should other older relatives interfere with parents' decisions concerning their sons and daughters?

26. Should a boy or a girl have a definite allowance?

27. How can a boy get his parents to understand that a fellow needs some spending money besides carfare?

28. How much should a boy or a girl know about family finances?

29. If a teen-age boy is working, what part of his salary should he give to his parents?

30. Should parents allow young people to choose their own friends?

31. How old should a boy or a girl be before being allowed to date members of the opposite sex?

32. How can a father be kept from interfering with a girl's dates?

33. What is the correct time to come home from a date?

34. Should a younger brother be allowed to stay out later than his older sister?

35. How can the time for coming home at night be decided when parents disagree on the time?

36. Should children make extreme sacrifices for their parents?

Many of these problems may seem trivial to the adult and cause him to smile at the seriousness with which they are asked, but to the adolescent nothing that would seem to interfere with his striving for adult status is unimportant. The situation becomes even more unmanageable if the parents or older members of the family do not realize what is going on in the thinking of the teen ager. Adults tend to criticize young people for becoming increasingly vocal in demanding their rights. It is unfortunate that some young people tend to place too much emphasis upon their *rights* and to ignore their *responsibilities*. However, it is much more wholesome for resentments to be voiced than for them to be repressed and allowed to fester, breaking forth later in the form of a warped adult personality.

The recognition of adolescent dissatisfaction does not mean that every young person should be encouraged to follow his own impulses and urges without proper guidance. It does, however, mean that adults should examine their own attitudes very carefully, so that they may achieve a proper balance in their thinking between the rights to which young people are entitled and the responsibilities that they should meet.

If parents themselves are emotionally disturbed, if their own marital relations are not well adjusted, if quarreling and bickering are the order of the day, then there is certain to arise within the adolescent member of the family a seething tempest, which may or may not find outlets. Such home conditions are likely to result in pitiful youthful confusion, conflict, and delinquent behavior.

Parents whose adolescent sons and daughters are achieving wholesome attitudes and habit patterns in their relationships with other people are meeting successfully the test of intelligent parenthood. However, many parents, as well as their teen-age children, need specific and practical assistance in the solving of the more or less serious problems of home adjustment. Each emotion-arousing situation must be considered on its own merits, as well as in its relation to the entire home-life pattern, and must be treated accordingly.

In the following pages you will find presented a number of stories of young people whose attitudes and behavior reflect a greater or less degree of conflict in the home. Parental over-protectiveness, apparent favoritism of one child over another, inability of parents to understand some of their children's adjustment difficulties, parental example of undesirable attitude or behavior are some of the factors that have militated toward adjustment difficulties of these young people.

As you read these stories and others throughout the book that describe adolescent struggle toward satisfactory life adjustment, it may be necessary for you to fill in for yourself some of the details that cannot be included in the sketches, because they are perforce relatively brief. You will probably be impressed, however, by the fact that some of these young people have done as well as they have in overcoming serious difficulties. Some, on the other hand, may cause you to wonder why a young person should become maladjusted in a home environment that seems to be not too undesirable.

You will observe that some of the young people described in these stories have been able to overcome their difficulties. This may be due, in part at least, either to the kindly interest in them of persons outside the home or to a change in their parents' attitude and behavior. No matter how carefully we may attempt to analyze human relationships into cause and effect sequences, we are forced to admit that certain subtle personality interrelationships cannot be analyzed out of a total situation and definitely tagged.

Competing with a Sister's Reputation

Margery is the third oldest of a family of eleven children. Her father is a hard-working, honest man, who finds it difficult, but not impossible, to provide a simple but comfortable home for his large family. Her mother is a sincere, placid woman, whose health has suffered as a result of childbearing. In general, the home relationships have been excellent except for the fact that Margery's sister Lenore, who is one year older than herself, has always been accepted as the beauty of the family and its most outstanding member. Consequently, Lenore was encouraged to give all of her time to study and was discouraged from participating in family duties.

It fell to Margery's lot to act as mother's helper for her younger sisters and brothers. She enjoyed housekeeping and often took more than her share of the responsibility for the household chores. She loved her mother intensely and did all she could to ease her mother's burdens.

The two girls attended the same high school and both earned excellent grades. Because of her attractive personality, the older sister was a school leader and gave a great deal of time to out-of-class activities. Margery was much more quiet than her sister and felt that she was needed at home as soon as school day was over. As a result, she took no part in the social activities of the school and, consequently, was not well known among the teachers and students.

Among her other activities, Lenore had been elected to the honor society of the school. When Lenore was a senior and Margery a junior, the latter also received an invitation to become a member of this honor society. At her interview, she exhibited an extremely antisocial attitude. She told the committee of student interviewers that she did not wish to join and that the only reason they were inviting her was because she was Lenore's sister. She asserted that she was tired of being reminded of Lenore's virtues. With that she left the interview and, as a result, was refused membership in the society, since personality as well as scholarship was a requirement for admission.

Until this incident occurred, her school advisers had known her as an excellent student who had elected a commercial course instead of the academic course, which was being taken by Lenore. They were not acquainted with her as an individual. Her behavior at this time brought her to the attention of her adviser and a warm friendship began, which has continued. At the end of that school year Lenore was graduated and entered college, where she continued to be as successful and as well liked as she had been in high school. During Margery's senior year, her adviser was able to develop more self-confidence in her by encouraging her to realize that she was just as able as her sister and that she gave promise of becoming equally attractive. At this adviser's suggestion, Margery was again invited to join the honor society and accepted.

When Margery was asked her reason for electing a commercial course, her answer was that it would be impossible for all the children to go to college. Since Lenore was the brighter of the girls, she and the boys should be given this opportunity, and it was her, Margery's, duty to help finance them. Margery was persuaded that Lenore could take care of her self, he that further training would increase Margery's fin ocial o help her younger brothers. She was urged t wn a course requirements for college entrance as a p e.

Margery became enthusiastic about this plan and completed two years of mathematics and one year of language in six months, earning honor grades. She was admitted to the college in which her sister was then a sophomore. College advisers were very much interested in Margery and gave her individual attention. Her first two years were successful. However, her sense of home responsibility persisted. A new baby had arrived and her mother's health was worse. Although Lenore's attitude had improved somewhat toward home chores, she still gave most of her free time to college activities. As a result, Margery gave so much of her attention and time to her home duties and to her part-time job that she left herself no time for study. Consequently, she failed in some of her subjects and left college in order to accept an excellent position in a bank.

She became a changed girl. In the past, her clothes and appearance had always been neat and clean, but she had done little to add to her physical attractiveness. After a few months of full-time employment, she emerged as a stylishly dressed and well-groomed young woman. The realization that she was making a definite contribution to the family budget and that in so doing she was superior to Lenore seemed to give her a self-confidence and assurance that worked wonders in her attitude toward life.

In the meantime, Lenore was graduated from college and married almost immediately afterward. Margery herself became engaged and took Lenore's place as the outstanding girl of the family. Later, Margery returned to college (evenings) in order to complete her college education.

At the last meeting between Margery and her former high-school adviser, the girl waxed enthusiastic concerning Lenore's baby and his soldier father. There seems to be perfect accord between the two sisters. Several of the boys are now in the service and are making excellent records for themselves. Margery's pride in her family is as great as it ever was, with this difference—in the past it was *they;* now it is *we*—evidencing her consciousness of herself as one who has done much to maintain family prestige.

Differing Effects of Environment upon Two Sisters

Nellie has had a long history of lack of cooperation and nonconformity with rules and regulations. Her father deserted the family when she was a small child, and her mother was recently committed to a hospital for the mentally ill. There has always been a struggle for existence, and the home was dirty and uncared-for. Various agencies, such as Catholic Charities, the Catholic Guidance Institute, The Bureau of Child Guidance, and The Society for the Prevention of Cruelty to Children, have worked with the family. No one was able to help the girl.

Because of her attitude and behavior, she was committed for a time to the Children's Society, but when she returned to school she showed no improvement. She created disturbances in her classroom, refused to do the work required of her or to wear the uniform required for her vocational work. When she could not do as she pleased, she resorted to swearing and other undesirable language. Her program was changed, in order to discover if the trouble that she had in various classes might be caused by a clash of personalities. The result was the same. The girl could get along if everything went as she desired, but if her conduct was interfered with she would go off into a temper tantrum. She was then kept out of class and given special work to do, but there was no change in her attitude.

Nellie had been taking a course in beauty culture, but at her request this was changed to a commercial course, so that she might be prepared for a position in a business office. She seemed pleased by this change and agreed to cooperate. Before long, however, she caused so great a disturbance in the typewriting room that she was sent to the office and kept there for the two months prior to her sixteenth birthday. At that time, it was decided to discharge her. She had not been attending school and, when she was called in to fill in her employment certificate, she was most impertinent and indignant because the attendance officer had the "nerve" to bother her to come to school for this purpose.

An older sister, Kate, attended the same school and made an excellent adjustment. By working part time, Kate had been able to support herself until she was graduated and obtained a very fine position. She later left home to live in a girls' boardinghouse because she could not tolerate living with her sister.

After Nellie was discharged from school, she hung around the house. She not only threw things about, but got herself a dog, which added to the confusion. She was in the habit of taking the clothes that Kate had bought for herself. When the latter put her clothes into a locked trunk, Nellie broke the lock and took them.

After Kate left the home, the Community Service Society arranged to send Nellie to an agricultural boarding school for training, so that she could obtain a job on a farm. Nellie went to the school but left almost immediately and returned to her home city. She insisted that Kate allow her to live at the boardinghouse and also support her. Upon Kate's refusal to do so, Nellie took a position as usherette in a motion-picture house and lived in a small room by herself.

She is most resentful of Kate's refusal to do things for her and does not recognize that her own attitude is very bad. Recently, she has been running around with an undesirable group of boys and girls. The Community Society is following her case very carefully in order to prevent her getting into serious sex difficulties.

It is interesting that two girls of the same family and brought up in the same home environment should have developed such entirely different attitudes toward their social responsibilities.

Effect of a Dissatisfied Father

A father who thinks that the world owes him a living and an aunt who has no authority are poor guardians for a girl who has never known a mother's care and affection. This combination has resulted in Alice's having no regard for parental or school authority. However, her natural quickness has enabled her to reach her last year in high school, in spite of habitual truancy, cutting of classes, and lack of respect for her teachers.

Her health is not good. She has occasional fainting spells, but she capitalizes on this fact and uses the emergency room at school as a means of getting out of attending her classes. These fainting spells are often the result of her refusal to eat any breakfast, as she is afraid of becoming stout—a fear that has no basis in fact. Her father has promised his full cooperation in the matter of improved health habits for the girl, but he is so concerned with his own affairs that he soon forgets; and the aunt will not take the responsibility of guiding Alice.

When Alice was within two months of graduation, she suddenly decided to reform. With the help of her teachers she made up the work that she had missed through absence, and was regular in attendance. Even when she was really ill, she refused to take advantage of her illness as an excuse to be away from her classes.

She earned graduation and obtained an excellent position in a business office. She still delights in recounting her "troubles" to her associates as an appeal for sympathy. She has an attractive personality and is able to win friends. She should make a good adjustment in her job, unless her interest in it wanes after the novelty of it wears off and she begins to play up a frail physical constitution as a means of evading responsibility. Unless the improvement in her attitude is more than temporary, she will develop into a woman with many of the characteristics of her father and become a complaining and dissatisfied wife and mother.

James's Mother Will Not Cooperate

James's father died some years ago, and the boy is living with his mother. His mental ability is well above normal but he is a consistent failure in his schoolwork and appears unable to adjust to other people.

His behavior is markedly abnormal. He walks slowly through the halls at school, arriving at his classes late. He never speaks above a whisper; and, when he is questioned, he mumbles unintelligible words. At times he stands motionless, his lips moving as though he were talking to himself.

He has had difficulties of this kind since he was a child. He never causes trouble and is quiet and unassuming. If he can be encouraged to smile, his smile is warm and winning; but he cannot be induced to take part in any activity or to make friends with boys and girls of his own age.

. He definitely needs psychiatric treatment. If he could be helped, he would be a very worth-while boy. His mother, however, will not cooperate. She insists that there is nothing wrong with him and that she will not give her consent to having him taken to a hospital or a clinic for the care that he so desperately needs. As long as parental consent is needed for the treatment of a young person who is mentally ill, little can be done for him by those agencies which are interested in his welfare.

Abrupt Change from Sheltered Environment Leads to Maladjustment

Fifteen-year-old Arthur is a victim of infantile paralysis. After spending eight years in the sheltered environment of a home for paralytics, he was returned to his own home and admitted to a public high school. As a result, he was very unhappy and showed little interest in his studies, passing only a few subjects at the end of a year and a half.

At first his attendance at school was very good, but with the piling up of failures he started to cut school and ran away from home. The Travelers Aid Society found him and became very much interested in his case.

He had been using regular transportation lines to and from school. It was suggested to the parents that he use a special bus, but they refused to allow this. They believed that, since he had improved physically, he should be treated no differently from any other child. Ordinarily this would be desirable, but Arthur is immature emotionally and needs special care.

He again ran away and was returned to his home but is still badly adjusted. To date, his parents have not cooperated with the authorities in their recommendation that he be placed in an environment in which he can learn gradually to meet his social and emotional obligations. He is very much discouraged and is experiencing a feeling of futility, which is not being helped in his home.

Hilary Is Antagonistic to His Parents

Hilary's parents have no control over him. As a child he was very much pampered. At present, he is incorrigible. He remains out at night until one or two o'clock in the morning and refuses to tell his parents where he has been or what he has been doing. He steals money from the home, which the father believes is being used for gambling.

Hilary's father wants the boy to be placed in an institution. Since Hilary is seventeen years old and has not yet been up before the court for criminal behavior, this is difficult to do. The boy had no interest in school and was a constant truant. Finally, he received his working papers, but up to the present he has not been able to keep a job for more than a month.

The case is almost hopeless, because of the antipathy

between the boy and his parents. When he was a child, he was allowed to do as he pleased because that was easier for the parents than attempting to guide him. He has probably never known the meaning of love from his family. He is a little Ishmael, whose hand is against everyone and everyone's against his. He is a constant liar and it has been practically impossible to reach the inner boy.

Mabel Has Been Overprotected

Mabel is eighteen years old. For many years she has been extremely nervous. As a result of overprotection on the part of her mother, she has failed to develop any independence of behavior. For a long time she suspected that she was an adopted child, but her mother constantly denied that this was so. The tension that existed between the two affected the girl's behavior to such an extent that she became ill whenever she had an argument with her mother. She seemed unable to do her schoolwork, and she exhibited an antisocial attitude toward other young people.

The school and several social agencies cooperated in an attempt to improve the relationship between Mabel and her family. Her schoolwork was adjusted to her interests and abilities and she was treated by a psychiatrist of the Child Guidance Bureau. At this time she learned that she was an adopted child, but she met the situation quite well. She seemed more poised and in much closer touch with her surroundings.

However, her improvement was short-lived and her schoolwork became worse. Her attitude at home was so bad that she was separated from her mother and sent to live at the residence hall of a local branch of the Young Women's Christian Association. She also received her discharge from school and went to work. However, by this time she had developed a strong sense of guilt and felt that she did not belong to anyone. Although she has returned to her home, she is planning to get a job far away from her present surroundings.

She has developed a great deal more poise and assurance, but she is still badly adjusted. She is very unrealistic toward her future and her own possibilities. She refuses to recognize her own shortcomings and blames other people for her failures.

Bad Heritage and Home Environment

Rachael's father died twelve years ago, when she was five years old. She has two older brothers and one younger. Her home conditions are poor; and her mother, who is emotionally unstable, is very proud of her sons, who are completely spoiled, and resent Rachael.

The girl has been in high school for five terms and has passed but one subject. She is not dull mentally, but dislikes school intensely and is not encouraged by her mother to attend, as the older boys left school as soon as they could and do little more than hang around poolrooms. Rachael is very large for her age, heavy set, quite polite but indifferent. She is dirty and slovenly in her dress and her hair and head are never thoroughly clean. Her mother also is untidy and careless about her appearance.

Upon the mother's statement that Rachael was going to another state to live with an aunt, the girl was discharged. However, Rachael did not leave her home but spent her time hanging around the neighborhood. Rachael looks about five years older than her age and is very much interested in older men. She has been running around with such men and staying out all night. About six months ago, she left her home and has not yet been found. Her mother is not worried about her, claiming that Rachael is old enough to take care of herself. It is almost impossible to do anything for a young person who is the product of a heritage and a home environment as bad as are Rachael's.

Laura Could Not Make an Adjustment

"I can't stay in school. See these spots on my face. All the girls keep looking at me and that makes me nervous." This was the reason given by Laura, a fourteen-year-old high-school freshman, for not attending school.

Her mother, an overworked, anemic little woman, the caretaker of a row of flats, was unable to manage this, her oldest, child. The family history was not good. The mother had been married to an emotionally unstable man. After the birth of Laura and her younger brother, her father was committed to a hospital for the mentally ill as a result of heavy drinking and abnormal sexual activities. Later, his wife obtained a divorce; married an honest, untrained laborer; and had another child, by him. Her husband was very kind to his stepchildren and did all that he could for them. However, although the younger children made a good adjustment to the home situation, Laura presented a problem that the parents were unable to meet.

The girl was graduated from a parochial elementary school and entered a public high school. Although she was bright, she was unsuccessful in her school subjects, with the exception of English, in which she excelled. Her previous school was small and she had been well acquainted with teachers and pupils. Here she was bewildered by the large student body and developed an abnormal shyness. She refused to participate in school activities, giving as her reason the fact that she was ashamed of her skin condition.

As a matter of fact, the girl was attractive and the skin rash was a very slight attack of acne. Her tendency to withdraw had a mental rather than a physical basis. Her adviser was able to keep her at school by filling her program with manual subjects, such as clothing, foods, and ceramics, thus diverting her attention from her classmates. For at least a year her teachers escorted her personally from class to class, lest she attempt to escape. A close, friendly relationship developed between Laura and her adviser and the girl gave many confidences. Laura was interested in writing and started innumerable stories, many of which had definite literary promise. However, she could not take criticism of her writing and, instead of rewriting one story or poem, she would start another.

She gradually developed an abnormal interest in the opposite sex and was accustomed to recount long tales of her adventures with married men, visits to men's rooms, drinking parties, and the like. Investigation of her activities indicated that her adventures were imaginary—attempts at attention getting. As her complexion improved, she became aware of her prettiness and thought that she was being followed on the streets because of her great beauty.

There was close cooperation between the home and the school. The mother and father tried to do all they could to improve Laura's attitude but, since they were uneducated, they were not successful in their efforts. Laura refused to help her mother with her work, gave up her church affiliations, and, believing that her mother had not divorced her first husband, insisted that she was living in sin. This was not true.

Finally, through patient and persistent encouragement, the girl was graduated from high school, but she was incapable of holding a job. She would come late, leave early, refuse to follow directions, and think that everyone was jealous of her great beauty and attractiveness to men. After several unsuccessful attempts at placement, her mother, who for four years had resisted any suggestion that the girl be sent to a hospital for observation, finally gave her consent and the girl was committed to a hospital for the mentally ill, suffering from dementia praecox. At the hospital she gradually showed a slight improvement. Because of the crowded conditions in the hospital, she was discharged at the end of nine months. She suffered a relapse, and several months later was again committed, this time for life.

Laura was a victim not only of a bad biological heritage (since both parents were emotionally unstable), but also of parental ignorance. Psychiatrists who examined and treated her agree that if Laura had been hospitalized when she first exhibited symptoms of emotional disturbance she could have been helped to make a normal adult adjustment. More than that, she might have earned success through her writing, as she had both creative ability and unusual power of expression. This is a case in which an early and correct diagnosis was made, but parental understanding and cooperation were lacking.

Ada's Parents Understood Only Physical Illness

The fact that Ada's parents both work and that they cannot understand any kind of illness except physical diseases is in large measure responsible for the girl's lack of adjustment. At school she had no interest in any of her subjects, was a truant, had an antagonistic attitude toward anyone who tried to advise her, and was belligerent and uncontrolled in behavior. She forged records, cards, and letters. She showed a general negative response to all efforts of teachers to have her study or come to school.

It was recommended that Ada should be treated at a guidance clinic. Her parents admitted that they recognized Ada's instability, but they were unwilling to have her go to the clinic, as this might make her "crazy." Mental hygiene was not understood by them. The school then tried to guide her. After many painful interviews, Ada said that she was interested in aviation and wanted to join the flying club. Hence, she was invited to make model planes with the boys and girls and seemed happy and cooperative while at this work.

The improvement was temporary, and she returned to her former undesirable habits of behavior. Her parents supervised her homework as much as possible and denied her certain privileges when she misbehaved. However, the girl made no progress and became openly defiant. As a result, she was transferred to a private business school, in order that she might gain enough training for a simple office job.

She is now attending that school but is not showing any particular interest in her work. Her attitude seems to be that, since both her parents are working, it is their responsibility to support her until she marries.

The Cards Are Stacked against Homer

Homer is the third oldest of ten children. His mother is distracted, excitable, inadequate, noncooperative, and antagonistic. The father, who is a veteran, is ill and a heavy drinker, and abusive to the mother and children. His family believe that he is mentally unbalanced, especially when he is under the influence of liquor and threatens his wife's life and his own. The children are under great stress when he is in this condition, and they often do not get sufficient sleep because of the disturbances he creates.

The home consists of six rooms, which are poorly furnished and inadequate. There is haphazard supervision of the children. The mother does not know how to control her large family, and the father disappears from the home for several years at a time. Moreover, an immorality charge was brought against him for his behavior toward one of his daughters.

Homer entered high school when he was fourteen years old, but was a consistent failure as a result of his many absences and his refusal to study. It was thought desirable to transfer him from an academic to a vocational school, but he would not make the change. The mother upheld him in his decision and explained his absences in terms of various types of minor illnesses. Finally, she refused to give any reason for his absence and reprimanded the attendance officer for calling at the house. She informed the officer that, in the future, she would not allow him to enter her home. She added that she was going to keep the boy home whenever she felt like doing

so, because "I have so many worries and cares I'll go crazy."
The younger children repeated her admonition never to enter
the home again; and, as the attendance officer drove away,
threw mud at his car.

Homer is consistently sulky. He evades all attempts at
friendliness, resents outside help, and is emotionally upset.
He hates his home and hated school. As soon as he was sixteen
years old, he applied for working papers and received a job,
which he was unable to hold.

Homer has not yet done anything to bring him into conflict with the law, but it is impossible for him to make any
kind of desirable adjustment in his present home. The future
holds no promise for him or for his sisters and brothers, unless
a way can be found for getting them out of their unwholesome
home and neighborhood environments.

As you read these stories, you no doubt were impressed
with the importance of the home in the life of the teen-age
youth. In many of these cases, one cause of the maladjustment
can be found in the fact that the young person himself displayed characteristics possessed by one or another of the
parents. The home environment resulting from parental
incompetency or indifference acted as a further factor for the
intensifying of the young person's undesirable attitude toward
the world in general.

Many of our educational and community leaders recognize
the need of removing children from unfavorable conditions
before uncooperative or delinquent behavior patterns become
fixed. This is difficult to accomplish, since foster parents
cannot be found easily for children of this type. One suggestion for meeting this problem is that of the setting up, at
community expense, of well-equipped and well-staffed boarding schools. However, it is almost impossible to provide a

home atmosphere in institutionalized living, no matter how informal and kindly the organization and supervision of a school of this kind may be. Thus the child is denied his right of experiencing intimate home relationships. If the home is unadjusted, institutionalized living may be the lesser of two evils.

Parents may get off to a bad start in their attitude toward their children, even though they themselves are basically normal in their behavior. Such parents usually respond to guidance given them by interested advisers. Hence, many young people who in their early years give evidence of a non-conforming attitude can be led toward satisfactory adolescent adjustment.

Before you consider the suggestions concerning parent-child relations that are discussed in the chapter that follows, you may wish to evaluate your own behavior in these relationships. For this purpose certain behavior practices are listed for your consideration. It is suggested that you read carefully and reflect upon each one. It is hoped that from this self-examination you will derive an increased recognition of your parental responsibilities.

Rate yourself on the self-evaluating questionnaire that follows. If your answer is found in the column numbered 1, give yourself a score of 1; if it is found in the column numbered 2, give yourself a score of 2; and if it is found in the column numbered 3, give yourself a score of 3. In checking your reactions, be honest with yourself.

WHERE I STAND IN RELATION TO MY SON OR DAUGHTER

Score yourself at the right on each item listed

	1	2	3	Score
I permit my son (daughter) to be late for meals.	Often	Sometimes	Never	____
I criticize my son (daughter) in the presence of visitors.	Often	Sometimes	Never	____

	1	2	3	Score
I set my son (daughter) an example of proper dress.	Never	Sometimes	Always	____
I set my son (daughter) examples of unnecessary worry about money.	Often	Sometimes	Never	____
I set my son (daughter) examples of bickering.	Often	Sometimes	Never	____
I set my son (daughter) examples of bad manners.	Often	Sometimes	Never	____
I keep our house neat and clean.	Never	Sometimes	Usually	____
I inform my son (daughter) about our financial problems.	Never	Sometimes	Often	____
I give my son (daughter) the social freedom necessary at his (her) age.	Never	Sometimes	Often	____
I give my son (daughter) guidance in the wise use of freedom.	Never	Sometimes	Usually	____
I give my son (daughter) definite work to do in the home.	Never	Sometimes	Often	____
I solve personal differences with my mate in my son's (daughter's) presence.	Often	Sometimes	Never	____
I expect my son (daughter) to accept my decisions.	Always	Never	Sometimes	____
I give less attention to my son (daughter) than to another child.	Often	Sometimes	Never	____
I treat my son (daughter) as an adult.	Never	Sometimes	Often	____
I advise my son (daughter) on his (her) personal problems.	Never	Sometimes	Often	____
I believe that I am misunderstood by my son (daughter).	Often	Sometimes	Rarely	____
I give reasons for denying my son's (daughter's) requests.	Never	Sometimes	Always	____
I plan with my son (daughter) in the expenditure of money.	Never	Sometimes	Often	____

	1	2	3	Score
I restrict my son's (daughter's) behavior.	Often	Never	Sometimes	___
I welcome my son's (daughter's) friends in the home.	Never	Sometimes	Often	___
I am confided in by my son (daughter).	Never	Sometimes	Often	___
I give in to my son's (daughter's) whims.	Often	Never	Sometimes	___
I give my son (daughter) examples of affection and comradeship.	Never	Sometimes	Always	___
I attempt to give my son (daughter) intelligent sex education.	Never	Sometimes	Often	___
I avoid gossiping about other people.	Rarely	Sometimes	Always	___
I advise my son (daughter) not to attend night clubs and roadhouses.	Never	Sometimes	Often	___
I interfere with my son's (daughter's) grooming.	Never	Often	Sometimes	___
I restrict my son (daughter) in his (her) choice of friends.	Never	Often	Sometimes	___
I permit my son (daughter) to make his own decisions.	Never	Sometimes	Often	___

Those items on which you have rated yourself a score of 3 indicate an excellent adjustment between you and your son or daughter. A rating of 2 indicates a good adjustment. Note particularly those items on which you gave yourself a score of 1. Then ask yourself what you can do to improve your attitudes and practices in these relationships between you and your son or daughter. The suggestions in Chap. 4, which follows, may help you.

Chapter 4

Suggestions for Improving Home Relationships

THE home wields a powerful influence over the attitudes and behavior of young people. Hence, men and women do not dare to take lightly their responsibilities as parents. Since parental influence upon a child begins long before he is born, young men and women should early prepare themselves for future parenthood. They should develop good health habits, refraining from participation in activities that may affect their physical constitutions. Excessive smoking and drinking, the keeping of late hours, insufficient or badly balanced diet, and promiscuous sex relations are not conducive to the bearing of healthy children.

Not only should young men and women prepare themselves for desirable parenthood, but they should also use intelligence and discretion in the choice of their mates. They owe it to their unborn children that both parents shall be healthy and virile individuals, who can give to their children a sound heritage.

Much has been done in recent years for the education of parents and prospective parents in the care and training of young children. Childhood conduct is the basis upon which adolescent habits and attitudes are built. A pampered child is often an irresponsible adolescent. Stubbornness, self-will, indolence, pretense, excessive timidity, carelessness, and the like do not suddenly change, with the advent of adolescence, into cooperation, industry, courtesy, poise, and carefulness. In fact, outstanding behavior patterns of childhood, whether they are good or bad, tend to become intensified as the individual develops and matures, unless environmental factors stimulate changes.

Adolescence is a training period for both the parent and

the child. If the parent is able to adjust his own attitudes and behavior to the needs of his growing boy or girl, the latter will be helped immensely in the solution of those problems which are inherent to the growing-up process. In the following pages, the problems of young people connected with their adjustment to home and family life are treated under six headings:

1. Rights and responsibilities of young people in the home
2. Effect upon adolescents of the marital attitudes of their parents
3. Relationships among sisters and brothers
4. Effect upon adolescents of the attitudes of grandparents and other relatives
5. The teen ager and family finances
6. Parental responsibility for the social life of young people

Under appropriate headings, suggestions are presented in as detailed and specific form as possible for meeting some of the common problems of adolescents in the home.

Rights and Responsibilities of Young People in the Home

Should parents treat adolescents as if they were still children?

It is very difficult for the average parent (especially the mother) to realize that a boy or a girl between the ages of twelve and twenty is gradually taking on the stature of young manhood or young womanhood, and that parental ties must gradually be allowed to relax. The young person is no longer satisfied (if he ever was) with "You should do this because Mother says so."

In school, he is expected to think things out for himself and is introduced to the relationship that exists between cause and effect. He is trained to exercise his own judgment, under guidance, in matters concerning his own welfare. He is constantly told that he is no longer a child. When a young person thus stimulated at school returns to his home, he cannot suddenly remove his attitude of growing independence as he would a coat. He is bound to resent attempts on the part of his parents to treat him as though he were still a child.

An adolescent should enjoy the same opportunity for self-direction in the home that he experiences in school life; and his opinions, crude though they may seem to an adult, should receive respectful attention. If his attitudes and opinions need guidance, this should be undertaken with the same seriousness on the part of the parent as is shown by the young person. Never should his opinions be met with a smile of tolerance, a laugh of derision, or a "What do you know about such things? You are too young even to think about them."

If an adolescent attempts to do something in the home that lies within his power of execution, he should be encouraged to continue the activity, even though his first attempts are inept or bungling. This procedure may try the patience of parents. It is much easier for them to say, "Here, let me do it. You are taking all day." The task will undoubtedly be done more expeditiously and efficiently by the parent; but the young person is thereby deprived of needed practice and the recognition of himself as an active member of the family group.

To encourage a young person to assume certain specific home responsibilities is desirable; but to expect an adolescent to shoulder complete care of the home is not only most unfair, but is sure to develop antagonism between parent and child, as well as possible youthful maladjustment. The story of Josephine, who had a tyrannical father, is a case in point. This father had no understanding of the rights of young people but overemphasized their responsibilities. He represents an extreme attitude; but some well-meaning parents, like Regina's father, also fail to realize that they are expecting too much of their adolescent children.

Josephine Has a Tyrannical Father

Josephine's father beat her, kicked her, and stepped on her because she had gone for a walk before she had put the spaghetti into the icebox, in spite of her explanation that the spaghetti was not cold enough for her to do so. This is one example of the man's attitude toward his four children—two boys and two girls, ranging in age from nineteen to fourteen. The mother of the children had died when the youngest was six years old. Frank, the oldest, had left home four times but returned each time because he realized that his younger sisters and brother needed protection from the father. The girls were expected to take complete charge of the housekeeping, including the washing and ironing and the cooking and cleaning. If anything did not suit the father, a beating was administered.

The three younger children, who were still at school, were given no time to do their school assignments. When their housework was finished, they were expected to help their father in his shop. The girls were allowed no social activities. The clothes that the younger children wore were paid for by their older brother or given to them by sympathetic neighbors, although the father could have afforded to supply them with anything that they needed.

Welfare organizations were asked by the school authorities to help in the situation. In spite of the father's prolonged and vocal objections, the two girls and the younger boy were removed from the guardianship of their father and were provided with a suitable home. Financial arrangements were made that would ensure the continuance of their schooling until they were prepared for good jobs. Frank was helped to find himself a pleasant home and a better job than those which he had gotten for himself. Within two years, Frank and the girls were working in excellent positions, the younger boy was doing well at school, and the four of them were living together in an attractively furnished apartment. Josephine is engaged to a fine chap. They are all very happy. Their only unpleasantness is caused by visits from their father, who claims that he is ill and needs their help. Among his friends he takes credit for having raised such a fine family.

A letter recently received from Frank by one of the social workers in the case reflects the fine attitude of these young people. After recounting their activities, Frank ended the letter by saying, "Thanks to you for your fine, courageous work. Without you I would not have been able to do anything. Thanks a million. You are a swell person. Write to us soon."

Regina Had Too Much Responsibility

Seventeen-year-old Regina is the oldest in a family of three girls. Her mother committed suicide about two years ago because of poor health. Her father owns a paint supply shop at his home address, but he derives very little money from his business and is forced to work as a painter in order to supplement his income.

Since his paint-supply store cannot be left unguarded, Regina had to be absent from school on the days of her father's work in other places. In addition, she was completely responsible for the care of her home and of her two younger sisters. As a result, the girl became very much discouraged. She felt that, unless she were relieved of her home duties, she could not endure the strain of her last year at high school, even though she was a good student.

Regina's father had been so much concerned about his responsibility for the financial support of the family that he had not recognized his daughter's difficulty. When it was brought to his attention, he blamed himself for his negligence and admitted that he had thought of remarrying, but had decided against it as he feared that his daughters might resent the intrusion of another woman in their mother's place. He discussed the matter with the girls and, to his surprise, found that they were more than willing to have him marry a woman who had been a friend of the family for a long time.

Since the father's remarriage, Regina has become much improved. She is doing well with her studies and expects to be graduated creditably. She admits that there are times when she does object to her stepmother's presence in the home, but she is intelligent enough to realize that this attitude is unfair to the woman who is doing all that she can for the family.

After graduation, Regina plans to go to work and to set up a home of her own, preferably in another city. There is still a little emotional maladjustment and a feeling of insecurity and frustration. It is probable that, when she becomes economically independent, she will make a very satisfactory adjustment.

In both of these cases, the young people concerned possessed potentialities which, when given an opportunity, led to excellent adjustments. However, the fact that Regina's father himself was able to rectify the undesirable home conditions when he was helped to do so has assured for his family a fine emotional attitude toward home relationships, which should be reflected later in his children's own homes. Josephine's father by his behavior has denied to his children the experience of home unity. As these young people set up homes of their own, the memory of their own childhood home may cause them to be too indulgent to their own children, lest the latter suffer feelings of frustration as they did.

At the present time, there are many families in which both the father and the mother are working away from the home. Consequently, a high-school daughter may be compelled to be responsible for the complete care of the home, the buying and preparation of food, and the family laundry. It is asking too much of a growing girl to assume the full responsibility for household chores and, perhaps, to look after younger brothers and sisters, besides.

An interesting story illustrative of this point has just come to the writer's attention. Ruth is an attractive, intelligent girl in her last year of high school. Both her mother and her father work; and an aged, crippled grandmother is in the home. Ruth's mother need not work but, since she enjoys her job, she is loath to give it up. Consequently, Ruth has been taking care of her grandmother and has had complete charge of a five-room apartment, besides going to school. The parents, realizing that this is too great a burden for their daughter, have suggested that the grandmother be sent to a home for old people. Ruth loves her grandmother and will not listen to this suggestion, but instead has decided to leave school, to which the parents have given their consent. Ruth's mother cannot understand that she should give up her job and encourage her daughter to finish her commercial course at high school.

A young person should not continue to be tied to his or her mother's apron strings. Even during childhood, it is undesirable for a boy or a girl to be too dependent upon his parents. During adolescence, it is inexcusable. An adolescent boy or girl should never be referred to as "Sonny" or "my little girl." Parents should in no way intimate in the presence of their friends that their son or daughter thinks he has grown up but that he is still "my baby." Adolescent pride causes resentment of this parental attitude.

The weaning process should be begun early and continued until, in early adulthood, the individual is completely independent except for such guidance as is needed by everyone at any age in time of crisis. Children who were delicate or unusually attractive during their babyhood are often the worst victims of parental protection. The experiences of Frances and Gordon are examples of the effect of overindulgence on the part of parents and too much dependence upon parental leadership.

Frances Responded to Sympathetic Guidance

Frances had more than average ability, but her schoolwork was not good. She seemed unable to concentrate and was extremely nervous and emotionally unstable. Her actions were childish. She attempted to get the attention of her classmates by loud talking, pushing other pupils, and making pert remarks. She was easily excited and angered, and so temperamental that it was difficult for her to cooperate with teachers or fellow students.

She had been a delicate baby and, consequently, had never been thwarted. She was as difficult to manage in the home as she was at school. Her parents realized that she needed psychiatric attention, but they were hesitant to submit her to it until they were strongly urged to do so by the school adviser.

The girl responded to the psychiatric treatment and to the adaptation of her school program. Because of her interest in music, she was given an opportunity to play in the school orchestra. She also spent most of her free time in the dean's office, working with other students. The sympathetic attitude of her teachers helped her to overcome her feeling of complete defeat, since she realized that she was among friends.

Frances changed considerably, from an overemotional girl, easily given to crying and loud in voice and manner, to one who was much more quiet and subdued in manner, conduct, and appearance. Since her family needed her financial aid, she left school to take a defense job. She appears to be well adjusted, and the responsibilities that confront her challenge her to use her superior abilities. When she left school, her parting words were "You've all been swell, just swell, to me. I hate to leave school and not see my teachers any more."

Gordon Continues to Be a Spoiled Baby

Seventeen-year-old Gordon has been a discipline problem since his early childhood. As a baby, he was spoiled by his mother, with the result that neither she nor his father has any control over him. Although he has average intelligence, he was retarded in elementary school and did not enter high school until he was almost sixteen years old.

He has utter disregard for authority. He was a habitual truant and cutter at school. At one time he brought a carving knife to school, but his mother was unconcerned by this fact. She has been consistently uncooperative. Gordon is erratic and restless and shows neurotic tendencies. He paws his mother, and she seems to enjoy this.

When he reached the age of seventeen, he refused to attend school; but when he was given his employment certificate, he tore it up. He insisted that there was no need for him to work and he did not intend to do so. At present he is hanging around the house, visiting poolrooms, and the like. His parents are doing nothing about his activities. He has not yet committed any criminal offense; but, since there is no one outside the home or in the home to discipline him, he is running wild.

Parents, as they attempt to be objective in their attitude toward their children, need to be careful lest they cause their children to believe that they are unwanted children. One adolescent stated it thus, "My parents seem to reject me. They act as though I have interfered with their lives." It can be recognized that, once this youthful attitude has been developed, it may be difficult for the parents to regain the confidence of their child.

Mothers and fathers should encourage their adolescent children to think for themselves in matters that are within the realm of adolescent decision. They should allow young people to take upon themselves a reasonable amount of responsiblity for home welfare. Finally, by their words and actions, they should make it clear to their teen-age sons and daughters that they, as parents, are aware of their children's developing maturity and are proud of it, but are ready and willing to advise them whenever adult assistance is sought.

Should parents open their children's mail?

This question cannot be answered by an unqualified Yes or No. If there exist complete sympathy and understanding between the adolescent and his parents, letters received by him are shared with his parents. However, a young person should have the satisfaction of opening his own mail. If the family attitude is good, the contents of the letter are then read to the parents, or the letter is given to them for reading. The fact that a young person does not want his parents to read his letters or that a parent feels that it is necessary for him to open and read a letter before his child sees it indicates a fundamental difficulty of which the reaction toward the letter is no more than a symptom.

It is natural for a parent to be interested in his child's social life and to want to know what the latter's friends are saying to him. However, this understandable curiosity should be curbed until the recipient of the letter is present to open it. This is a right that accompanies the growing-up process. If the parent opens the letter because he is suspicious of its contents, his so doing is an acknowledgment of his own failure as a parent to train his child in desirable social relations.

The average young person resents the opening of his mail only because he wants to feel the same independence in his social relations as that enjoyed by older members of the family. He is usually eager to share the contents of his letters with his family if he has had the first reading of them. An adolescent who is afraid of his parents' reactions to any letter that he receives is thereby acknowledging that his relations with its writer are undesirable. A parent can usually recognize a situation of this kind. If he is intelligent, he will endeavor to win (not demand) his child's confidence and advise him concerning his proper course. If a parent is too insistent in his attempts at censorship, he is likely to encourage the adolescent to have letters sent to another address. There is usually an obliging pal who will help out in such a situation.

Are parents always right?

No. There is no person whose opinions are always right. Everyone, no matter what his age, training, or previous experience may be, should be big enough to realize and to admit that someone else, even though this other person may be younger and less experienced, may have a better understanding of a particular situation. If, during childhood, a young person has been led to recognize the reasonableness of his parents' decisions, there will be relatively little conflict between parents and child during the latter's adolescence. Then, when differences of opinion arise concerning desirable adolescent behavior, the young person will be likely to have confidence in parental judgment and be willing to be influenced by it.

Arguments in the home are sometimes caused by such factors as age differences, changes with the times in the general social pattern of behavior, differing cultural backgrounds and educational inequalities between parents and children, and the like. Such family disagreements, especially if the parents are dictatorial in their attitude, encourage young people to look upon their parents as intolerant or narrow-minded. Adolescents often express the wish that their parents could be more broad-minded. There is a fallacy in the thinking of these boys and girls. What they do not seem to realize is the fact that they themselves are often as intolerant in their attitude as they accuse their parents of being.

The fundamental difficulty in cases of this kind is that neither parent nor child is able or willing to understand the point of view of the other. The parent's stubbornness of attitude is duplicated in the child's. Consequently, compromise is difficult, if not impossible. Either the parent wins and the child becomes a thwarted or frustrated individual; or the parent gives up the struggle and allows his immature son or daughter a free hand, thereby depriving the young person of needed behavior guidance.

A parent is not always right, but his judgment is usually more far-reaching than that of his inexperienced child. When differences of opinion arise, the parent with the child should give serious consideration to the following questions:

1. Is the matter important enough to make an issue of it?
2. Is parental opinion based upon sound, practical reasoning and consideration of the best interests of the child?
3. Will the fulfillment of the child's wish harm him in any way or is parental denial of it based upon a personal whim or on an outgrowth of personal adolescent experiences?

Two girls in their late teens were discussing the bringing up of children. One of them, whose adolescent activities were completely dominated by her parents, stated definitely that her children would be given all the freedom of decision that they wanted. The other girl, whose parents were giving her almost complete freedom of action, retorted that her children would do as she decided, since she now realized the dangers connected with her own freedom from parental control. So, parents are always wrong! This is true only if they go to extremes in their attitude toward their teen-age children's interests and wishes.

There must be a possibility of compromise. In matters of

relatively slight importance, such as the suit or dress to wear, young people should be allowed an opportunity to feel that their opinion, attitude, or behavior is respected. However, if a young person's attitude, opinion, or behavior is harmful to himself or to others, the wise parent attempts to guide his child, and patiently but firmly indicates the reasons (which must be basically sound) for parental encouragement of adolescent acquiescence with parental wishes.

When and how should a teen-age boy's or girl's behavior receive parental disapproval?

Young people should rarely, if ever, be criticized by their parents for their behavior in the presence of others, except members of the immediate family. Even then the criticism should not take the form of a comparison of one child's conduct with that of another. Sometimes, public reproof is the only kind that the young person receives from his parents. Undesirable behavior in the home is overlooked because "anything goes" with the family. Discourtesy to parents or other members of the family by the adolescent boy or girl is not frowned upon, chiefly because good manners and consideration for the other person are not habitual in the family group. It is only when such parents see their son's or daughter's actions through the eyes of people outside the family group that they become excited about the undesirable behavior of their children.

If the same emphasis upon cooperative and controlled behavior holds in home relationships for all the members of the family as is expected outside the home, parents will have little occasion to be embarrassed by their adolescent child's behavior in public. Habits of courtesy, cooperation, and self-control, developed and practiced in the home, will then extend beyond the family circle, and parents will be able to feel confident that the son or the daughter will be habitually considerate and charming at all times. A boy or a girl who in the home is allowed to preempt the most comfortable chair, select the most desirable piece of meat, or dominate the conversation, cannot suddenly change into a model of propriety in public. If, for any reason whatever, an adolescent displays undesirable behavior in the presence of people outside the family group, the wise parent ignores such behavior until he is alone with the adolescent and then voices his disapproval and discusses with his child the reasons for his attitude.

The kind and extent of guidance that should be given to adolescents when their actions merit parental disapproval is important. More important is the fact that penalties should never be administered when the parent is in an emotionalized state. There is danger that a reproof or a penalty emotionally administered may not "fit the crime." The young person is quick to recognize this. He may accept the parental disapproval or he may try to argue himself out of it, but his private opinion will be that Father or Mother "is on the rampage again." Moreover, a parent who becomes emotionalized over his son's or his daughter's misdeeds may not be consistent in his attitude toward that which constitutes desirable adolescent behavior. Conduct which at one time may stimulate strong parental disapproval at another time may be completely overlooked. As a result the adolescent is alert in recognizing a parent's good days and bad days. Hence, parental guidance must be objective and consistent.

Parents are often at a loss to discover the attitude that they should exhibit toward adolescent misbehavior, in order that it may be reasonable, fit the seriousness of the offense, and be effective. Usually, the kind and effectiveness of parent-child consideration of an offense during the early years of the child determine the kind to be employed with the adolescent. In some homes, nothing more is needed than a quietly voiced expression of disapproval, with reasons. Long harangues, reference to the disgrace brought upon the family, or comparisons between the disapproved behavior and that of other children in the family or of the parent in his youth are seldom effective.

Perhaps one of the most desirable influences upon young people's behavior is the temporary denial of privileges when the girl or boy neglects to meet his responsibilities. There must be, however, a reasonable relationship between the seriousness of the misdemeanor and the severity of the denial. In every instance the penalty should be related to the misdeed. For example, a young person and his parents have agreed upon a specific time for his return home after a social engagement, but the adolescent arrives home late, with no valid reason for the delay. The first instance of this kind merits an expression of parental disapproval. The second offense should be penalized by the denial of permission tc attend one other such social activity. The boy or the girl should then be given another trial, with the reminder that he is to be at home at a certain time. If the young person is again late, he should be denied the privilege of going out with this particular group but should be encouraged to have social engagements with other groups, the members of which are also expected by their parents to practice punctuality.

It is the responsibility of an adolescent to respond with improved behavior to the suggestions of his parents. It is the right of an adolescent to expect his parents to agree between themselves upon the kind of adolescent behavior that is desirable or undesirable. If a father and mother differ in their attitudes concerning desirable teen-age activities, their discussions of this matter should be held when the child is not present. They must arrive at an agreement, so that they present a solid front to the adolescent. Too often, a young person bemoans the fact that, if one parent says it is all right to do a certain thing, the other parent may object. This divided parental attitude causes bewilderment in the adolescent. How can standards of conduct be determined if parents themselves differ in such matters? Usually, the young person plays up to the lenient parent, even though he may recognize the fact that the other parent's attitude is probably the correct one.

Either too much rigidity or too much laxity on the part of parents tends toward the weakening of adolescent confidence in parental judgment. Moreover, parents should not set behavior standards for their teen-age children which they themselves do not follow. In homes where parents themselves are controlled, considerate, and cooperative, adolescent children usually follow the same pattern of behavior, except as immaturity of judgment may cause them to err. Reasonable and objective guidance will soon improve such behavior.

To what extent should parents make decisions for their teen-age children?

Conflict often develops between parents and adolescent boys and girls because of the tendency of the former to deny to the latter any freedom of choice in personal matters. The attempt on the part of the parents to dominate the lives of their children is closely allied to the fact that the parents still consider the adolescent to be a child whose judgment cannot be trusted. A few of the most common conflict-producing situations are discussed briefly.

1. *Selection of Clothes.* A young child cannot be trusted to select his or her own clothes. Although he may be allowed a choice between two articles of clothing, both of which would be appropriate, final selection should rest with the parents. However, as the young person progresses through his teens, he should be given more and more freedom in this matter. By example and precept he should be trained toward an appreciation of suitability, attractiveness, and good value in clothes. He should also understand the limitations of the family budget. From that point on, the young person should be given considerable freedom of selection.

During early adolescence, a parent should accompany his child on shopping tours and, by suggestion, guide the buying. As the boy or girl advances into the upper teen years, he or she should be encouraged to do most of his shopping alone, except as the parent may be invited, as a friend would be, to help in the selection. If an article of clothing is bought that does not meet the parent's standards of appropriateness or good value, he must be tactful in his appraisal of it. He should be quick to recognize the young person's reason for the choice but he should do no more than suggest that, although the particular article has certain desirable features, he personally might have selected something different. The young person, as he wears the clothing, will probably come to agree with the parent's judgment. Although he is not likely to admit that he made a bad decision, he will probably exercise better judgment the next time.

This is an important phase of adolescent training. As an adult, the boy or the girl will need to use his own judgment in such matters, since he will not always have his parents at hand to give him advice. Hence, he needs practice in the selection of clothes while he is still in the position to do so under guidance. Moreover, most adolescents receive some training in high school concerning appropriateness of dress. They want to apply this training without too much parental interference. Also, an outstanding means of asserting one's developing maturity is through personal dress and grooming. Adolescence is the ideal time to help the young person to set up for himself (not to have set up for him) accepted standards of attractive appearance.

2. *Smoking and Drinking.* Parents are often concerned about the possibility of their teen-age children's developing the habit of smoking, or of drinking hard liquor. At present, these are difficult matters to handle. It is generally agreed that, for adolescents, smoking or drinking, even in moderation, is unnecessary and may be harmful. If parents smoke and if

they drink an occasional cocktail or glass of wine or serve these in their home, it is natural for young people to want to be included among those who take part in such activities. Not to allow the adolescent ever to smoke a cigarette or to take a drink when he sees his elders do so is very hard on him. It might be possible to encourage him to indulge once in a while on a special occasion, but he must know why his parents believe that it is undesirable for him to do this often. If parents themselves are controlled in their smoking and drinking, young people usually are willing to conform to their parents' wishes in these matters.

Parents who themselves neither smoke nor drink must be intelligent in their attitude toward their children's possible interest in doing these things. To attempt to give the impression that such things are the invention of the devil and that no decent person indulges in them will do no more than cause the son or the daughter to lose faith in parental good judgment. Young people are likely to meet fine and attractive adults who do smoke and, occasionally, drink liquor. Parents who are complete abstainers should admit to their children that some fine people do these things but that they themselves believe such practices to be unnecessary and perhaps injurious to the health. They should also stress the fact that they would like their children to use similar controls in their own health habits. Overindulgence in sweets, starchy foods, gum chewing, and the like can be similarly handled.

3. *Possession of Pets.* There is often disagreement in families concerning a desire on the part of adolescents to own pets. Frankly, there is no better way to develop attitudes of kindliness and responsibility in a young person than for him to own and care for a dog. If the home is in the country or in a suburban area where the animal has plenty of play space without encroaching upon the rights of neighbors, parents should encourage their young people to have a dog. In fact,

it is often desirable for children to own a dog even before they reach adolescence.

If the home is in the city, it is much more difficult to allow the child this privilege. To keep a dog confined in an apartment or in a small house on a busy thoroughfare is unfair; hence, the city parent must weigh the advantages and disadvantages of encouraging his child to have a dog, a cat, or any other pet around the house. However, if the adolescent is allowed this privilege, whether it be in the city or in the country, the pet should be the young person's personal possession, not only to play with but also to care for in every way. The purpose of an adolescent's having a pet is defeated if the child has all the fun, while the parents carry all the responsibility.

4. *Having One's Own Room.*   Fortunate is the boy or the girl who has a room of his own. More fortunate is the one who is allowed a reasonable amount of freedom in the decoration and arrangement of his room. This is an excellent medium of self-expression. A young person's ideal of attractively decorated walls or interesting color combinations may cause an adult to shudder. If a parent can live through the various phases of his adolescent child's developing appreciation of beauty, the room of the older adolescent will probably be almost austere in its simplicity. This last is especially true if other rooms in the house reflect parental good taste in furnishings and decorations.

Let the adolescent's imagination run wild if it must, but insist that the contents of the room be kept in a reasonable state of cleanliness and orderliness. Even though there are servants to do the heavy cleaning, the day-by-day care of his room should be the adolescent's own responsibility and pride. This should include the making of his bed and the picking up and putting away of his clothes. He must receive training in his parents' home that will help him to keep his own home neat and attractive. The generic "he" is used advisedly here, to include both boys and girls. Many mothers who give excellent training to their daughters in the care of personal belongings fail to give a similar training to their sons. Boys as well as girls should take care of their own personal belongings, learn to make their own beds, and help with the household chores.

Returning to the consideration of a young person's room, this place should serve as a haven of peace to its occupant. He should feel free occasionally to enjoy the privacy of his own domain without an anxious or curious parent's coming in to find out what he is doing. Of course, if the adolescent makes a practice of withdrawing from family activities to the solitude of his own room, there is probably something wrong. The retiring from the family group is probably the symptom of family maladjustment which requires the intelligent attention of parents. The boy or the girl should not be scolded or teased for his attitude, but the reason for it should be tactfully sought. He may feel that his presence is not wanted, or he may be passing through a phase of mental superiority, which causes him to be bored by the ordinary family conversation or activity. Whatever the cause, it is the responsibility of the parent to discover it and to draw the young person back into the family circle.

To sum up the discussion of the rights and responsibilities of young people, it should be emphasized that the habit patterns developed during adolescence and the guidance in decision making received during this period have a tremendous effect upon the young person's success as an independent adult. A dominated adolescent usually is a futile and indecisive adult. Parents who do not give teen-age children an opportunity to learn by their own mistakes are depriving them of a rightful heritage. A dominating adolescent tends to become an aggressive, self-asserting, and self-satisfied adult. It is the responsibility of parents to guide their adolescent children toward habits of cooperation and consideration for others.

EFFECT UPON ADOLESCENTS OF THE MARITAL ATTITUDES OF THEIR PARENTS

Should parents have arguments in the presence of their children?

The answer to this question is definitely in the negative. However, it is much easier to recommend this than to practice it. No human being is perfect. No matter how well a man and a woman may be mated, there are times when the actions of one will cause emotional disturbance in the other. It is natural and desirable to express dissatisfaction with the conduct of a spouse when it annoys or hurts. To have it out with the other person is far better than to nurse a grievance, real or fancied, and thereby develop a silent antagonism, of which the mate is conscious without knowing what the cause may be. However, such matters are the personal concern of the married couple. Children should not be drawn into the situation. Every young person, although he may occasionally resent the attitude of his parents toward him, has an inherent respect and admiration for both of them. Unless a parent, by his actions, has forfeited the good will of his children, young people are loyal to him. They may criticize their father or their mother among associates, but no one else may dare say anything derogatory about either one of them.

Consider the effect upon a young person who wishes to be loyal to both parents if, in his presence, these parents engage in emotionalized quarreling and bickering. Which parent is right? The adolescent on the side lines is mature enough to realize that both parents may be justified in some of the things that they are saying to each other but that many of the accusations made are foolish and even unjust. Shall he interfere? Shall he take sides?

Loyalties are strained and the young person is confused. His attitude toward the marital relation may be affected by the friction in the home. He may decide that he will never marry lest he inflict similar torture upon his own children. As he grows older, he realizes that family arguments are not necessary and he will probably marry; but he will carry with him into his adult life the scars of emotional upsets experienced during periods of parental friction. Moreover, as the adolescent listens to unfair recriminations of one parent against another, he learns to discount similar outbursts against himself. Like Evelyn, he loses faith in his parents' judgment and good intentions.

An Unfortunate Home Situation

Evelyn is a very capable girl who is not working up to capacity because of her emotional instability. She is very self-conscious and is constantly wondering what other people are thinking of her. She was a truant from school, against her better judgment, and therefore found it difficult to keep up with her schoolwork.

The home situation is most unfortunate. Evelyn hates her father, who does not seem to know how to handle her. She is antagonistic to her mother, who is mentally and physically ill and who tends to blame her husband for her illness. Evelyn is constantly under tension because of home conditions.

At one time the mother was in the hospital and Evelyn was placed in a girls' home by the Catholic Big Sisters, who were very much interested in her. However, when Evelyn's mother was able to return to her home, she demanded that Evelyn return also, as her help was needed. This was very unfortunate. The girl had been making a very good adjustment while she was away from the influence of the family.

As soon as Evelyn was old enough to be discharged, her mother insisted that she go to work. The father did not seem able to get and hold a job and the mother was not well enough to do hard work. Evelyn's personality and her lack of training are making it extremely difficult for her to obtain and keep a good job. This fact is increasing the conflict between Evelyn and her parents.

What are the effects upon an adolescent of a broken home?

Although a broken home is not the only or even the major cause of adolescent delinquency, it does create an abnormal home situation, which is likely to affect a young person's emotional development. Loss of a parent through death not only deprives the developing adolescent of the wise counseling and guidance of that parent but may develop too close a bond between the remaining parent and the child.

If the home is broken because of incompatibility between the parents, the young person is affected not only by the break itself but also by the parental friction that led to the break. If the boy or the girl has experienced constant parental disagreement and then is deprived of one of the parents through divorce or separation, he is exposed to further conflict without adequate emotional stability to meet it.

The parent with whom the child remains may be very bitter toward the mate who is no longer in the home. Hence, he is almost certain to make disparaging remarks to the child concerning the other parent. This is hard on a maturing young person, even though his loyalty may be given to the parent with whom he lives. If he really loves the absent parent, the situation is tragic for him. To expect an adolescent to be friendly with both parents, perhaps living with each for a part of the year or living with one and visiting the other, demands emotional adjustment to a degree that he has not yet attained.

Parents who are separated from each other (mothers

especially) often encourage their children to visit the other parent and then insist upon receiving a full account of what was said and done during the visit. If the separated mate has remarried, the young person may be catechized about the new husband or wife. The adolescent does not know how to meet a situation of this kind. If the visit was a pleasant one and he reports it truthfully, he may be faced with a fit of hysterics or accusations of favoring the other parent. In order to avoid a scene, the boy or the girl may give a wrong picture of his visit, leaving the desired impression that he did not enjoy it.

In this way an adolescent may learn to deceive his parent, and develop the habit of employing the same technique in matters concerning his own activities. The important fact is that the child has lost respect for his parents and is no longer willing to submit to their domination. He is like a ship without a rudder, unable to steer his way to the safety of home port. Hence, he may find his satisfactions outside the home. If he develops undesirable habits as he seeks to assert his maturing personality, he has no one to whom he can turn for wise counsel and emotional security. The whole situation is intensified if the adolescent cannot find a place in the life of either parent and is left to the care of other relatives or of strangers.

Many stories about young people give evidence of the tragic results of a broken home. The fears of Gertrude's mother that her daughter might display some of the undesirable traits of the absent father, Clorinda's switch of parents, and the effect upon Lois of her divorced mother's influence are a few examples of the adjustment difficulties experienced by boys and girls from broken homes. Fortunately, the three young people referred to have been helped toward the achievement of healthful adjustments.

Mother's Fears Restrict Gertrude's Activities

Gertrude, an attractive and successful high-school student, developed a serious skin difficulty as a result of asthma. This physical defect, combined with home conditions, led to the development of emotional difficulties. She is very artistic. Her father, who was an artist of exceptional ability, has been confined for the past several years to a hospital for the mentally ill. Previous to that, the father and mother had separated because of temperamental differences.

The father is Irish and the mother is a thrifty German. Since the separation between the two parents, the mother has worked in a factory. In spite of her low income, the woman keeps her home attractive and is very proud of it. She lives only for her home and her children. In fact, she admits that she is selfish about them and that she wishes to keep them for herself. She does not want them to marry, for fear that they may be hurt as she was. Therefore, she worries whenever Gertrude is out of her sight.

For many years the mother feared that Gertrude, who resembles her father, might have inherited his carelessness and extravagance. Consequently, she constantly preached the value of thrift to her daughter. All of this caused friction between the two. Moreover, Gertrude felt that she could take care of herself and that she did not need her mother's chaperonage to and from church meetings that were held in the evenings.

Each argument with her mother upset the girl and aggravated her skin condition. Consequently, it was agreed by the skin specialist in charge of her case and the school authorities that Gertrude needed to be away from the home environment for a while and that the mother needed some education concerning the treatment of an adolescent daughter. It was made possible for the girl to spend a month or more of her vacation at a near-by camp. At first, the mother refused her consent to this separation, but she was finally convinced that it was necessary.

Excerpts from a letter written by Gertrude while she was away from home revealed the value of camp life to her.

"I am having a wonderful time and don't want to come home at all. My skin is getting along nicely. My face is as clear as a baby's and I am feeling tops. It is beautiful up here. We have dancing three times a week, golf matches, and horseshoe tournaments. We also play some pool (but just for fun). Would you believe it, I am the champion pool player and horseshoe player in my cottage. I am just learning to play golf. It is much easier than learning history or bookkeeping."

By the time Gertrude returned to her home, her mother's attitude had changed considerably. She had discovered that life had continued, even though Gertrude was not close to her. The last year of Gertrude's school course was a happy one for her. Previous to this, her mother had forbidden her to major in art, but now Gertrude was given all the art work that her program would allow. Upon her graduation from high school, she continued her studies as an art student with a scholarship and has been progressing well. Gertrude's mother is now very proud of her daughter.

Clorinda Shifts Parents

Clorinda's parents separated when she was a little girl. Until two years ago she lived with her father, as her mother was out of the state. During that time she seemed to be a very well adjusted child and quite happy with her father. When her mother returned to the state, Clorinda was transferred to her mother's home. Since that time, she has been uncontrollable. Her early history at high school was good. She passed her work and was a cooperative member of her class. Now, she became a truant, walked out of her classes, and defied all the school rules and regulations. Her conduct at home was equally undesirable.

Although the girl's father was not living at home, he was very much concerned about her and anxious for assistance in managing her. The mother was helpless in the situation, since Clorinda was definitely antagonistic toward her. The father finally requested that the girl be committed to an institution. However, one of the school agencies and the pastor of the girl's church were opposed to this. Consequently, they asked that the girl be given another chance.

Clorinda finally admitted that she did not want to be dependent upon her mother and that her father should not have to support her. She decided that she wanted to learn a trade so that she could train for a job. Clorinda was transferred to a vocational school and has been working hard to complete her course.

Lois Got Off to a Bad Start

Lois's mother and father are divorced. Because of the mother's lack of responsibility, the court appointed the grandmother to be the guardian of the girl. This did not prevent Lois's mother from seeing her and continuing to have a bad influence upon her.

Lois was a truant. During her long periods of absence from school she was employed illegally, since she was only fourteen years old, but she earned good pay. At home she was uncooperative and stayed out until three o'clock in the morning. During one of her periods of truancy, Lois, in collusion with another student of the same high school, gave a false address, in order to escape follow-up by the attendance bureau.

Her grandmother and an interested aunt were asked to cooperate. As a result of several conferences with them and Lois, the girl's adviser was able to persuade Lois that she was not living up to her abilities. She gave up her job, has refrained from seeing her mother, does not stay out late at night, and has transferred from an academic to a commercial course.

At the present time, she is making a good adjustment, but realizes that she still needs guidance.

These three young people were able to work out a satisfactory adjustment, partly because of their own ability to do so. The help that they received from interested adults and the fact that there was improved understanding of the situation by at least one member of the family were factors that also contributed to the improvement of adolescent attitudes toward home and social relationships.

Some young people are not so fortunate. The cards are literally stacked against them. Resentful Harry, indolent George, and Henrietta, who wants a home like other girls, are examples of young people whose adjustment to normal living has been definitely interfered with because of the disruption of the home.

Resentful Harry

Harry, a fifteen-year-old boy, has lived with his maternal grandmother since his mother and father separated. The boy has no respect for his mother or his grandmother and is completely beyond their control. He has been known to throw books through the window of his home; strike his mother, sisters, and brothers; and set fire to the furniture. Once, when his grandmother refused him permission to leave the house, he demolished the front door of the apartment to get out. At another time, he broke a window for the same purpose.

He has had a poor attendance record at school, but he is pleasant and anxious to do his work when he attends. Here he is quiet and seems to get along with his teachers and fellow students. Because of his poor attendance and his resentful attitude toward his home, he has been treated by several agencies and has been encouraged to attend school more regularly and to earn success in his schoolwork. When he is absent, however, he brings no notes to school from home but claims that he has been to one of the clinics for treatment.

At home he is still uncooperative and blames his mother and grandmother for the broken home. He apparently has idealized his father; but, unfortunately, the father has shown no interest in the boy's welfare.

Indolent George

George was born out of wedlock of a mother who died of tuberculosis when the child was five years old. He has a low mentality and a tendency toward serious obesity. He early became the victim of his inheritance and the environment in which he lived. An older sister, also born out of wedlock, is confined to a mental hospital.

Since babyhood, George has lived with his grandmother in a dilapidated, unpainted, dirty, and unheated home, having meager furniture. The home is located in a slum neighborhood on a street that is narrow and overcrowded. His associates are members of homes little, if any, better than his own. George has always been large for his age, dirty, and lazy. Because of his stupidity and unattractive attitude, he has had to choose his companions among boys and girls of his own kind.

He has consistently shown a dislike of schoolwork and of any other form of activity. His manner has been insolent, both to his grandmother and to other adults. The grandmother apparently wants to do the right thing for the boy but does not know how to go about it. In addition, she is unable to work and has to depend upon relief agencies for support.

George's excuse for failing in his schoolwork is the fact that the subjects offered him are too simple. He claims that if he could elect subjects like Greek and philosophy he would be an excellent student. His failure to adjust socially is also explained by him as resulting from the lack of opportunity to meet the right kind of fellows and girls. He has never recognized his own responsibility for his shortcomings but has always placed the blame for his failures upon other agencies, including the church and the government.

Physical examination indicates that glandular treatment is desirable, but George and his grandmother are too indolent to follow the treatment prescribed, even though it would cost them nothing. At the age of eighteen, he was compelled to leave school but refused to accept a job within his abilities. Moreover, his grandmother has been able to have his relief allotment continued on the basis that he is ill and unable to work.

He has not come into conflict with the police, mainly because he is too indolent to get into serious difficulties. He hangs around the neighborhood, entertaining groups of younger boys with stories of his prowess. This activity may lead eventually to his being taken into custody. The boy is sick and should be treated, but as yet no one has had the authority to compel the grandmother or himself to have him accept the needed treatment.

Henrietta Wanted a Home Like Other Girls

Henrietta's parents have been separated since her infancy. She has had a good home with her grandmother, but as she grew older she felt the lack of family life and began to resent the fact that she did not have a home "like the other girls." Consequently, she has been wayward, a truant, and has shown no respect for authority. Her explanation for her conduct is that her parents did what they wanted to do, so why can't she?

She was a consistent failure in her schoolwork and at one time she ran away from home and was placed in the custody of the children's court. The fact that she has always been a delicate girl intensified the problem, as the grandmother is overprotective, although most cooperative with the agencies that have been trying to help her granddaughter.

At the age of sixteen, Henrietta received her employment certificate and was employed in a cafeteria as a waitress. Later, she contracted pneumonia and was sent to a hospital, where it was found that she has diabetes, for which she is now under treatment.

It is true that one cause of adolescent maladjustment or delinquency may be found in the fact that the children of broken homes have inherited those personality characteristics of either or both parents which caused the marital friction and the final break. However, the broken home itself deprives adolescents of any supporting props that might have kept them straight. For this reason, some writers claim that the family unit should be kept intact, even though parents cannot get along together. If both parents are unstable, the adolescent has little potentiality of normal adjustment. If one parent is definitely responsible for the discord in the home and the other is emotionally stable, a young person would probably have more chance of achieving desirable adjustment if he remained with the emotionally stable parent and the other were completely removed from the situation. The sensible solution is for both parents to take their marital and parental responsibilities seriously, so that the home may represent closely knit family unity.

In this connection, Baber presents several ideas concerning the meaning of the broken home. He also draws an interesting comparison between the possible effects of divorce upon children and life in a family where there is constant bickering between the parents.[1]

Another worth-while discussion of children's relations with their parents and young people's reactions to discord in the family and the presence of stepparents can be found in "The Adolescent in the Family."[2]

What should be the relationship between adolescents and their stepparents?

The presence in the home of a stepparent is often the basis of emotional unrest among young people. It is a family situation in which great tact and understanding must be practiced by everyone. The bringing into the intimate relations of family life of a comparatively or completely strange person, entitled by his position in the family to a certain amount of authority, is likely to cause some degree of conflict, no matter how cooperative each member of the family may be. The period in the child's life in which the stepparent comes into the family, the cause of the actual parent's absence from the home, and the attitude of the child toward the latter are factors which must be considered in a discussion of this relationship.

No matter how much independence of action a young person may consider to be his right, it is normal for him at the same time to desire security and affection in his home relationships. The presence in the home of an uncooperative or disagreeable parent, the absence of one or both parents, or the presence of a stepparent may seem to deny a child that feeling of security which he craves.

If one parent is removed from the family by death, parental separation, or divorce, the effect upon a child of this

[1] Baber, Ray E., "Marriage and the Family," pp. 488–495, McGraw-Hill Book Company, Inc., New York, 1939.

[2] Burgess, E. W., chairman, "The Adolescent in the Family," Report of the Subcommittee on the Function of Home Activities in the Education of the Child, White House Conference on Child Health and Protection, pp. 116–157, D. Appleton-Century Company, Inc., New York, 1934.

breaking up of normal family unity may be either that the child becomes more closely bound to the remaining parent or that the void caused by the absence of the other parent leads the child to experience a feeling of great loneliness. The latter condition is likely to occur if the absent parent had been much loved by the child.

The bringing into the home of a kindly, understanding stepparent may do much to bring back the atmosphere of family unity, especially if the child is young enough to form new attachments and thus gradually forget the absent parent. As half sisters and brothers appear in the family, the attitude of the older child toward them is influenced to a great extent by the parental attitude toward him in relation to the younger children. If all the children are treated alike, especially by the new parent, many half brothers and sisters are as devoted to one another as are real brothers and sisters.

It is more difficult for an adolescent to adjust to new family relationships than it is for a young child to do so. The older girl or boy has become accustomed to certain routines of family behavior and, consequently, he may be unwilling or unable to include another person in the family unit. A strong bond of affection may have developed between the teen ager and the remaining parent. Hence, the new parent may be viewed as an interloper who is robbing the son or the daughter of the love or attention that is rightfully his. Or, the adolescent may have built up an ideal image of his absent parent, which causes him to be very critical of this new person who is attempting to take the place in the home of the beloved parent. Great anguish may result from the sight of this "stranger" sitting in the favorite chair of the absent parent or using articles around the house that are closely associated with memories of him.

As has been said earlier, maturing adolescents tend to resent too great restriction of their conduct. Even in well-adjusted family units, parents find that it is not always easy to guide their teen-age children toward socially desirable behavior. It is often very difficult for a new parent to win the cooperation of an adolescent stepchild in matters concerning the latter's activities. No matter how tactfully and sympathetically the young person is approached, there is likely to be a suspicion of adult motives.

One resentful seventeen-year-old boy admitted that his new stepmother did not interfere with his activity. In fact, she was more lenient with him than his mother had been. "But," said he, "I am just waiting. She is a regular snake in the grass. She is all smiles and honey now. She thinks she can fool me and make me forget Mother, and then she will tell me off. She can wind Father around her little finger but I'm on to her game." As a matter of fact, this woman had known and admired the boy's mother. The two women had been close friends, and, during the last illness of the mother, the latter had asked the other woman to look after her husband and son.

This stepmother was genuinely sorry for the boy and very fond of him. She also respected his loyalty to his own mother. She was not able to break down his antagonistic attitude toward her until she herself became ill as a result of nursing him through a long and critical illness. As a result, they became fast friends, but the boy's feeling for her is that of a boy toward a loved older sister rather than a mother.

Not all stepmothers or stepfathers are so wise or so well equipped to meet a situation of this kind as the woman just described. The stepparent of an adolescent is often afraid of his new son or daughter. Sometimes, the more he tries to win over the young person, the more mistakes he makes. The stepparent may be too lenient. One of the reasons for Ralph's waywardness was the fact that his stepfather hesitated to discipline the boy, for fear of endangering the friendship that existed between them.

Ralph's Stepfather Was Too Kindly

Until he was sixteen years old, Ralph was a fine lad. He was making a good home and school adjustment and had reached his senior year at high school. Then, for no apparent reason, he changed. He became boisterous and a constant source of trouble. He was abusive, argumentative, and given to truancy. He became involved in difficulties with other boys and was accused of being the father of an unborn child. Although he denied this, he did admit that he had had illicit relations with girls. The boy seems unable or unwilling to distinguish between right and wrong.

His own father had died when he was young, but he and his stepfather were very friendly with each other. The stepfather has always been interested in the boy and very kind to him but, in order to avoid the development of any antagonism between them, was always a little hesitant about disapproving of the boy's actions. Ralph's mother is very much concerned about her son's behavior and feels that it might have been better if her husband had exercised his authority, even though it was that of a stepfather. Ralph may fail to be graduated if he does not improve. He does not seem to be bothered by this fact, but neither is he interested in leaving school to go to work.

Again, stepparents, no matter how honest their intentions, are normal human beings, with all a normal person's emotional reactions. They are sometimes driven by their stepchildren's attitude to lose their own emotional control. This may cause family disagreement, not only between themselves and the children but also between themselves and their mates.

If there is disharmony between the adolescent and the new

parent, the cause may be found in the uncooperative attitude of the young person himself, of the new member of the family, or of the remaining parent. Sometimes the real parent may be torn between his loyalty to his child and his love for his new mate. Consequently, an attempt at compromise between the two loyalties may lead to a tension that is recognized by all three and resented by the two victims of the disturbed emotional attitude. Sometimes, a situation of this kind cannot be adjusted until the young person leaves the family home.

Adolescents are often uncertain as to how they should refer to the new mother or father. This problem may arise, even though there is a very good relationship between the stepparent and the adolescent. The young person dislikes to call the new parent by the term that was used for the actual parent. One of several procedures can be followed. If the stepparent is not much older than the adolescent, the use of the first name seems to work well. If the latter had been accustomed to call his actual parent Mother or Father, the terms "Ma" or "Pa," or "Mom" or "Dad" can be used.

Another factor that needs consideration is whether or not a child should assume the surname of the stepfather. This is a legal matter, but no general rules can be given for making the change. If the child is very young when the mother remarries, this may be wise. If, however, the child has reached adolescence, he may wish to continue his own identity by using his own father's surname.

The introduction of a stepparent to friends and acquaintances may also lead to embarrassment, unless the young person can be objective about it. If the surnames are different, the mother can be introduced in this fashion: "My mother, Mrs. Brown," accompanied by a comment concerning the stepchild's esteem for the new parent. If the stepfather is to be introduced, the boy or girl should say, "This is Mr. Brown, my second father. He is just grand!" or something to that effect.

RELATIONS AMONG SISTERS AND BROTHERS

What should be done about quarrels among brothers and sisters?

If disagreements among adolescent brothers and sisters are not too frequent and if they are not born of fundamental resentments, they are both natural and desirable. Sister-brother relationships give a young person opportunities for practice in adjusting to his peers. An only child misses this fundamental social training, in that he is denied exercise in adjusting to differing personalities and slightly different age interests in the intimate relationships of the family group.

Even though young people are the children of the same parents and are exposed to relatively similar environmental stimulations, all the children of a family do not possess similar temperaments, share similar interests, or think similar thoughts. There are bound to be differences of opinion about many things. However, if courtesy and consideration for others is the habitual attitude in a home, there will be no lasting resentments among the young people, and a temporary disagreement will very soon become a subject of amusing reminiscence.

Age differences may be the basis of sister-brother discord. Younger children tend to resent domination of them by older children, no matter how well-intentioned such apparent domination may be. The older boys and girls often think that the little ones are "getting away with murder" because the latter seem to be enjoying privileges that had been denied the teen agers when they were children. The tendency on the part of children to tease older brothers and sisters is another cause of quarrels.

Parental attitude is an important factor in the relationships that exist among the children. If parents are careful to accord to each child the rights and privileges to which he is entitled and at the same time expect individual responsibilities to be assumed cheerfully, there is usually an excellent attitude among the children toward one another. No member of the family should be granted privileges that are denied others, unless there is a valid reason for the denial and all the children understand the situation. The same principle holds for the granting of special privileges.

In the stories that follow, Adele's parents probably were correct in limiting her freedom during early adolescence, but they handled the matter badly. Olive's father did not really favor her sister, but the latter was more cooperative and the father was not by nature a pleasant person.

Adele Craves Affection

Adele is small, unattractive in appearance, and of slow mentality. She also suffers from instability of the knee joints, owing to patellae that slip to the side. This condition is not serious if she is careful not to exercise too much. At the age of eighteen, she was still a second-year student at high school but convinced that she would be graduated eventually and become a teacher.

She is the oldest of five children and is very unhappy at home. Adele has always been antagonistic toward her father, claiming that he dislikes her and will give her no privileges because of the fact that some years ago he had an affair with a woman—an incident that Adele resented. Neither parent is very intelligent, but both have always felt that Adele did not have enough good judgment to be allowed too much freedom. Consequently, they denied her privileges that she thought were her rights, and she developed a deep resentment toward them.

The girl's behavior at school was pathetic. She reminded one of a young puppy anxious for attention and affection. She had a definite crush on her biology teacher and persisted in sending her flowers, being underfoot at school, and standing in the street outside the teacher's home, gazing up at the windows.

Adele also struck up a friendship with a girl who is very much younger than herself and very bright and attractive. Their common interest was their admiration for the biology teacher and a resulting deep enthusiasm for science. Adele persisted in visiting this girl, Jane, at the latter's home, in spite of the disapproval of Jane's parents. Adele's parents also frowned upon this friendship. Consequently, Adele would tell her parents that she was visiting the biology teacher, but would meet Jane.

There is nothing vicious about Adele. She is gentle, courteous, and law-abiding, but she is the victim of her own physical unattractiveness, mental slowness, and parental attitude. Recognizing her defects, she realizes that she lacks the appeal of a normal adolescent girl. At the same time, she craves attention and affection.

As a result of conferences between her parents and her adviser, the former allowed her greater liberty in her social activities, especially those connected with her church. At school, she was persuaded to give up her ambition of becoming a teacher of biology and to prepare herself for general office work.

When she was graduated last year, at the age of twenty, it was possible for her to obtain a fairly good job in a reliable business house. She has not been given work beyond her capabilities, and her conscientiousness and fine spirit of cooperation have earned for her the respect of her employers. She has developed an air of assurance, and recently announced her engagement to a boy who is in the Army.

She is still very eager to win the friendship of people who seem to possess the qualities that she admires intensely but that she herself lacks. However, she has learned to control her emotions and is more careful of her behavior toward her "ideals." Her fiancé is at present in Europe. Whether or not they will marry is of course uncertain. At least, her engagement has done much to satisfy her craving to belong to someone.

Olive's Troubles Are Emotional as Well as Physical

Olive is very unhappy at home because she believes that her father favors her sister and denies her privileges that he permits the other girl. Her mother expects her to stay at home with her all the time and will not allow her to attend motion pictures, the girl's favorite form of recreation.

Olive also has a hearing difficulty, which tends to exaggerate her suspiciousness of people. Besides, her teeth were in very bad condition, because the family was unable to pay for their treatment.

The girl was taking a dressmaking course in an academic high school, but she refused to attend classes. She was called to court by the attendance officer, but neither she nor her parents appeared. Her case was referred to the Bureau of Child Guidance and she was interviewed by a psychiatrist. In this interview, she claimed that she wanted to be a nurse but that she had been told that she would be more successful in a vocational school. Unfortunately, her sister, who is brighter than she, was attending the same school and was doing good work. Although Olive herself did not object to a transfer to a vocational high school, her parents felt that she should do as well as her sister and that it would be a disgrace to the family to have a daughter attending a vocational school.

Neither the family nor the school had any control over the girl. She was negative, evasive, stubborn, and resentful. She would have gained a personal satisfaction if her father had been forced to go to the court because of her behavior, since she bitterly resents the beatings that he has given her. Her attitude at home became so antagonistic and her work in school so poor that her parents finally agreed to Olive's transfer to a vocational school, where she could learn how to operate a power machine.

Olive is making a good adjustment in her new school and is grateful to her former advisers for having arranged the transfer, although she will not admit it. Her teeth are being taken care of and her teachers have been advised of her hearing difficulty. Her school attitude has improved markedly, but her attitude toward her family is still most undesirable. She is made to feel that she is the black sheep of the family.

The only solution for this situation seems to be for Olive to leave home when she has received sufficient training to enable her to earn her own living. However, as soon as she is able to help with the family finances, the family attitude toward her may change.

Parents should not dare to "play favorites" with their children. They must be careful that their attitude toward each child is such that antagonisms are not aroused. A delicate baby does not necessarily remain a delicate child and adolescent. As soon as he gains normal health, he should be expected to receive the same treatment as is given to the other children in the family. There should be no ugly duckling or Cinderella in the family.

Much has been said and written about girls' being the father's favorites and boys' the mother's. This situation does not necessarily exist. If a child, whether boy or girl, looks like or has the personality characteristics of a beloved mate, there is a tendency on the part of the parent to feel especially drawn to that child. It is equally easy to discover and dislike traits in a child that are disliked in a mate. An amusing corollary of this fact is the quickness with which a parent may be heard to say, "He is just like his father!" or "That is her mother all over again!"

Must an only child be spoiled? Not necessarily. Because of a common belief that only children are pampered and petted unduly, parents of only children are sometimes tempted to be overobjective and almost too strict in their guidance of an only child. According to a study reported in "The Adolescent in the Family," by Burgess,[1] only children are emotionally more closely tied to and more dependent on their parents than are other children, but they also tend to be better integrated into the social group and to follow social codes more fully than do other children. Middle children seem to have more social contacts than do other children, but they may feel more self-conscious. In general, however, it is probably true that family relationships are dependent upon many factors and that no one factor can be held accountable, of itself, for any family adjustment or maladjustment that may be apparent.

Unless parents themselves set an example of quarreling or give in to one child to the exclusion of others, there is little stimulation for dissension among young people. If a quarrel does arise over individual rights or responsibilities, the parent should keep out of it, unless one child is definitely unfair in his accusation of or demands from another. The parent must always stand on the side of justice. If an older brother teases a younger brother or sister, tempting as this may be, the parents should discourage rather than encourage such an attitude on the part of the boy. No adolescent is always right, and very often an adolescent must be taught to recognize this fact.

Should brothers and sisters borrow one another's possessions?

No one should use anything belonging to another person except by permission of the owner of the borrowed article. In

[1] Burgess, *op. cit.*, pp. 242–243.

many homes a definite policy is established to the effect that brothers and sisters, and even parents, may ask for the loan of something that belongs to another member of the family, provided that the article is returned in good condition to the owner.

Many sisters make a practice of wearing one another's clothes, thus providing each with a more extended wardrobe. Carried out in the spirit of comradeship, this practice is highly desirable. If, however, the borrowing is one-sided, if it is against the wishes of the owner, or if the article borrowed is not returned in good condition, a parent should discourage this activity and explain his reasons for doing so to the member who persists in the practice. Under no condition should anything be used without the knowledge and consent of the owner. The right of personal property, as well as a mutual give-and-take, should be stressed in every home.

What is the extent of an adolescent's responsibility for the welfare of his younger brothers and sisters?

An adolescent should be an example of desirable behavior to the younger members of the family. Most adolescents recognize this responsibility and try to live up to it. However, they dislike intensely to be held up by their parents as a model. They do not want their actions to be under constant scrutiny and criticism in the light of the possible effects of their behavior upon little Johnny, Mary, or Joe. Neither do they take kindly to criticism from the younger children. Parents should not allow the latter to interfere unduly with the activities of their older brothers and sisters. It is the parents' responsibility, not the children's, to decide whether or not their adolescent sons or daughters are doing desirable things.

Similarly, there are limits to the right of older boys and girls as they appoint themselves to be guardians of the morals of their younger brothers and sisters. In general, this practice is not desirable. A few years' advantage in age does not give a boy or a girl the right to dominate a younger child. This, again, is the parents' responsibility. It is permissible for an older child to suggest to a younger one that certain conduct is not desirable, but that is all. If an older boy or girl notices that a younger child is developing a bad habit, he should take up the matter with his parents. Where there is a mutual attitude of liking and respect among children of different ages, suggestions made by either to the other are usually accepted in the friendly spirit in which they are given.

In large families, it is sometimes necessary for younger children to be placed temporarily in the care of older ones. At such times, the authority of the older child should be as definite as that of the parent; but the latter must be sure that this temporary authority is used with discretion.

Parents must not expect too much from their adolescent children in the matter of taking responsibility for the care of the younger children. A teen-age boy or girl should not become a slave of the family. Adolescents should rarely be asked to take younger children with them to social engagements. Each group should have social activities suited to its own age interests. Five years' difference in age is significant when one is fifteen and the other is ten. There is no appreciable age difference when one is forty and the other thirty-five. Parents must remember this fact and discourage a young child from tagging along with his adolescent brother or sister.

No boy or girl objects to giving up some of his free time in order to care for younger children, if this does not happen too often. One member of the family (often the oldest girl) should not always be the one to sacrifice her plans in order to stay home with her little brothers or sisters. This is especially annoying to a girl if an older brother is never asked to make a similar sacrifice. Parents have failed to plan an equitable distribution of family responsibilities if adolescents resent the younger children and if they look upon each new baby as a burden on their own shoulders. Of course, a mother's unexpected illness may make it necessary for an older daughter to take charge of household affairs. This situation should be no more than temporary; and all the members of the family, including the father, should share in performing home chores until the mother is well again or until other arrangements can be made.

At this point, a word should be said for the overworked mother. Although children should not be asked to assume an unfair share of family responsibility, every adolescent should be expected to give his or her mother some assistance in the care of the home. The mother should not be expected to do everything. Father, as well as children, should help with the household chores, marketing, looking after younger children, and the like. Even little tots should be trained to take care of their own toys and to perform simple little tasks around the home. If routine duties are well organized, the doing of them can be turned into a kind of game in which each member of the family vies with others in doing his job well and cheerfully. In such homes there are rarely neurotic mothers, disgruntled fathers, or resentful adolescents.

EFFECT UPON ADOLESCENTS OF THE ATTITUDES OF GRANDPARENTS AND OTHER RELATIVES

Why do relatives cause dissension in the home?

Much has been written concerning the effect upon children of interfering relatives. The problem may be serious during the childhood of an individual. Some doting grandparents or aunts or uncles intentionally or unintentionally spoil the child. Others are very generous with their advice to parents concerning the proper rearing of children. On the whole, a young child is not usually too much affected by this interference except to the extent that he may learn to wheedle out of his relatives certain privileges that are denied him by his parents.

During adolescence, however, there may be a definite clash of personalities. It is often difficult for an adolescent to accept parental guidance of his behavior. It is almost impossible for him to tolerate any attempts at control of it on the part of other relatives. Moreover, if a grandparent lives in the home of the adolescent, there may be a constant rivalry between the teen ager and the grandparent for the attention that each craves.

Too often, a grandparent demands little attentions from an adolescent, which in themselves are unimportant but which loom large to the older person if they are not granted. An intelligent parent usually learns to accept his growing child's apparent dislike of demonstrated affection. A grandparent may not be able to accept the will for the deed, and he may become unduly miserable because of his grandchildren's apparent neglect of him. If he voices his hurt, the young people are torn between pity for the older person and annoyance at the criticism of their own behavior. At one and the same time, an adolescent may feel that a grandparent is a nuisance around the house and experience a consciousness of guilt because of this feeling.

Grandparents and other adult relatives outside the immediate family circle are prone to be very much interested in the social activities, dress, and manners of their adolescent relatives. Too often they feel called upon to give well-meant advice as they criticize both the adolescent and his parents for the young person's attitudes and behavior. In this way, many a family disagreement has been started, especially if the relative tends to place the blame for adolescent misbehavior upon the in-law parent, thus stimulating bad feeling between the parents, which in turn is reflected in adolescent attitudes.

What can be done about relatives who interfere in family life?

It is probably unpsychological to offer suggestions in the form of specific dos and don'ts, but a few seem necessary in this connection.

1. Relatives should not live with the immediate family of adolescents. There are instances that would seem to give evidence of the desirability of having grandparents live in the home of a married son or daughter. These are rare. Whenever there appears to be an excellent adjustment in an arrangement of this kind, this usually has resulted only after struggles, or because the members of the family are unusually stable persons. All old people should be enabled to have their own homes and to pay for the care that they may need in time of sickness. The feeling of independence thus stimulated will make it easier for them and their families to remain good friends. There will then be less likelihood that the family will suffer from attempts on the part of old people at a kind of domination that is really the overt expression of a basic feeling of insecurity and dependence.

In general, it is also undesirable for uncles, aunts, cousins, or married sisters and brothers to live in the close family circle for a long period of time. The presence in the home of persons who are at the same time both like and unlike the members of the immediate family creates an abnormal situation. To what extent should the relative share in household chores? Whose interests or wishes should be given first consideration—those of the immediate family or those of the relatives? These and similar problems may arise and be difficult to solve tactfully.

No matter how friendly the relationship may be, there is usually some degree of strain caused in the home by the presence of other relatives. Family discussions of personal matters cannot be so free as they otherwise would be. Family activities may have to be adjusted to meet the interests of the relatives. The sharing of family expenses, the vying for attention, and the guiding of adolescents in their behavior may all contribute to possible family dissension.

2. When young people marry, an agreement should be arrived at with the parents and other relatives of both that any children that may be born are to be reared by the parents

themselves. Grandparents and other relatives should offer no suggestions or advice unless requested to do so. This is a difficult agreement to make in the early days of marriage, when each mate is anxious that his parents will approve of the other. An objective attitude on this subject can be achieved only through education, as it touches people of all ages.

3. Both grandparents and teen-age children must be given to understand that parents, and parents alone, are responsible for the guidance of their adolescent sons' and daughters' behavior. Grandparents and other relatives should not tell young people what to do; nor, unless they are authorized to do so by the parents, should they criticize the younger members for what they have done. Adolescents must learn that they should not go to their grandparents or to other relatives for consolation if their parents deny them certain desired privileges.

4. Adolescents should be held up to a consistent standard of consideration and courtesy in their dealings with their relatives. Young people should be ready and willing to do things for members of the larger family group; but they should no more be expected to be slaves to the whims of their grandparents, uncles, and aunts, than of the whims of their younger brothers and sisters. Demands upon the time of young people for care of and attention to other members of the family should be met by the teen agers to the extent that such demands are not excessive or likely to interfere unduly with schoolwork or with rightfully earned recreational activities.

5. Young people should be expected to be on friendly terms with all members of the family and to visit them occasionally. However, parents should not demand that their adolescent sons and daughters give up their own plans in order to be present at every meeting of the older members of the family group and to be responsible for entertaining these older people, whose interests may be very different from those of teen agers.

Some of these suggestions may seem too objective and cold-blooded as applied to the relationships of people who are bound not only by ties of blood but also by ties of family affection. This possibility of criticism is granted, but it is for the preservation of family good will and affection that the suggestions are offered. Fortunately, in many homes, family interrelations are excellent. There are respect and affection on the part of the young people for the older relatives. The latter do not in any way interfere with the lives of adolescents except insofar as they show friendly interest in teen-age activities. In such families are found well-adjusted people living happy lives. There are too many family groups in which this fine adjustment has not yet been achieved, and where there are resulting friction, conflict, and unhappiness. It is to the members of such family groups that these suggestions are offered.

THE TEEN AGER AND FAMILY FINANCE

Should an adolescent have a definite allowance and how should it be used?

One of the most important responsibilities of adult life is the management of financial affairs. The handling of money is a part of the growing-up process, and every boy or girl needs experience in using money, in order to develop a better understanding of its value. An adolescent must learn that before money can be used it must be earned. If money flows too freely into the hands of a young person, he may develop a wrong notion of its worth. Hence, every teen-age schoolboy and schoolgirl should be given an allowance and should receive definite guidance in budget making.

The size of the allowance depends upon the expenses that are to be covered by it and upon the source of income. The adolescent should gradually be given more money and greater freedom in spending it. The allowance should be set up for definite purposes. Before the amount is decided upon, one or both of the parents should work out with the son or the daughter a weekly budget of expenses. If the purpose is to cover school expenses, that fact should be definitely agreed upon, and the use of the money should be restricted to that purpose.

It might be desirable to have the budget include small articles of wearing apparel, such as gloves, handerchiefs, ties, and the like. Rarely are coats, hats, suits, underclothing, etc., included in the weekly budget. These are seasonal items and cannot well be included in the weekly allowance of relatively untrained young people. However, as a boy or a girl approaches the late teens, especially if he is attending college, it might be desirable to change the weekly budget to a monthly budget, making it large enough to include most of the personal expenses. The budget should include a definite sum to be used for recreational purposes and a small amount for emergency spending, with the understanding that if the money is not needed it will be deposited in a savings account, either through the school bank or in a personally arranged account in the local savings bank.

An adolescent should be held to a strict accounting for the expenditure of his allowance. Rarely should he be allowed to borrow on his next week's allowance; nor should he be encouraged to solicit funds from members of his family. An alert parent watches his child's spending. If it appears that the allowance is not large enough to meet reasonable expenses, it should be increased. If the young person needs money for gifts, club dues, or philanthropic purposes, the parents should expect some of this money to come out of his regular allowance. The remainder can be supplied by the parent as a gift of money to son or daughter.

The size of an allowance is less important than the training derived from its use. Many generous parents feel that an allowance is cold and objective. They prefer to provide the money whenever it is needed or to supply it in the form of gifts. Although a young person so treated may receive more money than the one who is given an allowance, he is denied thereby the satisfaction of spending his own money and of acquiring the education that is possible through this activity.

Should adolescents be informed concerning family finances?

Yes. Adolescent boys and girls have a right to know the economic status of the family. Too many parents seem to feel that they should grant all of their son's or daughter's requests for money, even though doing so involves foolish personal sacrifice. "Keeping up with the Joneses" is a bad attitude to encourage in a young person. The state of the family exchequer should not be kept a dark secret. Young children should know that parents cannot afford to satisfy all of their wants. Adolescents should be fully informed concerning the family's financial limitations. They should be included in family conferences relative to what should or should not be purchased in terms of available funds. Such matters as rent, cost of clothes, and the amount to be spent for a summer vacation should be discussed frankly and intelligently with teen-age members of the family.

A son or a daughter should sometimes enjoy the privilege of deciding what should be done with any extra money that is available. Young people should have the opportunity to sacrifice some of their own interests for the benefit of other members of the family. Of course, they need parental guidance in such matters. One young girl insisted upon giving up her college course when her father died, believing that it was her duty to support her mother. Since the girl was thoroughly acquainted with the state of the family finances, her mother was able to convince her that, if for a few years they denied themselves certain accustomed luxuries, the girl would be able to complete her education so that they both could enjoy the larger income that would result from the extended training.

Whether there is much or little money in the family, its members are drawn closer together if they share a full knowledge of the extent to which occasional extravagances or temporary denials of wants are in order. If parents are sincere in their desire to do all that they can for their children within their financial limitations, young people usually reciprocate by modifying their own desires to meet the family income.

What should a teen ager do with the money earned from a part-time or a full-time job?

Young people who are engaged in a full- or a part-time job often are much concerned over what proportion of their wages they should give to their parents. Some parents expect a working child to turn over to them the entire salary. The boy or the girl then is given an allowance by his parents. Other parents do not require their working sons or daughters to give them any part of the money earned. These procedures are both unwise. Half of the satisfaction of earning money is gained from the management of it. On the other hand, no young person should be allowed to expect his parents to support him entirely if he is in the position of earning money toward his own support. It is true, however, that an adolescent who earns money needs guidance and supervision in spending it.

A gainfully employed adolescent should share with his parents the cost of his living expenses. The amount of money that he should give to his parents for board or room will depend upon the size of his pay check and of the other expenses that must be covered by it. A high-school or a college student often works at a part-time job in order to defray some of his school expenses. If his parents do not need his financial assistance, the amount of money that he gives to them may be very small, perhaps no more than fifty cents a week. However, even that small amount may stimulate in the adolescent a feeling of pride that he is a wage earner in the family.

If the adolescent is working full time, he and his parents should agree concerning the amount of his salary to be turned over to them. The remainder of the money should be his to budget in terms of his needs and interests. In this way he develops gradually an understanding of the value of money and a feeling of financial independence.

Most adolescents are enabled through guidance to use money with discretion. The story of the twins presents an excellent example of adolescents who demonstrated ability to meet financial, as well as other, difficulties; and, although Anna was disturbed by the change in her family's financial situation, she was able to meet this problem, as well as her health condition, because of the fine attitude that existed among the members of the family.

Twins Make Good

John and Paul, twin brothers, achieved scholastic success in spite of frail health and disturbed home conditions. At the age of sixteen, they were honor students in their senior year of high school. All their schoolwork was excellent, but they were exceptionally able in science.

Shortly after the birth of the twins, their father had his neck broken as a result of an accident on the job. Because of the lack of competent legal advice, his case was settled for $500. Since the accident, he has been suffering from periodic amnesia. He wanders away from the home at intervals and sometimes stays away for weeks. He cannot keep a job, because of his extremely nervous condition.

When the boys were fourteen years old, their mother died as the result of an accident, and a baby brother also died less than a year later. As the family had no relatives and practically no money, the boys tried to keep the home together by working at part-time jobs while going to school. They accepted their father's behavior with unusual understanding; and in spite of their great interest in science and their strong desire to continue their education on the college level, John and Paul decided that it was their duty to go to work, upon graduation from high school.

However, they were led to realize that their physical frailty and their lack of preparation for any specific type of work would interfere with desirable job placement. Because of their unusual ability in science, interested agencies made it possible for the boys to go to college and devote all their time to study, without the strain and distraction of part-time work. Their scholastic achievement has more than repaid those agencies for what they have done for these fine young men, who already are giving evidence of creative work in scientific research. Fortunately, the father's physical and mental condition has improved and he is now working and helping toward his sons' college expenses.

Glandular Disturbance and Home Difficulties

Anna was failing in her work because she could not concentrate. She was also suffering from a serious skin condition. To add to her troubles, financial conditions in the home were desperate. These were new experiences to Anna, for she had had a happy childhood as a member of a closely knit family of moderate means. Her father was a shoemaker, whose success in his own business had enabled him to provide a comfortable one-family house for his family.

When Anna was about thirteen years old, her father contracted typhoid fever and was advised by his physician to live in the country for a few years, in order to regain his health. Consequently, he purchased a farm and found a job in a near-by town, to which he traveled daily. The cost of his illness, combined with his lowered income, made it impossible for him to keep up his payments on his properties. Hence, the holders of his mortgages on his home and his farm fore-closed. As a result, the father's mind was affected and for several years he was a patient in a hospital for the mentally ill.

Meanwhile, the mother, with the aid of welfare organiza-tions, struggled to support herself and her three children. The father, after his release from the hospital, opened a small shoe store, from which he derived a very modest income.

Anna was a bright, conscientious girl, but she was dis-turbed by the home situation and by the fact that not only had her skin become worse but a marked growth of hair had begun to develop on her chin. Through her school adviser, it was made possible for Anna to be examined at an endocrine-gland clinic, where it was discovered that she was suffering from pituitary imbalance. Treatment was provided for her at very little expense to the family. So rapid was her improve-ment that she was soon able to concentrate upon her studies and her skin condition was corrected.

Anna was graduated from her high school with a good rating. She secured an excellent office position and has been able to finance her sister's college education. Anna has become a very attractive young woman and is now engaged to a handsome young soldier. She and her family are pathetically grateful to those who helped her in her adjustment.

There are homes in which material advantages are stressed beyond the more subtle but fundamental ideals of stable home influences. Parents may sacrifice their own as well as their children's chances of experiencing normal family relations, because they are too eager to supply their children with unnecessary luxuries. Unfortunately, conditions may arise that necessitate a mother's working, away from the home. However, in many cases of working mothers, the family unity would be increased by the mother's staying in the home, even though the family style of living might be simplified thereby. The story of Eric is an example of too-great emphasis upon the accumulation of money.

Eric Is Neglected by His Parents

In spite of a high intelligence quotient, Eric failed in all his subjects during his first term in high school. He was a truant and cut his classes. If he did come to school, he arrived late. He constantly denied that these things were true, gave false excuses for his conduct, pleaded illness, and would not face reality. According to the Rorschach test, the boy showed definite emotional disturbance.

Eric has a bad home life. Both parents work and no meals are prepared at home. The parents seem to be unable to supervise the boy and are very little concerned about him.

Although the parents were informed of the boy's need for affection and a normal home life, they made no effort at adjustment. As he was sixteen years old, they encouraged him to leave school, even though there was no financial need. At present, he is an apprentice electrician at a navy yard but is not succeeding very well, as he is still concerned about the home situation.

Many other examples could be cited as evidence of the effects upon maturing young people of the economic status of the home and the family attitude toward it. It is no disgrace to be poor. It is no special honor to be rich. Whatever the economic status of the home, young people should be aware of it and, with their parents, should adjust to what they have. If improvement is needed, they should do their share in working toward it.

Parental Responsibility for the Social Life of Young People

Should parents allow teen-age boys and girls to choose their own friends?

In general, the answer to this question should be in the affirmative. Parents need not be too much worried about adolescent friendships if, during childhood, the son or the daughter has been encouraged to have desirable playmates and if the family live in a neighborhood in which the adolescent is brought into contact with desirable young people.

When a parent is tempted to criticize the companion of a teen-age son or daughter, he should make sure that he has a valid reason for his attitude. Too often fathers and mothers (especially mothers) dislike to see their children form associations that tend to exclude the parents themselves. It is this fear of losing the child's complete loyalty that may cause a parent, sometimes unconsciously, to find something objectionable in the young person's new pal. The difficulty in such instances lies not in the adolescent's choice of friends but in the adult's attitude of possessiveness. If this attitude is present, a young person is quick to recognize and resent it.

A young person who has confidence in his parents' judgment is eager to have parental approval of his friendships. In those cases where the interest in the undesirable companion is so strong that parental disapproval is not heeded, one of the best procedures to be followed by the parent is that of encouraging the son or the daughter to bring the friend to the home, where he may meet other members of the family and other friends of the adolescent. Usually, a person who is brought into an environment in which people act differently from the way in which he himself behaves is at a disadvantage. Hence, the son or the daughter sooner or later tends to recognize those characteristics in his friend which are displeasing to his parents, and the friendship may end. Many parents have used this method very successfully. Although it is difficult to welcome an undesirable person into one's home, the results are usually worth the effort, since little if anything is gained by a parent's demand that a young person give up an undesirable friendship. In fact, parental objection may actually increase the bond between him and the person of whom the parent disapproves.

The situation is especially trying when an adolescent becomes too much interested in a member of the opposite sex of whom the parents do not approve. The surest way to throw a girl into a boy's arms or to stimulate a boy toward a deep interest in a girl is for parents openly to disapprove of the relationship. The fact that the boy or the girl in question may be of a different faith, national group, or economic or educational level does not constitute a valid reason for parental objection to a friendship. An adolescent may not be at all interested in a particular member of the opposite sex as a possible mate unless or until adults put the idea into his head by an expression of their fears.

Young people should not have their friends selected for them by their parents. That is the right of the individual himself. Too much parental praise of a certain boy or girl may cause an adolescent to be repelled rather than attracted toward the object of all this approval. The spirit of developing independence cannot be coerced. As was suggested earlier, the extent to which parents and their children can agree concerning the latters' choice of friends is a part of the whole parent-child relationship. If a parent wishes his adolescent child to select desirable companions, he must start to work toward this end during the young person's early childhood by developing in him desirable attitudes toward his playmates.

*At what age should young people be allowed by their parents to
date members of the opposite sex?*

No definite age can be given as the most desirable one for
young people to start to "date." Judging by some of the
young people one sees strolling along hand in hand on the
streets of any town or the roads of any rural area, it would
appear that age has nothing to do with it. To adult question-
ing of their behavior, some young adolescents cite the case of
Juliet, who at the age of fourteen died for love of Romeo. The
argument that those were different days has little effect upon
the person in his early teens who is going through the puppy-
love stage. One way of meeting the situation is that of
providing for and encouraging so much participation in interesting group activities that the young person has little time
for individual dating until he is mature enough to be intelligent about it.

The above suggestions are directed toward those parents
who recognize the fact that, sooner or later, normal boys and
girls have the urge to pair off, and that for emotionally controlled young people this is both wholesome and desirable.
Now a word to those parents who refuse to allow their adolescent children any association with members of the opposite
sex until they are old enough (in their parents' opinion) to
marry. This attitude is often found among possessive parents
who cannot tolerate the thought that a beloved son or
daughter may develop loyalty to or affection for anyone
except themselves.

Another type of parent who holds this attitude is the one
who himself grew up in an environment of close chaperonage,
especially for girls. Such parents are unwilling to allow their
teen-age children to engage in any social activities except in
parental company. They will not allow their adolescent
children to bring friends to the home, nor will they permit
them to go outside the home for social relaxation. They are
then shocked if they discover that the young people are

engaging in the denied social activities without parental knowledge. An ingenious young person can find many opportunities for deceiving his parents. Why force him to do so?

At what time should an adolescent be expected to return home from a date?

The answer to this question depends upon many circumstances. In a small town, social activities can start early and end early. In large cities, where long distances between homes and places of amusement may require several hours for traveling, time schedules must be adjusted to meet such conditions.

Policies rather than specific clock requirements can be suggested. During the school week, an adolescent's social interests should be subordinated to his study needs. On his free evenings, the time schedule of his social activity should be determined by the kind of activity in which he is engaging, the distance that he must travel, and the attitudes of the group with which he is associated. A young adolescent should rarely be allowed to return home later than midnight unless he is accompanied by his parents or other responsible adults. For older adolescents, the time of return is less important. If a young person wishes to indulge in undesirable social practices, there are plenty of opportunities for him to do so at any time of the day. At present we are living on a twenty-four-hour schedule. Streets and transportation lines are used by people at all hours during the day and the night. A parent's concern need not be directed so much toward what time the young person returns home as toward where he has been and what he has been doing. However, if the parent sets a time for the adolescent's return, the latter should be expected to be punctual.

Parental attitudes toward the social life of their adolescent sons and daughters is one phase of the whole pattern of teen-age social adjustment. Many of the questions asked by young people concerning their relationship with other young people are directly or indirectly connected with their home relationships, not only from the point of view of their parents' own social activities but also in terms of family approval or disapproval of teen-age interests.

It has not been possible in this chapter to consider all the possible problems that may arise as parents attempt to guide their teen-age children's social adjustment. More detailed consideration of these problems will be found in Chap. 10.

Those parents who wish to read further on the subject may want to consult the following books:

Bossard, James H., and Eleanor S. Boll, "Family Situations" (especially, Part II), University of Pennsylvania Press, 1943.

Lloyd-Jones, Esther, and Ruth Fedder, "Coming of Age," Chap. III, Whittlesey House, McGraw-Hill Book Company, Inc., New York, 1941.

Wood, Leland Foster, and John W. Mullen, ed., "What the American Family Faces," The Eugene Hugh Publishers, Inc., Chicago, 1943.

SCHOOL ADJUSTMENT OF
YOUNG PEOPLE

Chapter 5

Teen-age Problems in School Life

A GROUP of men and women, leaders in their community, were working as volunteer helpers in a barn of an Ohio farm one summer day, sorting and packing sweet corn. Most of the members of the group were college graduates, some of them specialists in their respective fields—chemistry, journalism, education, etc. The presence of several educational leaders in the group caused the conversation to turn to a consideration of educational values. In a spirit of fun, a chemist started the discussion by asking one of the educators whether or not all his years of study were making a better corn sorter of him. This question resulted in much good-natured give-and-take. However, the conversation took on a more serious note as the younger members of the group, high-school and college students, began to ask pertinent questions concerning their own educational and school problems.

Among the questions brought up for discussion were the value of continued education versus learning on the job, the relative merits of various types of schools, the choice of majors, the extent to which students should participate in the social life of a school, teacher-student relationships, the extent to which young people should consider their parents' wishes concerning the choice of school, vocational selection, and the best methods of study. The exchange of ideas was interesting.

One or two members of the group, partly in jest and partly in earnest, contended that much of the content of high-school and college training seemed to be of little value in later adult activities. However, the educators defended their profession, and it was finally agreed that schooling gives power to an individual that an unschooled person may gain eventually, but usually only after many years of struggle and expensive failure.

The problems that arise out of an individual's school experience were not and could not be ignored or minimized in this group discussion. The questions asked by the younger members of the group are common to all young people who take their school life seriously. To meet such problems, the time, energy, and money expended by community and national leaders toward the improvement of educational facilities in America should be and are constantly increasing. Farseeing experts are preparing for the future educational needs of which many young people already are aware.

Present educational theory and practice are far from perfect and require constant revision and improvement in order to meet the needs of the group and to satisfy the interests and abilities of the individual. No matter how well the school is organized, how excellent is the curriculum, or how proficient the teaching personnel, problems will arise as individual students attempt to adjust to school life.

The American ideal of the right of every citizen to avail himself to the fullest extent of those educational opportunities which fit his needs and his interests has resulted inevitably in mass education. Large schools, oversize classes, quickly and sometimes inadequately trained teachers, too little understanding of child and adolescent psychology, a bewildering array of elective subjects on the high-school and college levels, an orgy of experimental teaching methods—all combine to develop a state of educational chaos, of which too many young people are the victims, resulting in general dissatisfaction with schools and school people.

We are now attempting educational reorganization. We believe that we are learning from the mistakes of the past and that we may be able to develop gradually throughout the nation a series of educational offerings that will meet the individual needs and interests of young Americans. We hope that our teaching techniques and teacher attitudes will be so improved that, through efficient teaching and sympathetic guidance, every boy and girl will be able to profit from any schooling into which he may be guided. We have gone a long way toward the realization of this educational ideal, but there is still much to be done.

At one time, a young person's school life was more or less divorced from his home life. Parents felt that their responsibility for the schooling of their children went no further than to have them enrolled in a school. The child's teachers were expected to carry on from that point. In the same way, school authorities excluded parents from the educational program of their pupils, except as an individual boy or girl appeared to be unwilling or unable to meet study requirements or school regulations.

There is now apparent a definite trend toward pupil-parent-teacher cooperation. Parent-teacher organizations function successfully in many communities. Through such organizations, parents and school people together are enabled to study the needs of young people and to devise ways and means of best meeting these needs.

More important, perhaps, than the formation of such parent-teacher groups is the fact that an increasing number of parents, teachers, and young people are recognizing the value of individual conferences that include the pupil, his parents, and his teacher or school adviser. It is through such conferences, started early in a young person's high-school life and continued throughout his course, that friendly relations are maintained between home and school. In this way a young person's interests, abilities, and school and future plans can become a cooperative activity. This type of intimate home-school relationship gives all those concerned a much better understanding of the importance to the growing boy or girl of a well-adjusted school life than is possible if parent, school adviser, and pupil attempt to carry out their own ideas concerning educational values independently of one another.

In the past, school administrators and curriculum makers often failed to keep pace with community progress. Consequently, many an adolescent did not get the kind of education that would best fit him for continued success in school or in his later adult activities. Tradition is an important stabilizer, and school tradition should not be treated lightly. However, traditional school practices should be continued only when such practices find their place in a changing civilization.

Our adolescent school population are fully aware of the problems connected with their schoolwork and they come to us for help. The following questions, asked by them, give an indication of some of the problems with which adolescent boys and girls are faced as they attempt to adjust themselves to successful school living. Like the questions raised by teen-age boys and girls relative to home life, these have been selected as typical of the many questions asked by them concerning school life.

1. Should a boy or a girl choose the high school that he will attend?

2. Should a boy or a girl be allowed to choose his own college?

3. Should a boy be forced to go to college if he prefers to go to work?

4. Is it better to go away from home to college or to attend a local college?

5. Why are postgraduate courses not given in high school for students who want to take special courses but who do not want to go to college?

6. Should a student who has pursued a commercial course make up subjects for college entrance or go directly to business?

7. What are desirable study conditions in the home?

8. What can be done to stop the family's loud talking or playing of the radio when one is studying?

9. Should we be given so much homework that we have no time for rest and recreation?

10. Would it be possible to allow us to do all our work at school, since home chores and a part-time job interfere with after-school studying?

11. How can a boy or a girl learn how to study?

12. How much time should a high-school student spend on homework?

13. Is it possible to be very successful in one subject and to fail in another, even though you try?

14. Is it a good habit to memorize the things that one does not understand?

15. What is wrong with study habits if a student does good classwork but fails in most of his written work?

16. Why is it hard to get up and speak in class?

17. What are the best subjects for a boy or a girl to study in college?

18. Should a student be compelled to go into an honor class if he believes that it is too difficult for him?

19. Why can't we take the courses that we want to take?

20. Should we be forced to take subjects in high school that seem to have no practical value?

21. Why do we not have more guidance when we enter high school?

22. Could the high-school course be so planned that a student could change his course after two years without losing credit for some of the work that he has completed?

23. How can a boy or a girl gain friends in high school?

24. Do you consider being very friendly with classmates a hindrance to school success?

25. Why are some students popular and others either unpopular or ignored?

26. How can one learn how to work with a group?

27. Why won't high-school students make friends with a younger boy or girl who is in the same class?

28. Why should we join clubs in high school or in college?

29. How can one get into school activities?

30. In how many social activities of the school should a student participate?

31. Should there be religious clubs in a high school?

32. What should I do to get along with teachers?

33. What can a student do about a teacher who constantly nags?

34. Can a student do anything about a teacher who has a "pet" and is unfair to other students?

35. Would it not be a good idea for students to have the same teacher in a subject for several terms?

36. Why do teachers not have more faith in their students and listen to both sides of a story?

37. Is it very serious to have a "crush" on a teacher?

38. How friendly should teachers and students be with one another?

39. What can a student do if he loses interest in his schoolwork?

40. Does part-time work interfere with school success?

When a young person enters high school, he has many adjustments to make. Learning to adapt himself to new teachers and schoolmates, deciding upon the course or subjects that he should elect, and training himself to accept personal responsibility for his success beyond what was expected of him in elementary school—all these combine to create bewilderment and perhaps serious discouragement unless there is available much sympathetic guidance and assistance in the meeting of such problems.

Further, a young person's decision concerning after-high-school plans must be given serious thought. Should he continue his education on the college level? Which college should he attend? What should be his field of major study? Should he enroll in a specialized school of higher learning? Would it be desirable for him to go directly to work after graduation from high school? Here again the influence of parents, advisers, and friends is potent.

After a young person has been admitted to the school of his choice, he is faced by problems that are closely connected with his achieving success, not only as a student but also as a member of the school group. Efficient methods and conditions of study, examination-passing techniques, value of curricular offerings, participation in extraclassroom activities, and the desirability of engaging in part-time work while attending school may cause anxiety in the high-school or college student.

Equally perplexing to these young people may be questions that concern their relationships with their teachers and fellow schoolmates. How friendly should be their attitudes toward their teachers? What may they expect from their teachers and advisers? To what degree should they engage in the social activities of the school? To what extent should they form intimate relationships with fellow students?

We must keep in mind that an adolescent brings to his school life a set of habit patterns and interests that have been developing gradually through his childhood and that have been and still are much influenced by his home relationships. Often, a young person's habitual attitude toward himself and other people may make his attempted adjustment to his school life very difficult.

The following stories of actual young people who found adjustment to school life difficult may assist the reader in recognizing some of the factors that militate against successful and happy school experiences. Fortunately, some of these adolescents were helped to make satisfactory school adjustments. Others of them had to find their adjustment outside the school. Still others are so emotionally disturbed that little or no adjustment, either in or out of the school, seems possible at the present. They need special mental-hygiene treatment.

John Knew All the Answers

At fifteen, John was tall and attractive but stubborn and self-willed. He knew all the answers. His mother and aunts, according to him, meant well but did not know what it was all about. His teachers merited nothing but contempt. The only one who deserved any respect was his policeman father, except that John was not quite sure that his father was quick enough on the trigger.

At home his attitude was one of silent tolerance. In school he maintained a habitual attitude of passive resistance to any suggestion to him that he use the ability that he possessed. His answer to almost every question put to him was a shrug of his shoulders and "I don't know." He appeared to doubt the sincerity of anyone who wished to help him and was suspicious of adult intentions. The longest speech that he made to his school adviser was to the effect that all teachers were crazy. He had read it in the newspaper and "the psychologists say so." He was intelligent enough to admit that he knew that success could not be won without work, but he was not interested in success.

His family expected him to go to college, but he was negative in his response to their suggestions. It was finally agreed by the family and the school adviser that his attitude be ignored. At home, he was never requested directly to do anything nor was he drawn into family conversations or activity. At school, he was treated the same way. No comment was made concerning unprepared homework. He was not called upon to recite in class and his examination papers were not returned to him.

After about five months of this treatment, John walked into his adviser's office and said, "Lay off and call the family off. I've had just about as much as I can stand and I've brains enough to know when I'm licked. Fix up my program. I am going to college, and believe me, I'm going to be on top."

He carried out his promise. He was graduated from high school with honors and is now doing very well at college. His younger brothers are complaining that no child could be so good as he expects them to be. They have to do everything that their parents or teachers say, or he settles with them.

A Victim of Parental Ambition

"Speak up, Jean. Why don't you answer the teacher? She is always like that. I have to do all of her talking for her. Now stop sitting there looking at us as if you did not know how to talk English. What can I do with her? She embarrasses me wherever we go." And on and on went Jean's mother, as she sat in conference with Jean and Jean's school adviser. Jean, an attractively well-groomed girl and a doctor's daughter, looked much more adult than her fifteen years. However, she wilted visibly as her mother continued her harangue.

The interview had been called because Jean seemed to be suffering from a stutter, either actual or affected. Some of the girl's teachers suspected that she was using this stutter as a means of covering up lack of school preparation. However, there were times when Jean seemed so overcome by fear that it was decided that the stutter was real, but functional rather than organic.

The economic situation of the family was excellent. The father, a successful physician, attempted to dominate the destinies of his children. He had forced one boy to prepare for medicine, in spite of the lad's interest in art. Another son had run away from home because his father would not allow him to study mechanics. Jean herself was expected to finish high school and then to marry a wealthy older man, whom the father already had selected. Jean's mother was ambitious, nervous, and temperamental. She looked upon her daughter's lack of interest in social advancement as a punishment for some sin which she (the mother) must have committed but which she could not recall.

It is little wonder that a girl should become emotionally maladjusted in such a home situation. Left to herself, Jean was a charming and unspoiled young person. It was only when she was reminded of the fact that she was a disappointment to her parents that she became disturbed. She wanted to do well in her studies and attempted each evening to prepare the home assignments carefully. However, her mother was accustomed to burst into the girl's room, reminding her that she should be sure to have her work well prepared for the next day and that she should talk up in class so that her father would not be angry. Consequently, when Jean attempted to recite in class, she recalled not the subject matter that she had studied but the admonitions of her mother. She would then become so emotionalized that it was impossible for her to speak.

The only solution seemed to be that of sending Jean away from home to a boarding school, where she would be free from the emotionalized atmosphere. Her parents were loath to accept this suggestion, as they feared that Jean would go to pieces if she were away from their watchful care. It was only when the emphasis was laid upon the social advantages of a select boarding-school education for their daughter that parental consent was obtained for the change.

A school was found that met the parents' social standards and, at the same time, was known for its excellent attention to individual students. Jean is now attending this school, where she is making slow but satisfactory adjustment. Her letters to her adviser indicate that she is happier now than she has ever been. Her one worry is that she may be expected to spend her vacations at home. In her last letter she begged her adviser to recommend a camp to her parents that would be fashionable enough to suit them. Her own words were "Please pick a camp where I can have a good time with real boys and girls, but make Mother think it's the last word in style."

Lulu May Came Out of the Fog

At fourteen years of age, Lulu May decided to leave school. She was tall for her age, very attractive, and exceptionally bright. Her mother, a widow, was heartbroken by the attitude of her only child. Any plea that she give better attention to her studies was met by sullenness or the complaint, "What, again! I have told you a thousand times that I cannot concentrate."

Since she was too young to leave school, her advisers gave her special attention, helped her with her home assignments, permitted her to be an assistant in the school-guidance office and, in general, treated her more as an adult than as a child. She gradually began to improve in her work. Each high mark was treated by her mother and school advisers as a great personal victory. Although she still insisted that she was going to leave school as soon as she could, her bad moments became less frequent as she continued to earn creditable promotion from grade to grade.

When she was sixteen, she became so interested in arranging a program that would earn graduation in three and one half years that she forgot her repeated desire to leave school. Upon graduation, because of her maturity, ability, and attractiveness, she was able to obtain a very good office position, where she soon earned promotion.

About a year after her graduation, she asked her former high-school adviser about the desirability of her taking a few courses at an evening college, so that she would not "get stale." By the end of another year, she decided to give up her position and use the money that she had saved to start her on a full-time college program. She is making excellent progress in preparing herself for merchandising. She and her mother are extremely happy and her favorite expression is "It's a good thing I came out of the fog."

Handicapped but Not Discouraged

Mary, the youngest of four children, has suffered from birth with a congenital cataract. Her father and mother, her older sister, and two older brothers all worked in the clothing industry. Consequently, even as a little girl, Mary was expected to take almost complete charge of the housework.

In elementary school, Mary was in a sight-conservation class, but when she entered high school she insisted upon taking a commercial course (including stenography) because she had to get a job as soon as possible in order to help with the family support. She was a conscientious and able student, but the eyestrain connected with her studying and the care of the home presented problems that were too much for her, in spite of her eagerness to cooperate.

Social agencies became very much interested in Mary and wanted to arrange for her admission to a state school for the blind. Her parents minimized her condition and insisted that she leave school as soon as she was sixteen years old, in order to go to work. Mary, herself, very much wanted to continue her education, but she felt that it was her duty to follow her parents' wishes. The conflict between ambition and duty was so great that for a while she wished she were dead or completely blind.

After a long struggle, parental consent was finally obtained and Mary was given an opportunity to complete her high-school course at the state school for the blind. She made an excellent adjustment and was very popular with students and teachers.

Her course included preparation for both college and commercial work. In a little over a year, Mary was graduated with honors and admitted to a local college, in order to prepare herself as a teacher of the blind. She is also working part time. This bright and happy young woman is looking forward to a career of service, with deep gratitude to those who made her present success possible.

The postscript of a letter written to one of her former high-school advisers is an indication of her excellent attitude. "It makes me laugh when I think of the ten times I had to leave this letter before I could finish it. All the girls seem to be coming to me for one thing or another. Say, if I am not mistaken, my house mother is calling me now. Goodbye till next time."

Fred Was Mechanical Minded

Against his own wishes but at the instigation of his parents, Fred elected the academic course when he entered high school. Although he was above normal mentally, he was not interested in his work and became a habitual truant. He was very unhappy but was unwilling to discuss his problem. It was not until his adviser discovered that his only successful subject was art that he admitted that his one interest was mechanical drawing.

His academic program was scrapped in favor of one consisting of mechanical drawing, shopwork, and physical training; and the cooperation of the chairman of the mechanical arts department was enlisted. The boy's improvement was surprising. He no longer cut classes. His school grades were excellent, and he gave valuable service to the school.

Since the economic conditions of the family were poor, it was necessary for him to leave school for a job in his uncle's printing business. Here he is both successful and happy. Since he realizes that he can advance himself in this work if he has the proper training, he is continuing his studies at an evening high school. He is extremely grateful to his teachers who discovered his problem and who helped him with his vocational adjustment.

A Victim of Circumstances

Eugene had careful bringing up. His parents, who were professional people, gave particular attention to the setting up of a wholesome home environment. Eugene was a quiet and serious child. By the time he reached high school, he showed definite leadership ability and was selected by the faculty and the student body to direct many student activities. For example, he became president of the school traffic patrol, a much-coveted position.

Eugene was a very active boy. Although he was not an unusual musician, he played the violin well enough to become a member of the school orchestra, which was selected one year as an outstanding orchestra in the United States. Also, with his brother, he sold newspapers, which kept him very close to a routine schedule and required that he arise at five o'clock in the morning in order to complete the route and get to school on time.

The boy carried out these and other responsibilities with dispatch, although his school grades did not reflect his excellent mental ability. His many interests and activities made it difficult for him to concentrate on any one of them to the point of exceptional achievement.

Upon graduation from high school, he was admitted to one of the leading colleges. Here he was as popular with the student body as he had been at high school. Among his friends was a son of one of the deans. These two boys, with several others, developed a strong interest (as bright college freshmen often do) in philosophical discussions of life and its meaning.

At one of these bull sessions, a member of the group scoffed at the idea of the existence of ghosts. This remark became the stimulus of a boyish prank that had serious consequences. One night, Eugene and the dean's son, with two other boys, decided that they would convince their doubting pal of the existence of ghosts. Consequently, the boys procured sheets, in which they wrapped themselves, and started for their victim's dormitory.

However, they encountered an experience that they had not anticipated. Some of the citizens of the town saw them crossing the campus and became very much frightened. In spite of the disturbance that the boys caused, they continued on their way that night and succeeded in frightening the doubter.

The attitude of the townspeople acted as a new stimulus. Therefore, the next night they paraded across the campus and into a near-by cemetery and were rewarded by exciting the entire town. They got more than they bargained for. The civil authorities investigated the incident. The boys were apprehended by the police but were released to the custody of the college. Following this experience, Eugene's work at college was poor. However, by this time he had reached the age of eighteen and was inducted into the armed services.

In the Army his superior intelligence and fundamentally fine character were recognized and he was given an opportunity for special training, in which he earned considerable success. Eugene's story is an example of a boy who, as a result of excellent heritage and fine home training, had developed too great a control of youthful spirit of adventure. This incident at college during his first year away from home was a natural reaction. Because of his inherently fine ideals, the effect upon himself of the consequences of his acts might have been very serious if he had not been given an opportunity to direct his abilities and interests toward worth-while ends.

There Was Not Enough Activity in School for Donald

As a child, Donald suffered from epilepsy and gave the impression that he was mentally unbalanced. However, he completed his course in the elementary school and was admitted to high school at the age of fifteen. There he seemed unable to adjust to school rules and regulations. He wanted his own way and became violent if he was thwarted. His misdemeanors included fighting and disorderly conduct, assaulting a student guard, excessive tardiness, leaving school without permission, and some truancy. At the end of two years he had failed in all of his subjects except one term of physical training.

Neither parent seemed able to cope with the boy, and his father was definitely indifferent to the lad's welfare. Psychological examinations indicated that Donald was normal and could do good work. However, the only activity at school in which he showed any interest was swimming and the only teacher to whom he gave any respect was the swimming teacher. Since it was impossible to allow him to spend the whole day in the pool, he was discharged at the age of seventeen for "incorrigible behavior."

As soon as he was able to do so, he enlisted in the Merchant Marine and is evidently making an excellent adjustment. He wrote to the school expressing his satisfaction with his present activity. His letter was manly, straightforward, and surprisingly well written for a boy who had passed only one subject during his five terms in high school. He expressed a wish to have the school paper sent to him and his name placed on the school roll for servicemen. He had never intentionally obeyed a school regulation, but he wrote "Them's skipper's orders," as though he meant to obey them.

Violet Was Given Bad Guidance

Pretty and very intelligent Violet's father died five years ago, when she was eleven years old. Since that time her mother has been ill and has found it difficult to support the family. Consequently, there has been no one at home to control Violet's activities.

Until about two years ago, Violet was a good and cooperative student. Since then, she has been associating with undesirable companions. She became a member of a so-called patriotic club, stayed out late at night, and disregarded her mother's advice. She is inclined to use too much make-up and wears flashy clothes. She is also stubborn and sometimes impudent.

When she was transferred from junior high school to senior high school, she was advised to elect a commercial course, because of the family's financial situation. However, she was not interested in business and failed her commercial courses but was very successful in academic work. Before her brother went into the armed services, he was able to keep her in school; but after he left the home she became a truant, although she could do good work when she attended. Finally, resenting the financial aid that the family was forced to accept from welfare agencies and claiming that she wanted to make money and have a good time, she left school as soon as she was sixteen and became a model.

Here is a girl with superior mental ability, attractive and of good family background, who could have developed into an able and well-adjusted young woman if she had been steered in the right direction. Violet should have been encouraged, upon her entrance to high school, to continue with the academic course. If society had subsidized her in such a way that she could have continued her education and at the same time maintained her self-respect, she might not have made a mess of her life. Her own intelligence may still save her. Her present life may not satisfy her and she may continue her studies if she is able to save enough money to do so, thus enabling her to take the place in society to which she is entitled.

Marilyn Has School Troubles

Upon graduation from elementary school, Marilyn, a very bright but immature girl, was accepted for admission to the practice school of a local teachers college. This meant that she was separated from her friends who were attending public high schools and that she had a long trip between home and school. As she was only twelve years old, she found it difficult to adjust to her new school environment and was afraid to travel so far alone. Consequently, she became a truant and was discharged from the practice school. Her father, who was very much disappointed by her failure to take advantage of this educational opportunity, decided that she was not worthy of an academic education and had her admitted to a commercial high school. She did not like her course. She became very indifferent, both at home and at school, and refused to participate in any activities at the school or to associate with any young people.

Marilyn's father came to school periodically to check her attendance. His attitude was one of disgust and distrust. School advisers tried to convince him that he should give the girl a chance to make a new start and should stop acting as though she were a disgrace to the family.

After several conferences between Marilyn and her adviser, the girl began to show an interest in the life of the school. Since she had exceptional ability in English, she was encouraged to go to college. Some poetry that she had written indicated definite literary ability. This fact encouraged both the girl and the father. She has been transferred to an academic school and is taking a college-preparatory course. Marylin's father has promised her that if her high-school record is good he will allow her to continue her education at a college of her choice. The attitude at home has improved and Marilyn is now on speaking terms with her father.

Herbert Disliked His School

At the age of thirteen, Herbert was admitted to a public high school. He had attended a parochial elementary school and wanted to continue his schooling in a parochial high school. He showed his resentment toward his parents for not complying with his wishes by a complete lack of cooperation in the home and in the school.

His behavior included truancy, excessive tardiness, cutting of classes, losing of books as fast as they were issued to him and making no attempt to pay for them. When he was present in school, he flouted all rules and regulations and made no attempt to study.

He rates high in intelligence, but he refused to apply himself. His program was changed several times; but, at the end of two years, he was still in the first grade of high school. Herbert's parents and his parish priest finally decided that he should be transferred to the parochial school of his choice.

However, the change was made too late and he continued to be a truant and to defy school discipline. He was brought to court on the charge of truancy and sent to a farm school out of the city, where he is working and being encouraged to study. At present there seems to be little improvement in his attitude, but it is hoped that his own intelligence may lead him to cooperate in making a more satisfactory adjustment to life.

After reading these stories, you will perhaps agree that, in these cases at least, there is a definite relationship between family attitude and adolescent behavior. A feeling of insecurity in the home is reflected in a teen-age boy's or girl's attitude of distrust or fear of the school situation. Inadequate or unintelligent guidance during early adolescence or the necessity of subordinating one's own interests to the wishes of parents or advisers may have serious results.

It is only through frank and objective consideration with the young person himself of the latter's interests and abilities that satisfactory school planning can be done. It should be noted that, where adolescent readjustment seems desirable, best results are usually obtained when there is close and sympathetic understanding and good will between parents and school advisers.

Teen-age boys and girls live a very intense life in school and take themselves and their activities much more seriously than we sometimes realize. If we, as parents and educators, were to meet our obligations conscientiously and intelligently, many fears and worries of youth could be lessened or even eliminated. Thus, a more pleasant and profitable school life would be assured to adolescents.

As you consider the self-evaluating questionnaires that follow, reflect upon your responsibility for the school success of young people. A review of the items may help you to evaluate your own attitudes and behavior.

WHERE I STAND IN RELATION TO THE SCHOOL PROBLEMS OF MY SON OR DAUGHTER

In the column at the right, score yourself on each item listed

	1	2	3	Score
I encourage my child (teen-age) to be enthusiastic about his school.	Never	Sometimes	Often	___
I try to provide a quiet place in the home in which my child can study.	Never	Sometimes	Usually	___
I help my child to arrange a time schedule for his homework.	Never	Sometimes	Often	___
I insist upon my child's getting to school on time.	Never	Sometimes	Always	___
I encourage my child to co-operate with his teachers and fellow pupils.	Never	Sometimes	Always	___
I encourage my child to take courses in which he is not interested.	Never	Often	Sometimes	___
I encourage my child to settle his own school problems.	Never	Sometimes	Often	___

	1	2	3	Score
I pamper my child at home, even though this gives him a bad attitude at school.	Often	Sometimes	Never	____
I worry about how well my child will do in examinations.	Often	Sometimes	Rarely	____
I encourage my child to be critical of his teachers.	Often	Sometimes	Never	____
I advise my child to attend the school of my choice.	Often	Never	Rarely	____
I talk loudly while my child is studying.	Often	Sometimes	Never	____
I permit my child to neglect his schoolwork.	Often	Sometimes	Rarely	____
I expect a child to go to college, even though he does not wish to do so.	Often	Never	Sometimes	____
I am willing that my daughter attend a college away from home.	Never	Often	Sometimes	____
I help my child overcome his fear of examinations.	Never	Sometimes	Often	____
I am at fault if my child argues with his teacher.	Often	Sometimes	Rarely	____
I am partly at fault if my child does not choose the proper courses in high school.	Never	Sometimes	Often	____
I urge my daughter to go to college, even though she expects to be married.	Never	Sometimes	Often	____
I urge my child to go to college, even though his high-school grades are below average.	Never	Often	Sometimes	____
I urge my child to go to college, regardless of his mental ability.	Never	Often	Rarely	____
I think that my child should not be required to take a subject which he does not like.	Never	Often	Sometimes	____
I give my child a weekly allowance large enough to include his school-activity dues.	Never	Sometimes	Usually	____

	1	2	3	Score
I attempt, within my financial means, to have my child dressed as well as his classmates.	Never	Sometimes	Always	____
I expect my child to help at home as well as to do homework.	Never	Sometimes	Often	____
I think that my child should work part time while he is going to school.	Often	Never	Sometimes	____

After you have finished this questionnaire, note particularly those items on which you gave yourself a score of 1. Then ask yourself what you can do to improve your attitudes and practices in these relationships. The suggestions in Chap. 6, which follows, may help you.

WHERE I AS AN EDUCATOR STAND IN RELATION TO TEEN-AGE SCHOOL PROBLEMS

In the column at the right, score yourself on each item listed

	1	2	3	Score
I help pupils who are new to the school to become acquainted with other pupils.	Never	Sometimes	Often	____
I have a friendly attitude toward all my pupils.	Never	Sometimes	Always	____
I talk too much in class.	Often	Sometimes	Never	____
I encourage my pupils to get up and speak in class.	Never	Sometimes	Always	____
I think that a pupil should take a subject which he does not like.	Never	Often	Sometimes	____
I try to teach my pupils how to study.	Never	Sometimes	Always	____
I permit pupils to engage in as many school activities as they wish.	Always	Never	Sometimes	____
I attempt to create interest in the work of the class.	Never	Sometimes	Always	____
I encourage "crushes" on the part of the pupils.	Often	Sometimes	Never	____

	1	2	3	Score
I attempt to have all study done at school.	Never	Often	Sometimes	___
I am careful to explain difficult points in my subject.	Never	Sometimes	Always	___
I encourage pupils to memorize what they do not understand.	Often	Sometimes	Never	___
I give a pupil a chance to defend himself if he has created a disturbance in class.	Never	Sometimes	Always	___
I use sarcasm in disciplining my class.	Often	Sometimes	Never	___
I insist upon punctuality.	Never	Sometimes	Always	___
I carefully check daily attendance in my classes.	Never	Sometimes	Always	___
I believe that a pupil who is a bad influence upon other pupils should be expelled.	Never	Often	Sometimes	___
I encourage an able pupil to enter an honor class.	Never	Sometimes	Often	___
I am partly to blame if any of my pupils lose interest in my subject.	Never	Sometimes	Often	___
I believe that school should take first place in the interests of high-school pupils.	Never	Sometimes	Usually	___
I cause my pupils to fear examinations.	Often	Sometimes	Never	___
I am at fault if a pupil selects the wrong course.	Never	Often	Sometimes	___
I try to help my pupils learn to adjust to the realities of life.	Never	Sometimes	Always	___
I believe that high school should give postgraduate courses for pupils who want to do special work.	Never	Often	Sometimes	___
I believe that a pupil should attend a coeducational school.	Never	Sometimes	Often	___
I have the habit in class of talking about matters unrelated to my subject.	Often	Sometimes	Never	___

	1	2	3	Score
I nag certain pupils in my class.	Often	Sometimes	Never	___
I have "pets" in my class.	Often	Sometimes	Never	___
I believe that admission to college should be based upon individual ability rather than upon specified courses.	Never	Often	Sometimes	___
I encourage pupils to participate in school activities.	Never	Sometimes	Always	___
I believe that pupils should pay certain school dues.	Never	Sometimes	Often	___
I try to make school attractive to my pupils.	Never	Sometimes	Always	___
I help pupils to learn to live with others.	Never	Sometimes	Often	___
I believe that a pupil should be allowed to take the subjects that he wants to take.	Never	Often	Sometimes	___
I treat my pupils as my inferiors.	Often	Sometimes	Never	___
I give a pupil a second chance.	Never	Sometimes	Usually	___
I encourage pupils to join at least one school club.	Never	Sometimes	Usually	___
I try to explain the value of my subject to my pupils.	Never	Sometimes	Always	___
I try to give indirect training in character development.	Never	Sometimes	Always	___
I try to encourage independent thinking, within the ability limitations of my pupils.	Never	Sometimes	Always	___

A review of the items may help you to evaluate your attitude toward student-teacher relationships. If you scored 1 on any items, you might ask yourself what you can do to develop a better understanding of adolescent interests and needs relative to them. You may find some helpful suggestions in the chapter that follows.

Chapter 6

Suggestions for Improving School Relationships

OR the majority of young people, the beginning of adolescence and the entrance into the secondary level of their educational experiences coincide. The natural adolescent urges toward self-expression, independence of thought and action, and consciousness of themselves as individuals among other individuals of their own age cause young people's years at high school and college to become a proving ground in which they are prepared more or less adequately for adult living.

In all except small communities, new school environment, new faces, new subjects of study, and new social and recreational activities stimulate the young teen ager toward new forms of behavior. However, as he attempts to adjust his childhood behavior patterns to function in his new experiences, there may arise conflicts and accompanying emotional disturbances.

As you read the stories of young people who achieved a greater or less degree of adolescent adjustment, you probably noticed how intimately their school success or failure is related to their incipient or actual maladjustment. Parents, high-school and college administrators, teachers, and civic leaders must share the responsibility of helping young people to earn success in their school relationships.

The activities connected with school life should be the major concern of most adolescents. The years between twelve and twenty should be devoted eagerly to the development of those skills, knowledges, and attitudes which will serve the individual well during his adult years. It is unfortunate that such factors as health, economic necessity, inability to profit from school offerings, or a personal emotional blocking may prevent an adolescent's gaining a full and rich education through these formative years.

For those young people who are willing and able to spend their teens in school, there are offered by society excellent facilities to meet the differing needs and interests. Society attempts to provide adequate school plants, courses adjusted to the needs and abilities of all students, well-trained and emotionally controlled teachers, and recreational space and facilities.

Every adolescent should be guided intelligently and tactfully toward participation in well-planned programs of study and play, so that ample opportunity may be afforded for the successful direction of individual urges. A teen-age individual should not be left to flounder. He is entitled to receive the benefit of available guidance.

It must be remembered by those who are responsible for the education of young people that, although school life is extremely important, teen agers are living a home life and a life with other groups in their community. Not only should they be guided toward effective school living, but care should be exercised that all phases of their living should receive just and rightful consideration. This interrelationship of the various phases of adolescent life is sometimes forgotten by school people, with the result that the young person, unaided, may be unable to synthesize his differing interests. The pull of one or another interest then interferes with the development of a well-balanced personality.

The questions asked by young people indicate their need for help in adjusting to their adolescent school environment. The personality of their teachers and of their schoolmates; the study demands of their subjects; the dovetailing of their school, home, and community interests and activities—all these may become emotion-disturbing factors, unless adult leadership is wise and effective.

The suggestions in this chapter are based upon the more

common problems of young people in their school life and are discussed under the following six headings:

1. Selecting a school
2. Developing good study habits
3. The importance of the curriculum
4. Social life in school
5. Student-teacher relationships
6. Some factors that influence school success.

SELECTING A SCHOOL

Should a boy or girl choose the high school that he will attend?

In a small community young people usually attend the one high school that is available. In many communities, the high-school entrant is sent to the school that is nearest to his home. In large communities, however, there is a possibility of choice. There may be academic, commercial, vocational, technical, and industrial high schools. A few large cities include all-boy and all-girl high schools, as well as coeducational high schools. For boys and girls who live in large cities, the choice of high school is an important factor in their school and vocational success.

Too often, parents are tempted to choose a school in terms of what *they* want their son or their daughter to become, without considering the young person's interests and abilities. If a child has made up his mind that he wishes to attend a high school where he can prepare himself for a certain vocational field, he should be allowed to do so, unless it is evident that he cannot earn success there. Chloe, who wanted to be a doctor in spite of her low mentality, is an example of a girl who should have been counseled soundly by her mother concerning the inadvisability of attending an academic high school.

Chloe Could Not Adjust to Her Mental Limitations

Fourteen-year-old Chloe was a school problem. As a pupil in an academic high school upon which both the mother and her daughter had decided, in spite of the latter's low mentality, the girl was a constant source of trouble. She attended classes when she pleased, left her classroom without permission, spent periods in the lavatory or the lunchroom, ran up and down stairs if she thought someone was looking for her, insisted upon wearing a boy's coat, and was outrageously insolent to the teachers and the principal. She consistently demonstrated a lack of personal responsibility for her actions.

Chloe had shown the same attitude from childhood. She early developed symptoms of chorea, and has been under the care of a psychiatrist, with no effect upon her behavior. There is no father. Chloe's mother worked at night but, before leaving for work, saw to it that the girl was in bed; and an older woman friend stayed with the child while the mother was away. Although Chloe was not interested in staying out late at night, she was uncooperative in the home, refused to help with the household duties, and defied authority.

Chloe wanted to be a doctor or a chemist. Her inferior mental ability made this vocational choice impossible, but she was placed on the school laboratory squad, with the hope that this prestige might improve her attitude toward her studies. The patrolman assigned to the school also took a personal interest in the girl and tried to help her to develop self-control. No one of these methods gave satisfactory results. Her only interest seemed to be in active sports. She was a member of the school swimming club and took part in neighborhood games.

In order to help her adjustment to school, Chloe was transferred to a vocational high school, where she might learn a trade. However, the girl's behavior was no better there than it had been at the academic high school. She became so unruly at home that her mother cooperated with the school and social agencies in having her transferred to a reform school for girls. Her low intelligence, her emotional retardation, and her experiences to the present make any possibility of a rehabilitation doubtful.

For a parent to advise and yet not to dictate is a good procedure. A young person of average ability who has not yet discovered his definite interest should enroll in an academic, or general, high school, since there he may discover his interests. Even though he does not do this in high school, his academic or general preparation may qualify him for entrance to college, where later he will be able to determine the definite course of study in which he is most interested. There are many boys and girls, however, who, from the beginning of their high-school course, should be guided into specialized schools, such as technical, aviation, needle trades, homemaking, commercial, and the like.

A word of warning should be given here. Even though a young person is definitely interested in a special field, the school to which he should be sent needs to be carefully considered. For example, a girl may be very much interested in the field of home economics. However, if she is an unusually intelligent girl, she will want to continue her study on the college level and prepare herself to be a dietitian. This girl should attend an academic high school where she can major in home economics and at the same time prepare herself for college entrance.

Rather than that a child should be discouraged from selecting a high school that is best fitted to develop his potentialities, the parent and the child, with the help of a school adviser, should agree upon a school in terms of the young person's interests and abilities, availability of a suitable school, and later vocational opportunities in the chosen field. It is much better to select the right school and to complete a definite course in that school as a preparation for entrance into a college or into a desired field of work than it is just to go to high school. However, any high-school training within the limits of his ability is of value to an adolescent and should be experienced by every young person in his teens.

Should a boy or a girl choose his college?

Those high-school graduates who continue their education on the college level may or may not have formulated definite plans concerning the courses that they wish to pursue in college. Few college entrants have done more than to decide upon a large field of study, such as science, the arts, social science, etc.

The relatively small group of high-school graduates who, with the help of parents and high-school advisers, have made their decision concerning their specific fields of study, such as teaching, accounting, medicine, law, engineering, and the like, are more nearly ready than are others to consider and find answers to questions like the following:

1. Which colleges offer the courses in which I am interested?

2. Am I qualified for admission to any of these colleges?

3. Should I attend a college near home or go away from home to college?

4. Can my parents afford to send me to the college of my choice?

5. If I have not decided upon my course, what kind of college should I attend?

6. Should I choose a college for social or sports reasons?

Since the great majority of aspirants for college entrance are relatively uncertain concerning their ultimate vocational interests, such young people might do well to enroll in a college that offers during the freshman and sophomore years an opportunity for individual discovery of potentialities and interests. These high-school graduates must also consider such matters as qualifications for admission to a college of this kind, cost of the college course, and distance from home.

Some college-entrance aspirants find it most desirable to pursue a four-year course in a liberal arts college before entering their field of specialization. Still other young people unfortunately may choose their colleges for social or sports reasons.

Parents and advisers must be very tactful and understanding as they help young people decide upon the college to be chosen. To allow a young person complete freedom in this decision is unwise. To attempt to steer him into a college or a college course against his will may defeat the purpose of a college education. Parents must be sure that their advice is objective and that it is aimed at the best interests of their child.

To allow a young person to attend a college merely because of the social rating or the athletic reputation of the school is putting the emphasis in the wrong place. Some schools, especially colleges for girls, have long waiting lists. For that reason, a socially ambitious parent may decide that his child should attend that school, in spite of the fact that another type of college might be better equipped to meet the young person's interests. Again, a parent should not insist that the child attend his own Alma Mater, unless the child definitely wishes to do so.

The cost of a college education and the distance of the college from home are two problems that should receive careful consideration. If there is a college near home that is inexpensive and suited to the needs of the young person, parents of limited financial means and their children can well agree upon such a school. This is especially desirable if the sending of the young person away from home to a relatively expensive school will cause undue sacrifice on the part of the parents and will involve the necessity of the young person's engaging in so much part-time work that he will be denied sufficient time for study and social activities.

However, if the problem of finances does not enter, there is much to be said for the values to be gained by the teen-age young person in a college away from home. The social disciplines and pleasures of living in a dormitory with other students, the personal responsibility for day-to-day decisions, and the task of making and following time schedules without parental aid are experiences that do much for an individual in the later teens. He is thus enabled to develop an independence of decision and helped to achieve a broad understanding of people in group life. Moreover, his relations with his own family are placed upon a more objective basis.

A college, then, should be selected on the basis of suitability, location, and cost. An individual should attend that college which can best give him the training that he needs and that will fit him for adjusted social living. Further practical suggestions concerning ways of learning about colleges and other schools will be found on pages 205–207.[1]

Helping Adolescents Develop Good Study Habits

What are desirable study conditions in the home?

Effective learning usually comes to those who know how to study and who have desirable conditions for study. Above the elementary-school level, much of a young person's preparatory study for schoolwork is done in the home. Hence, parents are faced with the problem of encouraging their teen-age children toward concentrated study and of providing a place in which this studying can be done with a minimum of distraction.

[1] For further discussion on this topic see

Hawkes, Herbert E., and Anna L. Rose Hawkes, "Through a Dean's Open Door," Chaps. I–V, McGraw-Hill Book Company, Inc., New York, 1945.

An adolescent is fortunate if he has a room of his own in the home for study. A boy or a girl who is really interested in his school progress experiences great satisfaction in the feeling that in his home he has a place where, undisturbed, he can calmly and effectively pursue his studies. Desirable as this is, it is not enough. The boy or the girl must also be assured of the fact that his study time will not be interrupted by home interests or home chores. For this reason, parents should make it their responsibility not only to provide a place for study but also to encourage a time for it.

Although a young person should be expected to take his share of home responsibilities, his home duties should be so planned that they will not interfere with the time that should be set apart for study purposes. Nor should the combination of home duties and home study exclude a little time each day for relaxation and socialization with other members of the family. Every parent, therefore, should work out with his child a definite time schedule for study and other activities.

A possible time schedule is suggested below. It is based upon a school day that extends from 8:30 A.M. to 3:30 P.M. This schedule should be known by all members of the family and by the friends of the young person concerned. The schedule may have to be revised to meet individual needs. However, after a satisfactory schedule has been prepared, it should be adhered to closely and few, if any, exceptions should be allowed from day to day. This means that parents should cooperate in the carrying out of the study schedule.

SUGGESTED TIME SCHEDULE FOR STUDY

3:30–4:30 P.M.	Return to home; recreational activity, such as school club or home chores
4:30–5:15 P.M.	Study—one subject
5:15–6:00 P.M.	Study—another subject
6:00–7:30 P.M.	Evening meal, chores, and relaxation
7:30–8:15 P.M.	Study—another subject

8:15–8:30 P.M.   Relaxation—Socializing with family, listening to
                 the radio, etc.
8:30–9:15 P.M.   Study—another subject
9:15–9:45 P.M.   Final preparation, checking, and getting books and
                 material ready for the next day

A parent should make certain that he and the family by
their actions do not become major distractions. This does not
mean that the life of an entire family should be geared to the
interests and activities of one person; but too often young
people are forced to do their studying to the accompaniment
of a blaring radio, loud conversation (sometimes quarreling)
among members of the family, interruptions by younger
children, and the like. Within the limitations of the home
environment, study conditions should be made as conducive
as possible to success for the adolescent.

Ultimate success in college is closely related to the student's study habits throughout his course. If a college student
is living at home, the time schedule suggested for high-school
students can be used except for certain revisions in terms of
the amount of time spent at the college, special library assignments, and the like.

A freshman in college away from home may find it difficult to make an adjustment to the great amount of free time
at his disposal. Here, the providing of adequate study conditions and the guiding of students toward success-bringing
study habits become the responsibility of the college advisers.
If the boy or the girl lives in a dormitory, a study schedule
may be planned for him by the college administration. He
will then have a time and a place in which he may prepare his
classroom assignments. However, this studying is often done
in a room in which there are other students who by their
actions, such as sharpening a pencil, talking to a neighbor,
looking out of a window, etc., may distract the student from
his work.

If a college student lives away from the campus, he may

be tempted to spend so much time participating in the social activities of the school and of the neighborhood that concentrated study out of the classroom may be neglected. The early adjustments of the college student away from home are many. He has to devise a completely new life pattern for himself. Other interests may tend to encroach upon the time that should be devoted to study. However, if the young college student has followed a definite study schedule during his high-school days, he has thereby developed effective study habits that will serve him in planning his study at college.

The value of a study time schedule lies in the fact that it affords the student an opportunity for uninterrupted concentration upon study material. However, other factors in the immediate environment may act as distractors unless attention is directed toward their improvement. It is probably impossible to free an individual during his study time from all distracting stimulations. Such things as the pictures on the wall, the desk, the books on the desk, the lighting and heating arrangements, and the individual's own thoughts tend to attract attention away from study. However, minor distractions can be disregarded if the individual is really interested in his work.

How can parents and teachers help young people to establish good study habits?

Although the modern tendency in education is to offer young people more and more opportunities for learning by doing, much of the subject matter of high-school and college curriculums still requires book mastery. It is true that study in its widest interpretation includes the mastery of book material, the application of such material to the solving of problems, the practice of skills, literary and artistic creation, and the like. Before a boy or a girl can practice a skill or write a composition, he must have mastered certain material. Hence, fundamentally, study begins with an interpretation or an evaluation of what has been written or said by another. It is not easy for the young person to get the thought from a printed page unless he is helped to follow a definite plan of interpretation, evaluation, and memorization.

Teachers and parents as they attempt to improve the study habits of young people should be familiar with the basic principles of effective study that are listed below.[1]

The student should

1. Have the right attitude toward his study.
2. Focus attention actively on what he is learning.
3. Know why a particular assignment has been made.
4. Study with intent to recall.
5. Attempt to understand what the writer is presenting.
6. Raise questions as he reads.
7. Organize the ideas in his own mind or take brief notes.
8. Make intelligent use of repetition or review.
9. Know that some material is more quickly and easily mastered than are others.
10. Continue practice in skill subjects.
11. Be alert to the points emphasized by the teacher.

The writers frequently are asked for advice by parents who are sincerely interested in their children's school study program, even though study conditions in the home may be excellent. The young people are encouraged by their parents to spend all the time they need upon their home assignments. However, in spite of long hours of apparent home preparation, the school progress is poor. In many instances, both parents and the young people themselves are very much concerned

[1] For detailed discussion of study procedures consult

Crow, L. D., and Alice Crow, "Learning to Live with Others," Chap. XII, D. C. Heath and Company, Boston, 1944.

Frederick, R. W., "How to Study Handbook," Foster & Stewart Co., Inc., Buffalo, 1938.

Smith, S., and A. W. Littlefield, "Best Methods of Study," Barnes & Noble, Inc., New York, 1938.

over the situation. The difficulty appears to lie not in the fact that the subject matter is beyond the mental capacity of the boys or girls but rather in the young people's inadequate study habits.

It is not enough for a parent and a teacher to know that a student has devoted a definite amount of time to his study. They must also discover his methods of study and help him to make any improvements in them that may be considered desirable.

Many teachers, during the first week or two with each new group of students, help the latter to become acquainted with the most desirable techniques of learning the material of the course. Class periods are devoted to the preparation of home assignments and individual guidance is given in methods of study. Unfortunately, many parents are not well enough acquainted with desirable study techniques to be able to continue the study guidance in the home.

So much for the study of book learning! Now, a few words to parents concerning ways in which they can cooperate with their sons and daughters in the perfecting of skills learned at school, the application of creative learning, and the carrying out of group projects. A girl who is studying home economics may well be encouraged to plan some of the family's meals and to try her hand at the preparation of some of the food. A boy who is studying mechanics or carpentry may be given an opportunity to take care of minor repairs in the home or to renovate articles of furniture. The pride of young people as they demonstrate in a practical life situation what they have learned at school should more than compensate for some of the mistakes that they may make as they start to apply their learning to practical situations.

Many incidents in the lives of young people who enjoy parental cooperation in their creative efforts are illuminating as well as sometimes amusing. Fifteen-year-old Jane was very much interested in her high-school course in clothing and costume design. She was much impressed by such principles of dressing as color harmony, relation between types of figures and pattern of material, appropriateness of accessories, and the like. She suddenly decided that her mother was so inappropriately and unfashionably dressed that her father might lose interest in his wife.

Then began Jane's attempts to change her mother into a "glamour girl." A well-developed sense of humor and an understanding of their daughter's motives on the part of both parents saved the situation. Jane's mother suggested that she and Jane consult with Jane's teacher concerning desirable changes in her (the mother's) mode of dress, hair-do, and other details. As a result, this wise parent allowed herself to be used as a guinea pig for several class lessons on appropriate and stylish grooming for a middle-aged woman. Jane was delighted by the consequent improvement in her mother's appearance under the guidance of the teacher. She also learned in this practical and intimate fashion the difference between "glamour" and good taste in dress. Jane's mother was equally pleased and was heard to comment frequently, "My daughter has made a new woman of me!"

Sometimes a minor tragedy may result from a teen ager's attempt to apply his practically mastered skills. Robert was studying the elements of plumbing. During his father's absence from home, the kitchen sink developed a stoppage. Against his mother's advice, Robert attempted to make the needed repairs without first shutting off the water supply. When the father returned, he found his distracted wife at the telephone attempting to get a professional plumber, while water was streaming in all directions and a deflated young amateur sprawled on the floor gazing at various pieces of pipe, nuts, etc., which did not seem to fit together. In some ways this was a costly lesson. However, young Robert is now specializing in expert plumbing and already has several simple but excellent inventions to his credit.

Rather sad was Martha's experience with her family when she attempted to introduce them to the table manners that she had learned at school. Her efforts at improvement were resented by the members of the family and she was told that they had done very well for all these years and did not need her newfangled notions. Her comment to her teacher as she described her lack of success was, "I told them that if they want to disgrace themselves in public they can, but that I am going to mind my manners!" Who is at fault in a situation of this kind? To what extent should school training interfere with home standards? Certainly neither Martha nor her family exhibited tact; but an already bad home situation was not improved through this incident.

One more story may help to demonstrate the way in which learning by doing becomes a part of a young person's life into which the family can be drawn.

During one spring, Arthur's class in biology was studying spring flowers and blossoms. The members of the class, after several field trips, were encouraged to hunt for unusual specimens, on their own. Arthur's father, a good-natured man, who was interested in his son's schoolwork, volunteered to drive Arthur and some of his pals to places where unusual specimens might be found. Little did this father realize what he was bringing upon himself. First, he suffered extreme embarrassment because of his own ignorance concerning flora with which these young people seemed well acquainted. Secondly, he became so enthusiastic about helping them that he found himself not only reading up on the subject but also consulting the teacher and leading the young people far afield from home in search of interesting specimens. There was a little difficulty with other members of the family concerning the use of the family car, but the companionship that was developed between this father and his adolescent son was worth the effort and the energy expended.

THE IMPORTANCE OF THE CURRICULUM
What should be included in the curriculum?

A curriculum should be as broad as life itself. In a democracy, education should affect the physical, mental, emotional, ethical, and social development of every individual, no matter what his physical or mental capacity may be. Every citizen is entitled to training within the limits of his ability. For a democracy to function effectively, everyone must be given an opportunity to develop his specific talents so that he may make his contribution to the democratic way of life.

The success of a democracy depends upon the extent to which every citizen has been trained to think, to act, and to appreciate. School curriculums must be so diversified that every boy and every girl will be given an opportunity to become prepared adequately for effective citizenship. Curriculums must be adapted to the individual interests and abilities of all learners. They should also include the use of all available community agencies, in order that boys and girls may become acquainted with the various phases of life activities in which they, as adults, may be engaged.

An individual's education should be continuous, from his kindergarten days until he reaches adulthood. For that reason, a developing curriculum is so constructed that there are no gaps in the young person's educational process. His elementary schooling should give him the basic tools of interrelationship with other people. This is the period of common education. As soon as the child has mastered the fundamentals of reading, writing, and simple mathematical computations, accompanied by an understanding of the simple principles of group living, he is ready for specialization in the field of his choice.

There should be no definite break between the elementary school and the high school. The adolescent continues to improve and extend his skill in reading and writing. He is introduced to more complex mathematical relationships. He is given a broader understanding of scientific, social, and political principles. He begins his specialization.

The trend today is toward the experience curriculum, in which subject matter contributes to learning experience. The purpose of the experience curriculum is aimed at effective living and the preparation of students for further activity, whether the objective is college, industry, or home living. The habits, knowledges, attitudes, and ideals thus acquired should ensure success in the meeting of new responsibilities.

By the time a boy or a girl completes his high-school course, he should be prepared within the limits of his ability to think independently, to practice emotional control, and to recognize his responsibility as an active, contributing member of his social groups. If he is going into the world of work, he should possess skills that will assure him success in his chosen vocation. If he is planning to continue his education on the college level, he should be mentally and emotionally equipped to meet the demands of his new school environment.

The college is interested in the continued training of individuals who will be a credit to themselves and of value to society. The college curriculum, therefore, must be broad enough so that it may assist every student in the acquisition of those attitudes, ideals, and intellectual skills and procedures which will enable him to contribute to human betterment and to the establishment of a more abundant life.

What help should a young person receive in selecting high-school or college courses?

An individual student in high school or in college does not have sufficient background for the making, unaided, of wise selection of courses to be elected. Left to himself, he may select a course because he has a temporary interest in it, because he likes the teacher, or because he has learned that it is easy.

In small schools there is usually very little leeway in the selection of courses. Of necessity, such schools have a rather rigid curriculum, which must be followed by most students. With the increased size of a school there usually goes an increase in complexity of the school offerings. The individual student selects one of several or more curriculums, or courses, and then fills in his program with other free electives. These factors so complicate the problem for most individuals, regardless of their ability, that they desire help or guidance from parents, teachers, or special advisers in arriving at a suitable choice of course, or curriculum.

An individual may be guided in his choice by his chances for success in any study area and, therefore, will set his educational sails in that direction. For those students who want to make high school their last level of formal education there should be a wider range of subject choices than for those students who are preparing to continue their education on the college level. However, any individual who has pursued any organized curriculum, who has better than average ability, and who has done outstanding work in that area should be allowed to go to college, regardless of the fact that he may not have the specific courses that have been set as entrance requirements to a particular college.

A student should be discouraged from side-stepping a subject merely because he does not like it. If the subject fits into his program of education toward the development of a particular skill or for specialized training, he should be advised to include it in his program. If a student is extremely eager to elect certain courses, such as art, he should be encouraged to try them. If his progress is successful in the chosen field, this is proof that he should continue. The story of Doris illustrates this point very well.

Doris Finds Adjustment through Art

The third of a family of seven children, dark-eyed, petite, sixteen-year-old Doris seemed to be living in a world of phantasy. She adored her mother—an efficient, placid woman—but was very much afraid of her father, a stern, self-contained man.

At home, Doris was quiet, cooperative, and very helpful in the care of her younger sisters and brothers. At school, in spite of her superior intelligence, she was not succeeding in her studies. She was given to telling romantic tales to her classmates concerning her outside activities, to borrowing money from her teachers (which she did not repay) for gifts to her family, and to falsifying her report cards.

When the school authorities became aware of her un-adjusted attitude, she was told that the home visitor would talk with her parents. Thereupon, she claimed that she had intended to return the money but that her father had lost his job and that she had not falsified her report card but had merely entered marks in spaces that had been left vacant. She begged the home visitor to see her mother, but not her father and, on various pretexts, kept putting off the time of the visit.

The mother was very much shocked when she heard of her daughter's behavior at school and promised full cooperation with the school authorities, including an agreement with Doris's school adviser that the girl should not be punished by her father for her behavior at school. The mother kept her promise.

When Doris's adviser studied the girl's record, she noticed that Doris had done exceptionally well in her required art and suggested the election of an art major. Doris agreed to this with delight, saying, "I always wanted to study art but was afraid that people would think me silly." The girl showed unusual talent in her art work. She became so enthusiastic over her success that she not only improved in her other subjects but became one of the most trustworthy and popular student leaders in the social life of the school.

Upon her graduation, it was made possible for her to win a scholarship in an art school, where her work was most commendable. Upon the advice of her teachers at that school, she is preparing herself to continue her work on the college level, so that she may not only create, but also become a teacher of art.

Doris now looks back upon her difficulties at school as the expression of an artistic temperament struggling for release. She is an extremely attractive and stable young woman.

If a young person who gives no evidence of a special aptitude for a given course insists upon electing it, in order to be in the class of a friend or for any other superficial reason, he should sometimes be advised to elect another subject more nearly related to his fundamental abilities and interests. This is more likely to keep alive within him a desire for further education, since he will probably thereby be rewarded with a greater degree of successful achievement in the subject.

Very often a student is heard to say that he just can't see any practical value in the subject he is taking. Most students feel that way about most subjects at one time or another (often when they have done poorly in an examination). If young people emphasize the immediately practical value of all the subjects that they study, teachers and parents find it very difficult to defend every subject from this point of view. Young people need to take a long-range view of their schooling. They should be helped to realize that some of the values of education are so subtly woven into the adult life pattern that their influence is often felt without being recognized.

Social Life in School

How can an adolescent make friends in school?

For a young person to go to a high school or a college where he does not know any of his classmates, or many of them, may seem to him a challenge that he cannot meet and may cause him to wish to retreat from the situation. Both high schools and colleges are now engaging in numerous activities in order to orient young entrants in the new and, to them, strange environment. Elaborate trips of inspection and conferences for explaining the rules and regulations of the school are utilized. In conjunction with these efforts go planned social events, which are used as means of acquainting incoming groups with some of the upperclassmen.

No matter what plans are made in this way to help each young person to meet and become acquainted with other people on the campus or school grounds, every boy or girl must himself make a definite effort to acquire friends. School friendships based upon similarity of interest and experience are very much worth while. Joining clubs, participating in other school activities, becoming acquainted with the members of one's class, and maintaining a consistent attitude of friendliness will reap a harvest in friendships.

Many students ask the question, How can I gain friends? Parents and teachers can give young people much indirect assistance in the building up of fine school friendships. Parents can encourage their son or their daughter to bring schoolmates home or to visit the homes of other young people. Fundamentally, however, the parent's responsibility for his child's popularity in high school or college began long before the boy or the girl reached these school levels.

The young person who, in his relations with his family and with his childhood playmates, was guided by his parents toward the development of a fine attitude of cooperation, friendliness, and tolerance will have no difficulty in forming satisfactory friendships. Popularity must be earned. It cannot be bought. The girl or the boy who is allowed to be self-assertive, selfish, and domineering in the home cannot use these same techniques in his relations with his schoolmates if he wants to be accepted by them. Robert is an example of a boy who was unable to make or keep friends because of his unattractive disposition. His mother's attempt to bribe other young people to include him in their groups was pathetic, not only because of the futility of her efforts but also because of her apparent unawareness that she herself, by spoiling him, had contributed so largely to his unpopularity.

Robert Blames His Mother

When Robert was six years old, he fell out of a window and hurt his spine. His mother, a widow, who had completely spoiled her only child, was not at first aware that the child had suffered any serious injury from the accident. When a spinal curvature became noticeable, the mother wished to take the boy to a doctor, but he protested loudly and vehemently.

The mother gave in to his protests and nothing was done about the condition until the child was nine years old. The curvature was so bad by that time that the boy consented to his mother's buying him a brace, which was unsuitable and heavy. Although Robert suffered not only from physical pain but also from consciousness of the deformity, he refused consistently to have medical care. The boy became irritable, selfish, and quick-tempered. His mother, since the accident had been caused by her own carelessness, had developed a sense of guilt and gave in to his every wish, thus encouraging his unpleasant disposition.

By the time Robert was fourteen years old and a pupil in

high school, his physical condition had become extremely serious and his attitude unbearable. He was a very bright boy and found his only satisfaction in surpassing his classmates in school studies. However, he was uncooperative and disagreeable with boys and girls of his own age, was jealous of anyone who made a higher grade than he, and constantly accused his teachers of unfairness.

Robert persisted in his fear of medical treatment. He consented to a physical examination only after he was told that if he did not do so he would be discharged from school for physical disability. As a result of the examination, he was hospitalized for a year, but was allowed to continue his studies under private tuition. During his stay in the hospital he organized various activities among the young patients. Since he was the oldest patient there, he tended to dominate the younger children. Although his activities were good for the morale of the other children, his attitude was resented by them as it had been at school. His mother tended to place the blame for his unpopularity upon the jealously of the other children and begged that the boy be removed from the hospital. This was not done until Robert was well enough to return home and, with the aid of a well-fitting brace, to carry on his regular activities.

The boy returned to school for his senior year. Physically, he was much improved. As a student, he was excellent. As a member of a social group, he was a complete failure. His mother, desperate in the situation, tried to bribe other boys to associate with him and even demanded that the school authorities compel students to include him in their groups.

The boy was graduated with a good scholastic record, but resentful because he had not won honors in more than two subjects. He is now at college and is continuing his excellent scholarship. The fact that he is barred from participation in college sports has increased his bitterness toward his mother for having been the cause of his physical handicap.

Physicians have agreed that if the boy were to take a more wholesome attitude toward his physical disability he might eventually overcome it almost completely. It is hoped that his own intelligence may someday enable him to accept an adult attitude toward himself and his failings and that then he may be able to work out a normal social adjustment.

Edward, because of his childhood experiences, found it difficult to gain the admiration and respect of his school associates. Fortunately, the boy's intelligence and basic qualities of leadership are helping him toward a solution of his problem.

Edward Had Difficulty in Working With the Group

Edward was a spoiled darling. An adorable baby, an appealing child, and a charming adolescent—he was always able to get whatever he wished from his completely subjugated parents. He is a bright lad and can master almost anything in which he is interested. However, his early popularity completely turned his head. By the time he had reached the age of sixteen he had become so domineering and self-satisfied that he was considered a nuisance by everyone except his parents.

He was very much interested in social activities and was a member of many young people's groups, in both school and community. As soon as he entered a group he would attempt to dominate its activities. His ideas were usually good but, because of his superior attitude, they were rarely accepted. This developed in both Edward and his parents an attitude of resentment toward his young associates.

The final blow to Edward's pride was the fact that he was

not elected to the honor society of his high school, in spite of his high scholastic record. His mother went to the school and berated his adviser because of the "unfair" treatment that he had received, and then begged the adviser to demand that the group invite Edward to membership. Otherwise, he would have a nervous breakdown. Nothing could be done with the mother, but the adviser called Edward into conference and told him frankly the reasons for his rejection by his schoolmates. To his credit it must be said that he took it like a man. Apparently, it was the first time in his life that he was made to realize that the fault might lie in him rather than in others.

For a time the boy withdrew from all the social activities of the school. Fortunately, an older boy, who was an unusually stable lad and a recognized leader, became interested in Edward. Realizing that Edward could be a definite addition to a group if his attitude were better, he took it upon himself to give the boy certain responsibilities that would not bring him too much into conflict with other students.

Edward is gradually developing a fine attitude of cooperation and his parents are more careful in their attitude toward him. He has not yet made a complete adjustment. On occasions, he becomes impatient if his ideas are not accepted. At other times, he doubts his own leadership abilities. He will need careful and sympathetic guidance throughout the remainder of his high-school course and in college, if he is to make a completely satisfactory social adjustment.

A mother who constantly emphasizes the fact that she and her family are superior to the neighbors is very likely to foster in her son or her daughter an attitude of snobbishness and intolerance that will make it very difficult for the young person to gain popularity. Parents often fail to realize that unusual physical attractiveness, expensive clothes, and an abundance of pocket money are not an open sesame to popularity among high-school and college students. Unless the possessor of the special advantage is at the same time modest, his apparent advantages of looks, clothes, and money will cause him to be viewed with suspicion by the majority of the student body. He may be able to "buy" some young people, but these will not represent the better type of student.

Young people sometimes try to convince their parents that they will be unpopular among the students if they refuse to break school rules and regulations. This is not true. In every school there is a small group of individuals who seem to feel that school rules and regulations are made to be broken. These young people take great pride in such things as cutting classes, defying their teachers, using wrong stairways and exits, and the like. In every such case there is present an actual or an incipent maladjustment, which causes these young people to act as they do. To be popular with this group is not an honor. However, the weak boy or girl who cannot find a place for himself in the school's social life is sometimes tempted to join a group of this kind.

Parents lay the groundwork for a young person's popularity in high school, and teachers can do much to help young people find a place for themselves in the school. A boy or a girl may be so shy as to find it difficult to mix freely with other boys and girls. If this shyness is a symptom of a functional disorder, guidance toward normal social relationships requires much patience, with a possibility of failure to achieve the desired goal. Mary seems to exhibit some of these tendencies.

Mary Is Unsocial

Mary is a borderline mental case. She is extremely introverted and unsocial. She displays an abnormal amount of emotional dependence upon her mother, which is very distressing to the latter. As a young child, Mary was so timid that it was almost impossible to persuade her to look at other people. Her mother can remember no unpleasant experience in Mary's babyhood which might have caused this attitude.

She has made no friends in her neighborhood or at high school. Her classmates consider her different. She is nervous, tense, and frequently distrustful when she is talked to by other people. The girl was treated by a private psychiatrist for almost a year, but he was inducted into the Army. This psychiatrist became very much interested in the girl and seemed to be helping her. Mary's mother is trying to find another private psychiatrist whose fees will not be too high.

It is thought inadvisable to send the girl to a neurological clinic since this might intensify her fear. She had regarded the psychiatrist as a regular physician and did not know that she was being treated for a mental disorder.

The girl is bright and, as the result of an adjusted program and sympathetic treatment by her teachers, is making a good scholastic adjustment. Consequently, the school has been successful in avoiding an aggravation of her nervous disorder, but there has been no improvement in her emotional attitude among people in a social situation.

Teachers should help not only the shy young person but also the one who by his aggressiveness antagonizes other young people. Sometimes the apparent "cockiness" is a protective covering for inordinate shyness. Sometimes it is the result of family spoiling. It is the function of teachers to recognize the reasons for a young person's unpopularity with his peers and tactfully help him to make whatever adjustments are necessary, so that he may be accepted by the other students.

A word of warning to teachers is necessary. They must never pick out one student and give particular attention to him. To gain the reputation of being "teacher's pet" is the surest way of earning the disapproval of the majority of students. This is true in college as well as in high school. Whatever a teacher does for a young person must be done tactfully and individually.

Should adolescents join school clubs?

Adolescents should not only be allowed to join school clubs but they should be encouraged to do so. Every member of the school should belong to one or more clubs and take an active part in the work of the club. The real social living of the school, be it high school or college, is usually experienced through one or, another kind of extraclassroom activity. These clubs should be under the leadership of faculty advisers who know how to work with young people and who refrain from doing all the thinking and work for the members of the club.

The length of the list of clubs in most schools is being expanded yearly and is now reaching out to include every kind of activity and interest that is connected with school life. An individual who does not wish to join a club may be the very one who needs it most. He should be given special attention and helped to enter the social life of the school through these activities. An adolescent needs to learn to live with people. If he prefers not to join a club, he thereby may be indicating a fear of people or a lack of interest in his school. The experiences that he needs most should not be closed to him. He can and should be helped.

STUDENT-TEACHER RELATIONSHIPS

How can adolescents get along with teachers?

Every boy and every girl of high-school or college age wishes to get along with his teachers. Whether or not he does depends upon his attitude, which often is an outgrowth of home attitudes toward teachers. Parents should not habitually criticize teachers, but should develop in their young people an attitude of cooperation with all teachers.

If a young person is not successful in his schoolwork, it is very easy for a parent to place the blame upon the teacher's attitude toward his son or his daughter, rather than upon the adolescent's own inability or unwillingness to take his share in classroom activity. An extreme instance of this critical attitude will be used as an illustration. Ruth, a high-school student, had been compelled by her mother, against her own wishes, to elect algebra. The girl recognized her own mental limitations and realized that all forms of mathematics were difficult for her. Both Ruth and her teacher tried their best to achieve at least a passing mark for Ruth in the subject. However, the girl failed badly in her tests. Thereupon, her mother first wrote a letter to the teacher accusing her of being unfair to Ruth and then visited the school, demanding to be shown Ruth's test papers. When these were shown to her, she insisted that the marks on them meant nothing as a teacher tends to give a girl any mark that she wishes, regardless of possible errors in the work. Ruth was transferred by her mother to another school, again in spite of the girl's wishes. Peculiarly enough, Ruth herself did not share her mother's resentment toward teachers and was cooperative in her classes.

Since the classroom of the present is becoming more and more the scene of teacher-guided rather than teacher-dominated activity, there are fewer instances of old-fashioned fears and hatred of teachers. However, young people sometimes forget, as occasionally do teachers, that courtesy and cooperation are necessary in a classroom as well as in the home or any other group of persons, if they desire to be respected and admired. A domineering teacher or an indolent and uninterested student cannot expect to be popular.

A teacher is often accused of having a "pet" in class. It is easy to understand how this comes about. The student who cooperates gets a great amount of attention from the teacher. Somtimes, before either is aware of it, there has been established an understanding between the two that may become very close as the semester goes along. The teacher should not let his special interest in one of his students show itself. If desirable classroom attitudes are to be established and cooperation is to be secured from all the class members, every student should be made to feel that he is as important as every other student.

The relationship between students and teachers should always be friendly. Teachers exert a great influence upon young students and are often remembered by the latter for the influence they had upon personality development rather than for the help given in the learning situation. Sentimental emotionalism, however, is foolish and undesirable.

How friendly should teachers be with adolescents?

The relationship between a teacher of either sex and a student of either sex should always be friendly, but dignified. A student should never be invited to the teacher's home except for business purposes or as a member of a group. A teacher and a student should not habitually leave school together or engage in social activities together outside of school. No matter how much a teacher may admire a student and enjoy his company, the teacher-student relationship must be strictly adhered to. Any other behavior will result in the loss of the respect of other students for both the teacher and the student concerned.

High-school and college students (especially girls) sometimes develop "crushes" on a teacher of the same sex or become infatuated with a teacher of the opposite sex. This is a very embarrassing situation for the teacher. His method of handling it is an indication of his strength of character. If he is weak, he may be unduly flattered by the attention he is receiving and encourage a situation that is bound to become most disagreeable and sometime sordid. If he is strong and sincere, he will tactfully convince the emotionalized young person that he or she is wasting an affection that should be directed toward a person of his own age. If the teacher concerned is consistently objective in his attitude, yet kindly, and if he allows no privileges to this student that other students do not enjoy, he will find it relatively easy to bring about a change in the young person's attitude toward himself.

These abnormal interests of students in their teachers often become serious problems among college girls, especially if there are few or no young men on or near the campus. Some college girls give an appearance of being interested in their middle-aged college professors in order to flatter the latter into giving them good grades. This is a kind of glorified "apple polishing." Others become really attracted to their professors and may kindle a similar feeling toward them on the part of the professor concerned. Such situations are very unfortunate, especially if the man is married. Tragic consequences may result unless others connected with the persons involved show forbearance and are helpful in bringing the relationship to an end before the school authorities are forced to take drastic measures.

Some Factors That Influence School Success

How can fear of teachers, classroom situations, and examinations be overcome?

The adolescent who fears his teacher to too great an extent may trace the cause to his fear of anyone in a supervisory relation to him. Parents who are too strict or who are unwilling to explain reasons for their corrections of youthful misdeeds, or parents or older brothers and sisters who play up the teacher as a person to be feared, are often responsible for the development of this attitude in young people. Such fear attitudes are hard to overcome, even with the sympathetic help of teachers. The individual not only fears teachers but he fears anyone in a position of authority. This may include policemen, who have been regarded by these young people during their childhood as individuals who punish children rather than protect them. Consequently, a young person in whom these fears have been allowed to develop comes to the new environment prepared for the worst.

Usually he does not fear the teacher for what the teacher actually does, but rather for what he fears that he may do. He wants to feel secure in the respect and affection of the teacher. Consequently, he may be stimulated to study hard because he does not want to disappoint his teacher. He feels sorry when he cannot answer in class, not alone because he will get a poor mark but also because he fears that he thereby has lost the esteem of his teacher.

A student should be encouraged by his parents to learn to work with, think with, and get along with every teacher he may have. When right attitudes are present in both the teachers and the students, there is usually no abnormal fear. All efforts utilized to remove these fears from the classroom are rewarded by better and more effective learning on the part of everyone.

Some individuals so fear the classroom situation that, even though they know the answer to a question, they become tongue-tied and are unable to give it when asked to do so. These individuals need help in overcoming their emotional disturbance. They need to have their confidence restored. The best way to do this is to spoon-feed them at first—get a response from them and praise whatever there is in it that can be praised. Such young people should be called upon frequently to answer simple questions, so that they will develop the habit of talking in class. As they do this, the fear that they have been experiencing will gradually be replaced by a desire to answer, since they have found that they can express themselves and that, as they speak, ideas come to them. There is no place where the doing is so important as in the individual's activity in class. The teacher cannot answer for the student; other students cannot report for him; he must speak for himself, if he wishes to increase his enjoyment of class participation.

Sometimes, able students who do well in classroom recitations fear examinations. They become upset and either cannot eat or are unable to do effective thinking at the time of the examination. When this happens, there is usually found a history that ties the condition to the home, the pressure of the parents, the study habits of the individual, and the like. Most examinations are based upon the material covered in class, and students should approach them with eagerness to do something with the ideas previously discussed.

The young person who has prepared his lessons from day to day and has been regular in his class attendance has little cause to fear an examination unless someone is prodding him on to an attainment that is beyond the reach of his ability. Adolescents should be encouraged to do their best and no more. There should not be a goal set by their parents for them to reach, such as the top place in the class. A teen ager often becomes increasingly nervous in school because of pressures experienced in the home. In some instances, emotional disturbance has resulted in a speech defect, such as stammering.

Many young people *express* a fear of examinations that they really do not experience. This is a practice of high-school seniors when they are preparing for their final examinations. They know that very few seniors fail to pass these examinations. However, they talk much about the difficulties of the examinations and their fear of losing graduation because of failure in them. This is a kind of emotional preparation. They are thus impressing upon their parents the importance of this or that examination. Members of the family consequently become very much concerned about a young person who must cross such important hurdles.

Hence, when the news comes to the home that the examinations have been passed and that graduation is assured, there is much rejoicing, and parents who a few weeks earlier were very much worried are now inordinately proud of their successful son or daughter. The underlying reason for this display of fear of final examinations is often not realized by the young people themselves until it is called to their attention. They usually admit the truth of the accusation and discontinue their emotional outbursts.

If an individual talks too much about fearing an examination, a check should be made of his study habits. He should know how to prepare his daily work and he should know how to study for an examination. It is through review that a greater understanding of the material that has already been studied is attained. The review not only aids general understanding but specific memory as well.

However, in addition to being prepared for the examination, knowing how to approach it is helpful. This should be done with confidence, since the individual who has prepared his work is usually eager to tackle the examination. Teachers should prepare their students for major examinations by reminding them of some of the suggestions that are given here.

It is usually a good practice to read through the entire examination sheet, so that an idea will be gained as to the general requirements of its contents. Questions to be answered can then be selected and time can be allotted for answering each question. It is better to write something for each question than to spend too much time on one or two questions.

Special attention should be given to the directions for the questions and to the questions themselves. Both the directions and the questions should be understood before an answer is undertaken. If the directions call for an outline, that procedure should be followed. If the directions suggest a complete answer, that kind should be given. Questions should not be answered in outline form unless the directions specifically call for that form of answer. In giving the answers, technical language should be used only when needed. If examples will make clear the points that are being made, they should be used.

The best way to reduce fear of an examination to a minimum is for the student to give time and energy to daily preparation of his work, with frequent reviews. When this is not done, the individual is likely to cram at the last minute. Cramming of material that has not been studied consistently may enable the student to pass an examination immediately after the cramming process, but forgetting will set in very soon thereafter. The systematic review that the individual undergoes during the cramming is valuable for immediate recall, but he tries to cover too much material in too short a time and is usually upset by this. The result is added fear of tests and examinations.

Students should know that examinations are not administered in order to find out how little they know. Examinations are measuring devices for the purpose of discovering the ability of the individual to recall facts, to evaluate, to organize and use information in a situation in which others are participating at the same time, as a basis for further study.

How can interest be developed in schoolwork?

The earning of success is very important as a factor for the development of interest in schoolwork. Boys and girls should be helped to select curriculums and subjects in which they can be assured a fair degree of success in school. When activity is accompanied by success, there is interest in the activity. Today there are so many influences competing for the attention and interest of a young person that he often raises the question, How can I develop interest in school?

To the adolescent the motion pictures, the radio, sports,

social activities, and work opportunities are much more exciting and interesting than what he is doing in school. If he, then, is confronted with the possibility of failure and has to work under the guidance of teachers who do not vitalize their subjects, the boy or the girl has little motivation for the kind of study that will help him to develop an interest in schoolwork.

Each student should be encouraged to do something that he can do with a fair degree of success. With this success will go the roots of interest that usually carry through to other subjects that are fundamental to his growth and development. Many of the stories given in this book of young people who experienced adjustment difficulties indicate that a lack of success in their school subjects was one of the precursors of their difficulties.

The stories that follow illustrate the relationship which may exist between school failure and other factors of maladjustment. If Edith's parents (her father especially) had been able to resign themselves to the fact that Edith had definite mental limitations, her attitude toward herself, her parents, and society in general probably would have been very different.

Edith Has Ambitious Parents

Edith has a low intelligence quotient and is therefore incapable of mastering "book" subjects. Her mother is very ambitious for her daughter and insisted that Edith elect an academic course when she entered high school. Edith realized that she could not compete with the other girls, and her failure in biology and in history caused her to become very much discouraged. In addition, she is suffering from a severe kidney disorder, which does not seem to disturb her mother.

Edith is very well-mannered and eager to be liked by

people, but she is not allowed to have any friends, either boys or girls. She has no outside interests except the church choir, and she goes everywhere alone or with her parents.

At school, Edith has been tutored by the faculty and by members of the school honor society in order to give her an opportunity of earning a little success in her schoolwork and of meeting people in a personal relationship. She has been most appreciative for this help but has been unable to compete with the more able students in her classes. The constant prodding on the part of her parents has made her very unhappy and she has become progressively withdrawn.

Her mother finally consented to an examination and treatment for Edith by the Child Guidance Bureau, but the father made the mother withdraw her consent, with the assertion that he did not need anyone to tell him how to bring up his child. Finally, the father decided that the school faculty did not understand his daughter, were not interested in her, and were not able to teach her. He demanded that she be transferred to a private commercial school, where she is at present struggling to master stenography and accounting. She is still unhappy and more withdrawn than ever. Her nervous condition is intensified by the fact that her father constantly reminds her that her education is costing him money and that she must succeed.

Alfred's chances of successful school and vocational adjustment were made possible because of the fact that, in his case, the school authorities insisted upon his change of course. Unfortunately, the home situation could not be improved because of his mother's selfish ambition to make of her son a white-collar worker.

Lack of Parental Understanding

In spite of his poor work in elementary school as a result of inferior mental ability, Alfred was forced by his mother, at the age of fifteen, to enroll in an academic high school. Since the boy found it impossible to earn scholastic success in this school, he became defiant and abusive. He resented the fact that his mother had not allowed him to study mechanics at a trade school and he carried this resentment over into his attitude toward his teachers. He was sullen, refused to recite, made peculiar sounds when he was reproved, banged on the desk, and openly defied authority.

The mother was advised by the school adviser to transfer Alfred to a vocational high school. She refused to do this, although in other respects she was overanxious about him and attempted to protect him in every way. She could not accept the fact that Alfred was too slow mentally to succeed in academic work, but she did admit that the boy occasionally disobeyed her at home and made queer noises. However, she never resorted to physical punishment because she feared that he would be thrown thereby into a nervous state.

Since there was no possibility of parental cooperation, the school superintendent ordered the transfer of the boy to a vocational school. He is at present studying mechanics there and is showing definite interest and ability in his work. The boy is satisfied and happy in school, but is still having a conflict with his mother, who insists that he is bringing disgrace upon her by his unwillingness "to be brought up like a gentleman."

Poverty in the home and unintelligent handling of the boy by his mother, as well as her false ambition, resulted in Bernard's developing behavior patterns that will require long and patient guidance, if he is to make a satisfactory adjustment to society.

Bernard at Cross Purposes

Bernard has consistently refused to attend school except by court order. He was recently arrested, with other boys, for possessing indecent pictures. He responds to kindly treatment for brief periods by improving his personal appearance and his behavior. These periods of reform, however, are of short duration.

Bernard's mother is a widow and receives a Board of Child Welfare pension. She is elderly and shields all his illegal actions. Two older sons are in the Navy and their mother is inordinately proud of them.

Bernard knows that he can dominate his mother and resents their poverty. Consequently, he worked at nights in a bowling alley where he was earning at least three dollars per night and consorted with boys much older than himself. One reason for his truancy from school was the fact that he needed sleep during the day. Another reason given by him was his dislike for academic schoolwork. He wanted to learn a trade, but his mother had insisted upon his attending an academic high school. He was transferred to a vocational high school but, in spite of promises to reform, he attended that school as irregularly as he did the other.

The boy is a glib liar. He can lie himself out of any difficult situation. As soon as he was old enough, he left school with the expressed purpose of supporting his mother. His lack of training and his own instability have made it impossible for him to keep a worth-while job.

Cold logic on the part of parent or teacher will never encourage an adolescent to become interested in any school activity. To engage in the activity because it is good for him is a negative suggestion. He needs help that will get him into action. Every parent should encourage his child to elect those courses or subjects for which he is mentally and tempermentally fitted. Every teacher should try to present his subject in such a way that the members of the class will grow to like it, even though they have come to it with an attitude of dislike.

It is a fact that those students who are punctual and regular in attendance are more likely to be interested in schoolwork than are those who cut classes and are late, thus missing many ideas that are presented in class. However, very often the cutting is a result of the fact that the young person is attempting to earn success in a subject that is too difficult for him or in which he is not interested.

Sometimes adolescents feel that assignments are too long. If they must do other work, either at home or away from home, they are hard pressed for enough time to prepare their homework well enough to compete with the other members of the class. This leads to discouragement and a lack of interest in schoolwork. The school adjustment of such young people needs the cooperative help of teachers and parents. Either the after-school work should be lessened or the student's school program should be lightened.

Sometimes, during the regular recitation periods, adolescents allow their thoughts to wander to things that are of interest to them but are not directly related to the lesson. They find it difficult to keep their minds on the work of the class and often wonder what they can do to keep from day-dreaming. The mind tends to be carried to the things of personal interest at the moment, since in any discussion many such experiences may be called to the student's mind. He should learn to bring his thinking back to the subject under consideration as soon as possible. Teachers can be of real help in this by keeping all students interested in what is going on through motivated discussions. The alert teacher is quick to recognize whether or not his students are following the thinking on the topic under discussion at the moment. As teachers continue to keep the pupils motivated, students are thereby helped to break their habit of daydreaming, since they are being given something concrete and definite to which to direct their attention.

What has ability to do with success in high school or college?

Each individual brings to his high-school and college experiences certain definite abilities, which are the result of his inheritance and of his training up to that time. In the past, most schools were organized mainly for the purpose of educating those young people who had the kind of ability that would enable them to work successfully with abstractions and book learning.

Since more and more adolescents are now attending high school and college, there are included in all school registers some young people who do not have the capacity to master difficult book material. All except the very dull among American youth are entitled to an education on these higher levels. We need to do more in the way of adjusting subject requirements to the mental capacity of less able students, so that they can profit in a practical and cultural way from the time and energy spent on schoolwork.

There is little gained by a young person who attends school for an education but receives nothing but one failure after another. It is an educational crime to allow an adolescent to remain in an academic high school for two years without passing a single subject. The parents who insist upon such a young person's staying in this school and the school authorities who do nothing about having his course adjusted to the level of his mental ability to profit by instruction are failing in their responsibility to youth.

A careful analysis of the abilities of every boy and girl should be made to the end that each one is given something to do in school that will allow him a reasonable degree of success. The spur to stay in school and to continue education in some field of activity is based upon the success factor, and not upon the failure factor.

The introduction of many new subjects into high-school and college curriculums has done much to meet this youth need. Subjects which, twenty-five years ago, were not offered in high schools or colleges are now considered to be basic courses. Among these are such subjects as music, art, home economics, commercial subjects, speech, and many others, which gradually have found a place in the curriculum. These have been introduced, so that differing interests and abilities of students may be satisfied and developed.

Does part-time work interfere with school success?

A high-school student can gain much experience through part-time work. It is true that, if he has to work too hard or too long hours on the part-time job, he may not have sufficient time or energy left to give to his study. His schoolwork may suffer, and he may become discouraged and drop out of school. However, if the part-time worker is properly supervised and he is helped to plan a study and work schedule for his use in completing his daily program of activities, he can develop effectively in both areas. This is especially true of the college student in his later teens.

A part-time job can be of value to an adolescent for one or all of the following reasons: the insight gained through vocational tryout experiences, the information that can be gained only from work on the job, the gaining of a better understanding of money. and a keener appreciation of an education as a steppingstone to vocational success. An allowance that is *earned* by a young person will be appreciated in a way that is not possible if money is handed to him every time he asks for it. The interesting report of Frank shows the thoughtful interest that may be given to the value of money when an adolescent uses his own energy to earn it.

Practical-minded Frank

Frank was the younger of two brothers by slightly more than a year. The parents of these boys were as objective as they could be in their treatment of them, and both Frank and his brother were popular among friends and acquaintances of the family. Frank, especially, was very sociable and in his early years showed definite extrovert tendencies. He would approach people whom he did not know and ask them questions in such a way that he was never considered pert. He was very active and enjoyed being among people.

Since the parents allowed their sons a great deal of freedom of activity, Frank was well able to go places and do things on his own. For example, during one summer he visited the World's Fair alone almost daily and not only investigated every exhibit very carefully but met a great many different types of people.

When the boys were about sixteen and seventeen years old, respectively, they took a trip through Canada in an old Ford, unaccompanied by their parents. They traveled about three thousand miles and had many exciting experiences. Frank has always been interested in going places. It was this spirit of restlessness and desire for adventure that was responsible for an incident that might have had serious results.

During his senior year at high school he had an argument with one of his teachers. He was convinced that he had been treated unjustly. Consequently, one morning he went to school with his brother as usual and then, without reporting to the school authorities, returned home. He knew that neither his mother nor his father would be there. He packed a few clothes; took with him about seven dollars, which he had earned; and left. He was gone a total of forty-eight hours. According to his story, he hitchhiked a distance of about a thousand miles. He claimed that he would have continued his trip but that he was followed and robbed in a city about five hundred miles from home. By this time he was sleepy, hungry, and moneyless, so he decided to return home. In the meanwhile, he had not communicated with his parents; but he had given some indication of his plans to a pal, who told the parents. Knowing that Frank was resourceful and able to take care of himself, his parents were not too much worried about possible danger to him. When he reached home, they welcomed him without comment, accepted his story at face value, and sent him back to school.

He has always been interested in the value of money and, as soon as he was old enough to do so, began to work at jobs suitable to his age. In connection with a high-school project, he gave the following account of his work experiences:

"During my seventeen years of existence, my working experiences have been many and varied.

"Shortly after our family moved from a small town to a city (I was in the third grade at the time), I started selling magazines. Each night, rain or shine, snow or otherwise, I would go from door to door selling magazines. I can never remember making much money, but, from the small amount I did earn, I learned the value of money. Even yet, when I spend money, I think of how many houses I would have to go to to sell magazines enough for the prescribed amount of money. My next job along this line was a paper route. My first route was an afternoon edition, but when I became twelve years old I got a morning route. Getting up at five in the morning required going to bed early; a job that requires regular living is worth much more than its pecuniary returns.

"My grandparents live in a small town, where they operate a general store, a feed mill, and a coal business. They also buy large quantities of maple sirup. My first selling experience, that is, in a store, was in my grandparents' general store; selling groceries, hardware, and clothing. Also at their place of business I learned to operate a feed mill, to run grinders and mixers. Here I learned, by contrast, the value of a white-collar job. I also learned something about the process of making maple sirup, a product which I have been retailing in this city from door to door for the past year.

"Other relatives operate farms and I have had the opportunity of working on their farms. Learning many of the activities of a farmer has been quite interesting and healthful.

"I have spent many days caddying and working in a parking lot. These contacts with people have proved invaluable. During Christmas vacation I have worked in a post office, helping to deliver mail. An experience such as this is interesting at first but after a few weeks becomes dull and boring.

"My next job was helping a milkman deliver milk. The milkman has a rather hard job, with long hours starting at three in the morning. However, through this contact I learned the workings of a modern dairy.

"I've been working this summer while attending summer school. I first got a job in an ice-cream bar, selling cones, sodas, and sundaes. It did not pay very well so I got a position as a salesman in a Western Auto Store. This is rather interesting, as we sell 10,000 different items.

"The day summer school is over and until my college term starts, I expect to get a job as a coal passer on a ship on the Great Lakes.

"All the different types of work in which I have been engaged have been of great importance in helping me to determine my future lifework."

Upon graduation from high school that summer, he entered

a leading college, where he made a good record. At the age of eighteen, after a year in college, he was accepted by the Army.

Frank has earned several promotions since he has joined the Army. His interest in people, helped by his many work experiences, has been of value to him in his assignments as they require leadership ability. In thinking about his peacetime vocational plans, he admits that his decision will be in terms of the one which in the future will provide him the greatest monetary return in a "white-collar job."

Frank's story gives an excellent picture of the way in which study and work experiences combine in helping an adolescent to discover his vocational interests and the kind of educational program that will be most conducive to success in his chosen field. The boy exhibits an extremely practical attitude toward his future life plans. Perhaps we should not take too seriously his present emphasis upon monetary returns. He does know that his interests and abilities would probably assure successful achievement for him in one of two fields. In that respect he is fortunate. Too many young people of his age are still uncertain about their future careers. Frank's many work experiences have been of great value to him, at least in helping him to discover the fields of work in which he would not be interested, and have increased his interest and success in those college studies that will prepare him for his chosen career.

In general, school and college advisers have found that a part-time job tends to act as a stimulator of interest in school-work. Even a few hours of work per week during the school year or vacation jobs that are not too strenuous help a boy or girl to recognize the value of an education in its relation to the work world.

An increasing number of colleges and high schools are introducing a cooperative program of work and study. According to this plan, a student spends part of each week or month in the school, where he learns the techniques of his work and also studies related subjects, such as related English and related mathematics. He then spends the remainder of the week or month at work, applying the principles that he has learned at school to his actual practice on the job. There are many values to be derived from this combination of activities, even for young people who are preparing themselves for a professional career. Contact with other workers on the job helps the young person to increase his maturity of attitude. Moreover, actually working at a project for the success of which he is responsible gives the teen ager a better appreciation of his strengths and weaknesses than is gained through his achievement in school projects and tests.

Unfortunately, too many high-school students are satisfied with a mere passing mark. To such students the attainment of a minimum passing grade of 65 or 70 per cent means that promotion to the next unit of learning has been earned. They do not recognize the fact that they have failed to master the subject completely. The student worker realizes that his failure to complete satisfactorily that which he is assigned to do on the job can be traced to his failure to learn sufficiently well the related material needed for better performance. Hence, he usually is stimulated to do a better job of studying while he is in school, so that he may gain greater success in his vocational work.

In general, the adjustment of a teen-age person to his school experiences cannot be considered apart from his adjustment in his out-of-school life. It is true, however, that much of the success of an adolescent's school life can be traced to the suitability of his school curriculum, the attitudes of his teachers, and the kind and extent of the school guidance that is made available to him.

Parents and teachers who may be interested in reading a more detailed discussion of the application of mental-hygiene principles to the school adjustments of young people are referred to the authors' treatment of this in "Mental Hygiene in School and Home Life."[1]

[1] Crow, L. D., and Alice Crow, "Mental Hygiene in School and Home Life," Chaps. X–XV, XVIII, and XIX, McGraw-Hill Book Company, Inc., New York, 1942.

VOCATIONAL ADJUSTMENT OF YOUNG PEOPLE

Chapter 7

Teen-age Problems in Vocational Life

IF REPRESENTATIVE men and women who have been active in their respective professions, businesses, or industries for twenty years or more are asked how they happened to engage in their particular occupational activity, many of them report that they fell into the work quite by accident. They may have obtained their first job through the efforts of friends or because there was a need for workers at the time when they were seeking work. Some, of course, chose a certain occupation because of a real interest in it and started early to prepare for the vocation of their choice.

When occupational opportunities are plentiful, it is relatively easy for a person of average or more than average ability, with good habits of work, to find for himself, through the trial-and-error method, a field in which he can earn advancement and job satisfaction. However, as occupational qualifications become more technical and rigid, haphazard methods of vocational selection are ineffectual, costly, and time wasting.

We are fast becoming a nation of specialists. Specialization cannot be developed overnight, nor can any individual expect to become a specialist without an aptitude for the work. Furthermore, occupational history indicates that, at any one time, there is likely to be an oversupply of specialists in one field and a lack in another. This condition is often brought about by the fact that young people are influenced by success stories of adults in a particular field. As a result, a young person may hope to achieve a similar success in that field, regardless of personal fitness for the work or available opportunities in the field.

Furthermore, a temporary shortage of workers in one form or another of occupational activity may so excite community leaders that they bring undue pressure upon young people to enter that field. Such leaders are apparently unaware of the fact that, by the time the adolescents have finished their training, the need for that type of work may have lessened or that too many may have been encouraged to train themselves, with a resulting oversupply of trained workers in the field. Consequently, men and women have failed to earn vocational success because they were misfits in one field and were unable, because of financial responsibilities, to prepare for another field of work.

Parents are often at fault when their sons and daughters do not make wise vocational choices. It may be that the parent, in his youth, wanted to enter a certain field but was prevented from doing so by his parents' interests or by his own lack of ability or by financial limitations. The parent now wishes to see his personal ambitions realized through his child and persuades or compels the young person to enter a field for which the latter is unsuited and in which he has little interest. Again, it may be that a certain profession or form of business is a family tradition and that the young person is expected to follow that tradition, regardless of a specific aptitude for another type of activity. Too many sons and daughters, as adults, harbor deep resentments because they are unhappy in the vocational work that was forced upon them by their parents or relatives.

We as a nation have gone through many periods of occupational undersupply and oversupply. Engineering, teaching, medicine, nursing, law, commercial work, etc., have had their ups and downs, because vocational direction has lagged behind changing occupational needs. Many of our young people are very much disturbed over the present vocational situation. They are torn between selecting a vocation that now appears to be offering exceptional financial and promotion rewards and preparing themselves for an apparently less popular vocation, which may be more nearly related to their interests and abilities. Youth's confusion is increased by the fact that it is difficult to determine with any degree of certainty what the occupational opportunities may be ten, or even five, years from now. Parents, interested friends, newspaper and magazine writers, radio speakers, and vocational specialists are generous with their advice. Unfortunately, these groups do not always agree in their predictions concerning future vocational needs. Hence, young people are often hindered by such advice, rather than helped, in the making of their decisions.

Even though each young person were guided toward the making of a desirable vocational choice, he still would be faced by many problems. Training opportunities are becoming more extensive and better organized than they have been in the past, but there are still obstacles in the way of a young person's receiving adequate training for one or another particular kind of work. The cost of training, geographical availability of training facilities, traditional prerequisites for continued study, and a lack of trained teachers in certain fields make difficult the achievement of an ideal program of vocational preparation. Many a potentially good worker in a particular field has been lost because of his inability to receive adequate education.

Moreover, there are still some schools offering specialized training that are not honest with young people. In order to increase their enrollment, such schools encourage a girl or a boy to attend the school, in spite of manifest unfitness for the training, and then make promises of immediate placement upon graduation—promises which cannot be fulfilled.

An adolescent trained in his specific field finds that, under normal business conditions, it is very difficult without experience to secure a satisfactory job. Hence, he resorts to more or less reliable newspaper advertisements, to commercial placement agencies, to the assistance of his friends, or to his personal application without introduction, in his search for employment.

Fortunate is the young aspirant for a job whose school is equipped to place its graduates in desirable positions on the basis of training and proficiency. During a period of worker shortage, however, there is danger that a young person may disregard the placement efforts of his school and accept a job in terms of financial reward, rather than from the viewpoint of permanency of position in a stable and reputable organization.

The neophyte in the occupational world has many adjustments to make on the job. He must learn to adjust to his employers and supervisors, to his fellow workers, and to the requirements and conditions of the job itself. He must be able to distinguish between his just rights and his fair responsibilities as a worker. These adjustments are not always made easily, since during his school life he was both more dependent and more independent than he is on the job.

At school, his teachers were accustomed to rate his achievement in terms of his ability, and usually they were willing to help him with his difficulties and to excuse his failings if he appeared to be sincere in his efforts to learn. On the job, he sinks or swims as a result of his own ability and willingness to do efficient work. He cannot lean upon someone else for assistance. If his work is not acceptable, his supervisors, who cannot afford to spend too much time and effort upon his retraining, are likely to replace him by a more efficient worker.

On the other hand, the young worker is introduced to a

kind of personal freedom and independence that he did not experience in his school life. He is relatively on his own. He is given work to do and is usually allowed freedom in doing it, provided that the results are satisfactory. His after-work hours are his own to do with as he pleases. There is no school assignment to interfere with his home or social activities. This apparent increase in personal freedom often tempts young people to leave school and seek employment before they have finished their education, especially when jobs are plentiful.

A young worker is likely to have difficulties in his relations with older and more experienced fellow workers. At school, he had learned to adjust to his teachers and to fellow students of about his own age and school status. On the job, he must face the possible condescension and "bossiness" of older workers. He may stimulate jealousies among the workers, especially if he is enthusiatic and competent. He is introduced to the ambitious employee, the dissatisfied worker, or the shirker. He may be drawn into employee gossip, or he may not choose his worker associates carefully and thus may become a member of the wrong crowd.

In his relations with his employer or his supervisor, he may not be able to distinguish between just and fair work requirements and possible exploitation. His employer may be too lax or too rigid. If the worker is a girl, she is in danger of misinterpreting the friendliness of her employer or her supervisor, or may allow herself to be drawn into an undesirable relationship with a male employer or employee. There is a question in the mind of a young worker concerning the extent to which his or her social life should be interrelated with the work life.

As has been suggested in the foregoing, the vocational life of a teen-age boy or girl is fraught with problems of adjustment. Young people early become aware of these problems and seek advice and guidance. The questions that follow indicate the extent to which many adolescents are concerned about their work life and the kinds of problems that they are already facing or that they are anticipating.

1. Should a boy choose his own career or should his parents choose it for him?

2. How can a boy or a girl overcome family objections in choosing a career?

3. Is it right for a father to prevent a nineteen-year-old girl's taking a job in a store because he does not approve of some of the girls who work there?

4. How can school advisers help boys and girls to make their vocational choices?

5. Should a boy or a girl always take the advice of school counselors?

6. How can we learn about vocational opportunities?

7. What should influence one's selection of a career— prestige, power, or money?

8. Should a girl plan for a career?

9. How can a boy or a girl find out whether or not he or she possesses the right characteristics for a certain kind of work?

10. What professions are open to women, in addition to teaching or nursing?

11. What is the relationship between choice of a vocation and chance of success on the job?

12. What can I do if I am afraid that my employer will discover that I do not know as much about my work as he thinks I do?

13. What vocational training should a boy or a girl receive?

14. Should a fellow accept a job that is not mentally stimulating?

15. Which is better—a college education or a business education?

16. How can we learn about job opportunities?

17. Is it good to apply to agencies for positions? If so, what agencies are reliable?

18. How can one be helped to apply for a job?

19. If a girl seems young for a job but looks older than she is, should she give a false age?

20. How can one overcome a feeling of inferiority when meeting an employer for an interview?

21. How can one adjust oneself to a job quickly?

22. How should employers treat boys and girls who are working for them?

23. Do clothes play a large part in business success?

24. How can a girl tactfully decline invitations made by a man employer who is married?

25. Should a worker have rest periods during the morning and afternoon?

26. Should employees be permitted to talk on the job?

27. Why are some foremen such poor supervisors?

28. Why should a supervisor be so anxious to please his boss that he makes the rest of the employees under him nervous?

29. How can one overcome favoritism on the job?

30. How can a boy or a girl be helped to make a good job adjustment?

31. What type of boy does a boss usually want?

32. Should young workers be treated the same as adults or should they be separated and treated as children?

33. What should be the attitude of an employee toward his employer?

34. How can an employee be pleasant when the boss is always complaining about something?

35. How can one get ahead on the job?

36. Should an employer allow one employee to be so important that if the latter is absent the work of the office is practically stopped?

37. How can jealousy among employees be overcome?

38. What should be the attitude of a young worker toward his fellow workers?

39. How can one meet the problem of being taken advantage of by older employees when the supervisor is not around?

40. How do labor unions help young workers?

These adolescent questions indicate the extent to which the experiences of their older friends and relatives and their own part-time employment influence the thinking of young people. They become very much concerned about the many possible problems for which they may need to find solutions as they attempt to realize their vocational ambitions.

No one can predict, ahead of time, how successful or contented a worker may be in any chosen field. However, if there is brought to the work a sincere interest in it, as well as adequate training for it, the probability of job satisfaction is much greater than is possible if the worker is in a field that is not of his own choosing and for which he has not received sufficient or thorough preparation.

In some instances, job inadequacy is recognized early enough so that definite means can be employed by the individuals concerned for the betterment of their vocational status. However, many persons do not completely recognize the fact that they are misfits until it is almost too late to do much about the matter. Since vocational failure is usually a problem of adult adjustment, the following stories include not only cases of adolescent work difficulties but also examples of adults whose complete life pattern became one of serious, if not tragic, frustration of youthful ideals or ambitions.

Benjamin Is Nonconforming

Benjamin's emotional difficulties are very severe and he has been maladjusted at home and at school. A child of unstable and frustrated parents, his superior intelligence and physical overdevelopment have constantly thwarted him, because of the discrepancy between his size and his interest and age.

Benjamin showed marked nonconforming behavior at school. He was a truant, cut classes, paid no attention to his work, and ridiculed others who did. His behavior was so disrupting in the school situation that he was sent to a boarding school, but he was discharged for breaking house rules. He was then returned to a vocational school, where his behavior followed its accustomed pattern. As soon as he was old enough, he left school for a job.

He seems much happier than when he was at school. He lives with his parents and believes that the money he gives to the family for his support has improved home attitudes. However, he is unable to stay at any job for a reasonable length of time. He has had thirty different jobs in the last thirteen months. His nonconforming attitude gets him into difficulties wherever he works. He finds himself unable to get along with his employers because they "show discrimination" or are guilty of other behavior that he considers unjust or immoral. He cannot be silent when he sees an unjust act (according to his opinion) committed.

Although Benjamin discusses his antisocial behavior and attitude in complicated psychological language, he has little real insight into his personality. However, he is beginning to accept himself better than he formerly did. He is not under the care of any agency at present and does not feel the need of psychiatric attention.

At sixteen, the discrepancy between Benjamin's appearance and his actual age is not so great as it was a year or two ago, although he looks like a man in his late twenties. His present plans are to join the Marine Corps when he reaches the age of seventeen and to complete his education under the Marine Corps Institute.

Benjamin's future is uncertain. He explains his present erratic behavior on the ground that all his activity is temporary and that he will soon be in the armed forces. However, it is not likely that he will be accepted for enlistment or that he will meet the health requirements when, later, he is drafted. What then?

Lloyd Sent to a Farm for Adjustment

Life on a farm has done much to help in the adjustment of Lloyd. His early life was very unhappy. During most of the boy's life, his father had been confined to a hospital for the mentally ill. His home was disorganized. His mother had no affection for the boy, and he himself suffered from an unbalanced personality. Below average mentally, he was indifferent to schoolwork.

Since his home and school life were not satisfying to him, he ran away a number of times. He was transferred from an academic to a vocational school but made no better adjustment. Finally, he expressed a desire to get away from the city to the country. He obtained his employment papers and, at present, is making a very good adjustment as a farm worker.

Walter Needs Money

Constant friction in the home and ill health were responsible for Walter's failure to develop into a successful boy. Although the father is financially able to do so, he does not maintain the home properly and refused to care for the son's physical needs. Consequently, the boy worked after school until late at night but did not earn enough to give his eyes, teeth, and lungs the medical attention that they needed.

Because of his heavy work program, Walter lost interest in school and became a discipline problem. The mother and children have repeatedly threatened to take the father to court but have done nothing about it. Walter finally obtained his working papers and has obtained a good full-time job.

He is planning to take care of his mother and sisters and, as soon as possible, continue his education.

Edgar Adjusts through Work

Slow mentality, combined with the fact that he is very much overgrown and suffers from a peculiar facial defect, caused Edgar to be very unhappy in high school. Although he was sixteen years old, he had not yet passed the work of the first term. At school and at home he was a very well behaved boy and tried to cooperate with his teachers and his parents.

He did his best to earn success in his schoolwork, attended school regularly, and responded to the suggestions of his advisers. In spite of his fine attitude, he seemed unable to compete with the younger and more able boys in his class and, consequently, developed a fear and hatred of school. He was therefore allowed to leave school and take a job.

He is doing good work on the job and feels that he has at last found his place. He is also very proud of the fact that his earnings are helping to improve financial conditions at home. Edgar is now planning to attend an evening trade school, so that he may become a skilled worker and earn advancement. His present attitude reflects the fine cooperation that has been evidenced by his parents.

Slow but Persistent Dora

Short and stocky, slow in mentality, with a definite speech defect, Dora has managed to overcome her own personal defects, as well as the stimulations of undesirable home conditions. Because of the illness of her mother, she had the care of a large family of small children. Her father is a religious fanatic, who spends most of his time at revival meetings and seems unable to earn enough money to support his family.

At one time, Dora was much concerned about the behavior of two of her younger brothers, who were on the road to delinquency. With no aid from her parents, she enlisted the cooperation of the police and the court, in order to improve her brothers' conduct. She seemed to have an understanding that brought results. She was able to get these two boys back to school and to keep them there until one was graduated from high school and the other was able to obtain a good job.

Her mental slowness, combined with her many home responsibilities, made it difficult for her to pass her schoolwork. She persisted, however, and after six and one-half years spent in high school, earned a diploma at the age of twenty-two. Although her scholastic record bothered her teachers, her sincerity, cooperation, and persistency won their respect and admiration.

Upon her graduation from high school, she obtained, through her own efforts, a series of jobs. No one of them demanded too much intelligence, but each one offered better financial returns than the one she had left. Now she recognizes the fact that she has gone as far as she can without further education. She realizes that she is slow mentally and that she may not have the course qualifications for college entrance, but she is determined to qualify herself for entrance to a good college and use the money that she has saved in order to earn her college degree. She insists that she will realize her ambition, no matter how long it may take her to do so.

Although she has moments of discouragement, she is an unusual example of a person who knows his limitations but is willing to work in order to overcome these handicaps.

Parentless Ida Meets Many Trying Problems

When she was sixteen years old, Ida came to New York City from another state and was admitted to high school. Both her parents had died; and, although she had brothers and sisters scattered throughout the country, she had no contacts with them.

One sister, who lived in New York, supported Ida until a salary cut made this no longer possible. Since Ida was now homeless, she was given a part-time job by her school and a home was found for her. Unfortunately, the job was a temporary one. This discouraged Ida, and she wanted to leave school. Another job was obtained for her, where the working conditions were so bad that Ida could not tolerate them. She gave up the job but became very much discouraged and blamed herself for not being able to secure and keep a good job.

Embarrassed at the thought of facing her friends at school who had done so much for her, she failed to report to school and to the home in which she had been living. She spent the days looking for a position and the nights sleeping in the park. Ida's sister, not understanding the situation, became impatient and felt that Ida was old enough to take care of herself and should be left to her own resources.

Ida was found, finally, in a miserable condition both physically and mentally. Another home was found for her in a doctor's family, in which she was given her room and board, clothes, and spending money, in return for help around the house and in the doctor's office. Meanwhile she attended school. Although she was a little below average in ability, she developed considerable skill in secretarial work.

When she was eighteen, she left school before graduation and obtained a good secretarial position, because she felt that she was imposing upon the family with whom she had lived and thought that she should now take care of herself. However, so fine a friendship had developed between her and the family that she was persuaded to remain with them as a member of the family.

Ida could easily have got into serious trouble if she had not received help when she needed it and if she had not responded so well.

Ruth Is Not Discouraged by Physical Handicap and Poverty

"No, I don't eat breakfast. A girl must watch her figure." This was Ruth's laughing answer to a question concerning her extreme thinness. She did not explain that too often there was nothing in the house for breakfast. She was always neatly dressed, bright and cheerful, a good student, and unusually capable as a teacher's assistant. Her one physical defect was a bad case of strabismus (cross-eyedness).

Term after term, Ruth's teachers advised her to have her eye defect corrected, but the girl always managed to avoid commenting upon the suggestion. It was not until the beginning of her third year in high school that her distressing home conditions were discovered. When her adviser insisted that Ruth bring her mother to school to arrange for the eye operation, the girl broke down and told the following story:

"My father died two years ago and ever since then my mother, who is not strong, has had to work to support my brother and myself. In fact, I have been taking care of young children after school in order to buy my own clothes, schoolbooks, and odds and ends for my brother, who is three years younger than myself. I have tried to do all that I can in order to make mother's financial burden lighter. Next term I hope that my program will allow me to find an afternoon and evening position, so that Mother will not have to work quite so hard. I also want to work full time next summer and take some advanced courses during the evening, so that I can be graduated in three years.

"You see, I would like to become somebody in this world and earn a salary large enough so that mother can stop working. I want to help my brother through college, so that after that he can help me give my mother all the things she never had when she was young.

"I've talked to my mother about the operation and she

has given her consent, if it can be done with little expense. Mother feels the same way as you do about it. The only reason I don't want to consent is because I'm afraid. Friends of ours have had operations on their eyes and said that they could feel the doctors working on them and that, after the operation, their eyes pained them. So I'm afraid and wouldn't be honest with myself if I said I wasn't. I guess I will have to go through with it, because both Mother and you want me to."

It is needless to say that Ruth had the operation, which fortunately was successful. She was graduated from high school with honors in three and one-half years and obtained an excellent secretarial position. So intense was her desire to earn money enough to realize her ambition concerning her mother and brother that she gained the reputation with her employer of being mercenary. However, when he became acquainted with her ambition, he made it possible for her to gain several excellent promotions.

Ruth is a very happy girl. Her mother no longer works, and her brother is a college student working part time. She now eats her breakfast daily.

Not So Bright as He Seemed

Sometimes unsatisfactory vocational adjustment results from an overoptimistic evaluation of a young person's abilities. Godfrey and his parents shared high hopes for the boy's future, which were never realized because of the boy's inability to fulfill the promise of his early apparent potentialities.

As a child, Godfrey displayed exceptional alertness. The little fellow constantly surprised not only his parents but their friends by his precocious sayings and doings. His father, a professional man, had his son enrolled in a well-known private school, where everything went well until the boy reached his teens. Then the falling off of his school grades and the appearance of certain nervous mannerisms caused the father and the family physician to decide that too much pressure was being brought to bear on the boy in school, and he was transferred to another school, where the tempo was slower and student competition not so keen. In the new school Godfrey managed to complete his course, with grades that were average or below.

The boy was denied entrance to the college of his choice and had to be satisfied with acceptance in one whose entrance requirements were liberal. In spite of demonstrated inability to earn scholastic honors, Godfrey and his parents continued in their decision that he study medicine. By dint of hard work and parental pressure, Godfrey finally gained admittance to a medical school, but he just could not take it and was forced to withdraw.

The young man is now teaching science, with indifferent success, in a small high school. He still believes that his failure to achieve his original ambition is no fault of his own but the result of inadequate teaching in his preparatory schools.

Janet Is Too Ambitious

Janet is extremely versatile—in her own estimation, at least. She can dance, sing, and ice-skate. She is very artistic and also dramatic. Moreover, she can influence people and would excel as a social worker or a missionary. Her literary ability is also exceptional, if one were to accept her own evaluation of her talents.

In spite of her high self-appraisal, Janet was unable to complete her courses in mathematics, science, and foreign language. Her writing is ungrammatical and her spelling poor, but her ideas are interesting. Her artistic efforts are crude, although she does have some creative ability. She finally earned high-school graduation on the basis of easy electives, but this fact in no way lessened Janet's belief in her own inherent ability. Any evidence to the contrary is attributed by her to the fact that her eyes are not strong and that it has been necessary for her to engage in many hours of part-time work in order to help in the support of her family.

Since graduation from high school, Janet has drifted from one job to another—salesclerk, waitress, cashgirl, novelty-shop worker, etc. As explained by her, this constant change of job is caused by her impatience with "dead-end" jobs, not by her worker inefficiency. She is still planning to prepare herself for one of the many fields for which she considers herself fitted.

Unfortunately, Janet resists any attempt at guidance into a suitable field. She is attractive in appearance and has a certain amount of ability, although she is physically frail and her eyesight is not good. Here again, however, she refuses to follow medical advice, overtaxes her strength by working too strenuously at her current job, and stays up late at night reading heavy literature. She often collapses and is forced to take an extended rest period, during which time she keeps busy planning a new career for herself.

Here is a girl who possesses some excellent characteristics and who could be guided into preparations for one of several fields in which the work would not be too strenuous. However, her abnormal attitude toward life and her own potentialities make any such guidance practically impossible. In justice to Janet, it should be noted that she is the victim of a very weak heritage. Her father, a man of good family, made a mess of his life and is now a patient for life at a hospital for the mentally ill. Her mother is a well-meaning but ineffectual little woman, and her two older sisters have bad histories of vocational inefficiency and sexual delinquency. There is within Janet a constant urge to rise above the present family level, but she lacks the stability to work out her future along lines that are possible of achievement by her.

An Interrupted Career

Gerald's early educational and vocational history was excellent. Of good parental stock, he was an alert and well-adjusted student. Upon graduation from college, he entered teaching, the career of his choice. Here he was gaining expected success and advancement when he enlisted in the Army during the First World War and soon thereafter married an extremely fine and energetic young woman.

At the end of the war, he received his discharge from the Army and was ready to take on again his civilian duties. However, a slight gastric disturbance, which had started during army service, and an unwillingness to settle down to the routine of his former civilian life (characteristic of many returned war veterans) caused him to decide against a resumption of teaching as a vocation. He had dreams of better financial returns and more exciting experiences than are possible in the teaching field.

As a result of his decision, which had been approved by his wife, the two of them engaged in one business venture after another, no one of which brought him the economic security and the satisfaction that he craved. As he grew older, he became increasingly aware of the fact that his failure to return to teaching after the war had been a mistake. The accompanying emotional disturbance and worry aggravated his stomach condition, with the result that, for many years, his general health has been unsatisfactory.

Gerald has finally settled down as a maker of delicate tools. Since he is a very careful workman, his services are much in demand, but the sedentary life imposed upon him by this type of work is not good for him physically or mentally. He has become a fatalist in his thinking and has developed a general inertia and lack of interest in life that are most unfortunate. That he is a useful member of society cannot be denied, but he has not achieved the place of leadership that would have been possible if his original career had not been interrupted and if there had been someone available who could have given him the guidance that he needed when he returned to civilian life.

Duty Interferes with Ambition

Circumstances over which he has no control may interfere with a young person's vocational plans. Such was the case when Martin's father died. The family, consisting of Martin, his father and mother, and a younger brother, lived on a farm, which the father operated.

Martin was an unusually bright boy at school and was preparing to fit himself for the study of law, a field in which several of his relatives were earning commendable success. However, when the boy was about seventeen years old, his father died and his mother demanded that he leave school and take over the management of the family farm. There seemed to be no other course for Martin to follow, so he acceded to his mother's wishes, hoping that his brother, who up to that time had shown little interest in school, might later take over the farm, thus freeing Martin for the continuance of his studies.

The boy's ambitions were never fulfilled. His brother, who appeared to be the mother's favorite, was urged by her to prepare himself to be a physician, and Martin was expected not only to continue the support of his mother but also to finance his brother's education. This Martin did, although these obligations and, later, the support of his own family made impossible the furthering of his own vocational ambitions.

Martin was never able to adjust himself to farm life. He made several attempts to engage in other forms of business and left the management of the farm to his growing boys. However, as these boys and his daughters as well left home in order to continue their educational and vocational interests, he offered no protests but resumed the care of the farm with little interest and small financial return. His one outlet was reading, and in this way he satisfied his interest in study.

Fortunately, his children inherited his superior mentality and became leaders in their chosen professions. As an old man, Martin was able to gain a kind of vicarious satisfaction from the success of his adult sons and daughters, of whom he was very proud. He had reason to be proud of them, since much of the credit for their excellent vocational adjustment was the result of his attitude toward their interests and ambitions. Although he had never been able to do much for them financially, he had in no way interfered with their desire to work their way through college and achieve their vocational ambitions.

André Needed Guidance as an Adult

Born in France of a family that ranked high in French military circles, André continued the family tradition and at nineteen became an army lieutenant. His educational background was noteworthy, not only for its thoroughness but also for the excellence of this brilliant young man's scholastic achievements. He was not only a keen mathematician and well versed in science, but he also demonstrated exceptional linguistic and creative ability.

During a visit to America in his late twenties, he met and married an American girl and decided to make America his home. By accident, he obtained employment as an engineer, a field for which he had received training abroad.

However, he never adjusted satisfactorily to his work. His early experiences in French army life had not fitted him for success and happiness in American business. Moreover, he was by nature a scholar and an idealist. Hence, his restlessness urged him into the practice of several avocational interests, foremost among which was the writing of essays, religious articles and books, and plays, several of which were produced. He was an extremely religious man and at one time seriously considered the possibility of entering the ministry. However, he never actually did anything very definite about this, any more than he did about other possibilities of vocational change.

The one field in which he probably would have gained his

greatest success and satisfaction was that of college teaching. Unfortunately, this was the one field that he never considered. This man, with a wealth of potentialities, needed the kind of guidance that was not made available to him. As a result, he was constantly torn among conflicting interests, never made a success of any one of them, and died in the fifties, a frustrated and unhappy man.

The stories that you have just read give some indication of the many factors that may interfere with satisfactory vocational adjustment. The situation is especially grave when the recognition of the problem comes so late in the individual's work life that little can be done about it. This does not mean that some adults cannot shift their vocational activities if the need for doing so should arise. During the depression of the thirties, many men and women were forced out of their accustomed occupational work, with differing results. One group of such workers seemed unable to make an adjustment to another type of work. They were temperamentally incapable of change, since the new form of work often was much simpler than their former work and could easily have been mastered. Other victims of the depression sought and found opportunities for types of work that were quite different from those in which they formerly had been engaged. More than that, some of these workers in new vocations were able to advance themselves so satisfactorily in the new field that they never returned to the old field, even when excellent opportunities for doing so became available.

No one's vocational problem is exactly like that of another. Hence, no more can be done in the field of vocational guidance than that of making an honest effort to help remedy some of the most commonly observed causes of vocational maladjustment. Wider opportunities for gaining occupational information, more extensive and better equipped training facilities, and improved working conditions are goals worthy of attainment. However, the unpredictable human factor cannot be discounted but must be dealt with as objectively and as intelligently as possible, so that work experiences may be placed upon a stable foundation of unemotionalized service to society, with a minimum of problem adjustment.

A young person is certain to experience some vocational problems. He should not be expected to meet these problems unaided. Now, more than ever before, the efficiency and happiness of an individual depend upon satisfactory job choice. Every young person should receive wise guidance in vocational selection. Are you understanding and objective in the vocational advice that you offer teen agers?

A young person on the job is confronted by many new problems of adjustment, for the meeting of which he may not be prepared. He is expected to make adjustments to new people and to new conditions. Parents, what are you doing to help? Employers, what aid are you giving in the solution of on-the-job problems?

Your responses to the self-evaluating questionnaires that follow will help you to discover the extent to which you are meeting your responsibilities in the solution of these problems.

WHERE I STAND IN RELATION TO THE VOCATIONAL LIFE OF MY SON OR DAUGHTER

Score yourself at the right on each item listed

	1	2	3	Score
I help my son (daughter) choose his (her) career.	Never	Sometimes	Usually	___
I expect my son (daughter) to enter the vocation of my choice, even against his (her) wishes.	Always	Sometimes	Rarely	___

	1	2	3	Score
I encourage my son (daughter) to enter a vocation if he (she) is not suited to it.	Often	Sometimes	Never	___
I help my son (daughter) get a job.	Never	Sometimes	Often	___
I help my son (daughter) learn about vocational opportunities.	Never	Sometimes	Often	___
I advise my son (daughter) that all work that needs to be done is dignified.	Never	Sometimes	Often	___
I expect my son (daughter) of sixteen to work at least part time.	Never	Often	Sometimes	___
I advise my son (daughter) how to dress when applying for a job.	Never	Sometimes	Always	___
I advise my son (daughter) on the importance of correct dress in business.	Never	Sometimes	Always	___
I help my son (daughter) write a letter of application for a job.	Never	Often	Sometimes	___
I help my son (daughter) overcome fear of an interview for a job.	Never	Sometimes	Often	___
I help my son (daughter) adjust to his (her) job.	Never	Sometimes	Always	___
I advise my son (daughter) to consider the working conditions when he (she) applies for a job.	Never	Sometimes	Always	___
I advise my son (daughter) to give correct data in applying for a job.	Never	Sometimes	Always	___
I advise my son (daughter) how to behave with his (her) employer.	Never	Sometimes	Always	___
I advise my son (daughter) to be friendly with his (her) fellow employees.	Never	Sometimes	Always	___

	1	2	3	Score
I interfere with my son's (daughter's) getting a job if I dislike the employees of the firm.	Often	Never	Sometimes	___
I advise my daughter to accept social invitations from her employer.	Always	Sometimes	Never	___
I intercede for my son (daughter) when he (she) has difficulty on the job.	Always	Never	Rarely	___
I accompany my son (daughter) when he (she) applies for a job.	Always	Never	Sometimes	___
I encourage my son (daughter) to accept a job in terms of the length of vacation provided.	Often	Never	Sometimes	___
I am consulted by my son (daughter) in his (her) selection of a vocation.	Never	Sometimes	Often	___
I teach my son (daughter) to go to work every day that he (she) is well.	Never	Sometimes	Always	___
I encourage my son (daughter) to enter one of the professions.	Never	Often	Sometimes	___
I help finance my son's (daughter's) college education.	Never	Sometimes	Usually	___

As you review the items, try to determine whether or not you have a wholesome attitude toward the vocational problems of your children. It is as you become aware of your responsibility for their vocational adjustment that you will be able to strengthen any weak points that you may have. The suggestions offered in the following chapter may be of practical assistance as you and your child cooperate in planning for his success in the work world.

WHERE I, AS AN EMPLOYER, STAND IN RELATION TO THE VOCATIONAL LIFE OF YOUNG PEOPLE

Score yourself at the right on each item listed

	1	2	3	Score
I expect courtesy from all applicants for a position.	Never	Sometimes	Always	____
I expect accurate personal data from all applicants for a position.	Never	Sometimes	Always	____
I plan to have a personal interview with all applicants.	Never	Sometimes	Often	____
I give employees a chance to advance in my organization.	Never	Sometimes	Always	____
I try to employ the kind of person who is willing to work	Never	Sometimes	Always	____
I try to make an applicant feel at ease during an inview.	Never	Sometimes	Always	____
I expect applicants neither to overstate nor to understate their story about themselves.	Never	Sometimes	Always	____
I maintain friendly but dignified relations with my employees.	Never	Sometimes	Always	____
I am equally friendly with male and female employees.	Never	Sometimes	Always	____
I employ teen-age boys and girls without the consent of their parents.	Often	Sometimes	Never	____
I help my employees adjust to their job.	Never	Sometimes	Always	____
I encourage friendliness among my employees.	Never	Sometimes	Always	____
I expect my employees to be well-groomed and appropriately dressed.	Never	Sometimes	Always	____

	1 Never	2 Sometimes	3 Always	Score
I want my employees to respect but not fear their supervisor.	Never	Sometimes	Always	____
I praise my employees for work well done.	Never	Sometimes	Always	____
I discourage bickering among my employees.	Never	Sometimes	Always	____
I expect my employees to be punctual.	Sometimes	Often	Always	____
I recommend all worthy employees to other employers when requested to do so.	Never	Sometimes	Always	____
I help employees progress on the job.	Never	Sometimes	Always	____
I respect and make use of the opinions of my employees.	Never	Sometimes	Always	____
I allow adequate time for lunch.	Never	Sometimes	Always	____
I arrange for suitable rest periods during the working day.	Never	Sometimes	Always	____
I permit my employees to talk on the job.	Never	Often	Sometimes	____
I provide rest and recreational facilities for my employees.	Never	Sometimes	Always	____
I conform with labor laws.	Never	Sometimes	Always	____

We hope that you appreciate employer responsibility for teen-age adjustment and that you understand and practice sound employer psychology. In this connection you may find the next chapter both interesting and thought-provoking.

Chapter 8

Suggestions for Improving Vocational Life

VOCATIONAL choice and preparation, job placement, and job satisfaction combine into a complex life pattern, each phase of which must be broken down and analyzed in detail, if young people are to achieve success in their lifework. Each step of the way must be considered carefully as a young person in his early teens is started toward adult job adjustment.

Much can be done in this field. Hence, specific and detailed suggestions are presented here for the use of parents and advisers as they attempt the vocational guidance of adolescents. Many of the questions asked by young people are treated in detail, since vocational success or lack of success may have its roots in a decision or an overt response which, at the time, seemed of little significance.

Parents and employers can well check their own attitudes toward young people's vocational problems as they consider the suggestions presented below under the following headings:
1. Choosing a career
2. Training for a job
3. Obtaining a job
4. Adjustment on the job

CHOOSING A CAREER

To what extent should parents attempt to influence a young person in the choice of a career?

The fact that a young person may believe that his parents are interfering unduly with his vocational interests may constitute a serious problem of vocational adjustment for that young person. It is true that most young people go through phases of occupational interest. Beginning in early childhood, a boy may, in turn, want to be a candy-store owner, a fireman, a policeman, a baseball pitcher, a prize fighter, a big banker, a politican, a physician, or any other of a number of successful business, professional, or sports leaders.

A girl, at various stages of her childhood and adolescent development, may insist that she is going to be a schoolteacher, a nurse, an actress, a model, a writer. a missionary or a nun, or even a Dorothy Thompson or Claire Booth Luce. As the boy or the girl reads about or meets a successful member of any one of these vocations, his youthful tendency toward hero worship is stimulated and he sees himself winning the fame and honor that are being earned by his current idol.

These youthful enthusiasms are understandable, and most parents do not take them too seriously. Intelligent parents are able to recognize any special type of vocational interest that seems to persist in the young person. If they believe that he shows ability for that particular field, as well as interest in it, they encourage him toward definite preparation for it. However, parents must be able to distinguish between the temporary interests of their children and any deep-seated interest born of an incipient aptitude for the vocation.

Every parent, probably, has high hopes for the future success of his children. These hopes must have a practical basis of good common sense. No parent should consider a young person's future solely in terms of his own interests and ambitions. Nor should a parent, for purely selfish reasons, discourage a young person from following a reasonable vocational ambition. Rarely, however, does a parent recognize the selfishness of his reasons for denying to his child a desired freedom of vocational choice. Many a parent, like Sara's father, believes himself to be influenced in his judgment by praiseworthy and logical motives.

Sara's Thwarted Ambition

An operatic prima donna may have been lost to the world because of a puritanical father's fear that daughter might become a victim of designing males and night-life evils if she were permitted to follow the musical career for which she was so well fitted. As a result of her parent's attitude, the girl actually became a bitter and frustrated woman.

As a child, Sara was very well adjusted. The home atmosphere, although a little rigid and conservative, was pleasant and conducive to excellent character building. Sara and her older brother and sister were successful and happy at school. With their parents, they attended church regularly and participated in church activities. In fact, from early childhood, Sara had been a member of the church choir and in her teens was a much-admired soloist.

Although the girl had secret ambitions to be a concert singer, she recognized her parents' attitudes on such matters and acceded to their wishes that she prepare herself for a secretarial position. Perhaps her life would have gone along placidly, including work followed by marriage and the raising of a family, if a well-known musician had not happened to hear her sing and become very much impressed by her vocal potentialities.

It was not long before Sara was invited by a famous teacher of opera singers to become his student. The girl was thrilled by this opportunity, but her parents were shocked at the possibility of their daughter's becoming a "wicked woman of the world." In spite of assurances from those interested in Sara's career that Sara would have little time for frivolous activities, the parents were adamant in their refusal to permit her study of music.

Her early training in strict adherence to parental will impelled Sara to follow their wishes. She gave up all thought of a musical career and continued her secretarial course. Although she later obtained an excellent position and was very successful in it, she became a cynical and embittered woman. In her early thirties she contracted a spinal disease. Her intense suffering and subsequent death were regarded by her father as divine retribution for her ungodly ambitions.

A parent should encourage his child in a vocation for which the parent at one time had wanted to prepare himself, *only* if parent and child both recognize the fact that the latter gives evidence of ability for and interest in that field. An educator was heard to remark recently that he believes a study should be made of the number of lives that have been ruined by too much parental domination of young people's vocational choice.

The parent who attempts to dominate his child's vocational life is only a little worse than the parent who will assume no responsibility whatever for his son's or daughter's choice of lifework. A man or a woman is failing in his responsibilities as a parent if he gives no advice or shows no interest in his child's future, is unwilling to make any personal sacrifice so that his child may prepare for a desirable field, or interferes with his child's education by forcing the young person to give up his studies and go to work in a dead-end job, except in a serious financial emergency.

Adolescent career planning should be a cooperative venture on the part of both parent and child and should include the utilization of all available sources of vocational information. Some excellent vocational information may be obtained in the following ways, each of which will be discussed briefly.

1. Reading of books and pamphlets dealing with occupational opportunities and job analyses

2. Visits to business, industrial, and professional organizations

3. Investigation of training programs offered by colleges and specialized schools

4. Attendance at vocational conferences

5. Consultation with school advisers

1. Modern, well-equipped public libraries are likely to have available for the reader's use many good books dealing with vocational material. Some excellent sources of occupational information are

> "Dictionary of Occupational Titles," U.S. Department of Labor, U.S. Employment Service, Washington, D. C. Government Printing Office, 1939, and its 1944 supplement. A total of 21,653 occupations are included. The duties to be performed in each of these occupations are described briefly.
>
> *Vocational Guide* (a monthly publication), Science Research Associates, Chicago.
>
> *The Occupational Index* (a monthly publication), Occupational Index, Inc., New York.
>
> *The Vocational Guidance Magazine*, published by the National Vocational Guidance Association, Inc., New York.
>
> *Your Future* (published weekly), American Educational Press, Columbus, Ohio.

2. In many communities, civic, business, and industrial leaders welcome inquiries about their organizations from interested young people and their parents. Rotary, Kiwanis, Lions, and Exchange clubs often conduct planned programs of presenting occupational needs and offerings for the benefit of citizens. Other organizations, such as the Knights of Columbus and the Y's, parent-teacher assocations, and business and professional clubs, are also usually very helpful.

3. *a.* Some useful references concerning colleges and other specialized schools are

Marsh, Clarence S., ed., "American Universities and Colleges," American Council on Education, Washington, D. C., 1940.

(This reference includes a description of the courses offered in 727 accredited colleges and universities, entrance requirements, etc.)

Eells, Walter C., "American Junior Colleges," American Council on Education, Washington, D. C., 1940.

Sargent, Porter, "A Guide to Private Schools, Colleges and Summer Camps," the author, 11 Beacon Street, Boston, Mass., 1942.

"Directory of Private Business Schools in the United States," War Emergency Council of Private Business Schools, Washington, D. C., 1943.

"Handbook of College Entrance Requirements," *U.S. Office of Education Bulletin* 13, 1941.

b. College catalogues. Colleges and universities are glad to meet individual requests for information concerning their offerings. The following reference is also recommended.

Greenleaf, Walter, J., "Working Your Way through College and Other Means of Providing for College Expenses," *U.S. Office of Education Guidance Bulletin* 4, Washington, D. C., 1941.

c. Several books of more popular appeal for parents and young people are

Bennett, M.E., "College and Life," McGraw-Hill Book Company, Inc., New York, 1941.

Lovejoy, Clarence E., "So You're Going to College," Simon and Schuster, Inc., New York, 1940.

Tunis, John R., "Choosing a College," Harcourt, Brace and Company, New York, 1940.

Smith, Charles M., "After High School, What?" Burstein and Chappe, New York, 1940.

d. A personal visit on the part of parents and child to the schools or colleges is strongly advised. There is much that can be learned concerning the suitability of a training course through an informal talk with the persons who are on the ground. Reputable institutions are careful to discourage from attendance at their schools any young person who is patently unsuited for such training. On the other hand, trained faculty advisers of such schools are able to recognize potentialities in a young person of which he himself may be unaware. Hence, conferences of this kind often are very helpful.

4. An increased number of private and community-controlled organizations are attempting to help young people, parents, and school advisers in teen-age career planning. Some of these organizations, such as Vocational Service for Juniors, conduct periodic conference programs at which leaders in the field discuss with interested adolescents and adults many of the practical problems connected with vocational planning and adjustment.

5. An increasing number of schools include on their staffs trained vocational and educational advisers who, with the aid of a well-equipped vocational library, are in a position to offer excellent vocational advice. Parents and young people should avail themselves of these opportunities. No matter how objective a parent may be, the point of view of a person who is outside the family group is usually extremely valuable.

Since the occupational activities of men and, in the modern world, of women as well are so important in the complete pattern of an individual's entire adult life, planning and preparation for this phase of living should not be hasty or be influenced by such factors as temporary expediency or immediate satisfaction. A long-range program should be mapped out cooperatively by parent and child and should include the following considerations:

1. Demonstrated abilities and interests
2. Occupational opportunities in the field of interest, not only at the present, but also in the future
3. The amount and kind of training needed
4. The schools that are best equipped for this training and that are most accessible

What help should school advisers give to young people relative to vocational selection?

In every school there can be found individual teachers whose interest in all or some of their pupils impels them to become very much concerned about the vocational plans of their young people. Consequently, such teachers are often able to give excellent advice informally to individual pupils. However, if every boy and every girl is to receive adequate vocational guidance, every school should plan a practicable and inclusive program of guidance for all pupils. There are many vehicles available for the offering of such assistance to young people.

Fortunately, trained and experienced leaders in the field have organized in book form some of the programs and techniques that they have found through experience to be practical and successful. The suggestions to be found in such writings usually can be adapted to the needs of particular schools and are worthy of study and application.[1]

[1] The following books include not only a discussion of the philosophy of and principles underlying vocational guidance but also many and varied techniques of guidance, as well as copious references to other general and specific writings on the subject.

Forrester, Gertrude, "Methods of Vocational Guidance," D. C. Heath and Company, Boston, 1944.

MacGibbon, Elizabeth, "Fitting Yourself for Business," McGraw-Hill Book Company, Inc., New York, 1941.

Myers, George E., "Principles and Techniques of Vocational Guidance," McGraw-Hill Book Company, Inc., New York, 1941.

Although vocational guidance is generally considered to be the responsibility of secondary schools and schools of higher learning, certain groundwork can be done on the elementary-school level. The first six years of a child's school life are devoted primarily to the mastery of certain simple and fundamental skills and information and to the development of desirable appreciations and civic attitudes. However, included in the child's program of work and play are many experiences that offer a background of occupational awareness, which, at this level, is not definitely aimed at vocational guidance but which will be helpful to him as he gives serious thought, on the secondary-school level, to his vocational planning.

Moreover, well-kept cumulative records of the progress of elementary-school pupils and of any special interests or abilities will be of great value later. Elementary-school advisers should be constantly on the alert to recognize those vocational interests of their young pupils that seem to show some degree of permanency. These advisers should also take into consideration the mental and temperamental characteristics of the children. Upon the basis of these factors, elementary-school graduates should be steered toward entrance into the high school that is best suited to meet their vocational needs and interests. For the child who does not yet give evidence of any specific aptitude, a general high-school course is recommended.

The vocational-guidance service beyond the elementary-school level should be broad in its scope but so specific in application as to serve every student in terms of his needs and interests. The functions of an adequate program are well stated by Myers[1] as follows:

"A comprehensive program of vocational guidance in secondary schools is concerned with eight different services:

[1] Myers, George E., "Principles and Techniques of Vocational Guidance," p. 107, McGraw-Hill Book Company, Inc., New York, 1941.

(1) a vocational information service; (2) a self-inventory service; (3) a personal data-collecting service; (4) a counseling service; (5) a vocational preparatory service; (6) a placement service or employment service; (7) a follow-up or adjustment service; and (8) a research service."

You have already been given excellent references to detailed discussions of the various ways in which vocational-guidance services can be set up in the schools. In every school there should be organized, within the limits of financial and personnel possibilities, adequate reference materials and guidance facilities. However, it cannot be emphasized too strongly that a well-equipped guidance office, an extensive informational library, and the like, do not of themselves guarantee long-range, individually satisfying, and eventually successful vocational planning. Unless the problems of each young person become the concern of all those whose function it is so to plan together that the guided and the guiders work out practical and possible solutions of the problems, the guidance spirit will be absent, leaving only an empty form.

Hence, every young person should be helped through the use of testing programs, appropriate reading, radio and motion-picture presentations, visits to business and industrial organizations, a course in occupational information, and group and individual conferences to attain an intelligent understanding of his own specific strengths and weaknesses, his vocational interests, the fields in which he may be expected to make the best adjustment, and his advancement possibilities in that field.[1]

In connection with a course on occupational information, students should be encouraged to make detailed studies of specific vocations and then to share their findings with their classmates. A course of this kind might well include a discussion of the following topics:

[1] In this connection read Myers, *op. cit.*, pp. 125–247; and Forrester, *op. cit.*, pp. 261–278.

1. General fields of occupational work
2. Specific types of work within each field
3. Job and worker analyses
4. Financial remuneration
5. Work conditions
6. Opportunities for advancement

Another excellent way in which an adolescent can achieve appreciation of himself as a worker is his participation in work experiences on either a part-time or a cooperative basis. The values to the young person who is physically able to carry on a combined work and study program cannot be overestimated.[1]

Should girls plan for a career?

This is a question that is often asked by young girls. However, their interpretation of the word "career" may vary. It is sometimes used to indicate that a girl should prepare herself for a gainful occupation in which she will engage until she marries. It may imply that a girl is definitely planning to devote the remainder of her life to the achieving of success in a given occupational field. Advisers of girls need to be very tactful as they help their students plan for the future.

Every girl should be encouraged to prepare herself for the eventual career of wifehood and motherhood, no matter how she plans for the time that will intervene between her graduation and probable marriage. To that end, every girl should receive some training in home care, home nursing, care of children, home decoration and furnishing, planning and care of clothes, and household budgeting. No preparation for a career should be allowed to interfere with the training to be gained in courses that prepare a girl for the career of homemaking.

Besides the training in the care of the home, it is desirable that every girl receive some vocational training; and that, for a shorter or longer period in her late adolescence and early

[1] For a more complete discussion of this topic, see pp. 168–173.

adulthood, she receive some experience in a gainful occupation. There are several reasons for this.

1. The girl may not marry so soon as she expects to, and may need to support herself during the interim.

2. It is probable that a young woman who has had experience as a worker will usually be able to manage her household in a more businesslike way than can the girl who has had no such experience. Earning and spending her own money helps the girl better to appreciate the value of money, and she is likely to budget her household expenses with a minimum of extravagance.

3. The husband may die or become incapacitated for work, and the wife may be forced to become the breadwinner of the family. If she has a vocation for which she has been trained and in which she has worked previous to her marriage, she will probably find it relatively easy to obtain gainful employment. An incapacitated father and an untrained mother can do little for their children.

4. As the years pass, the husband may become very much engrossed in his own business or profession and the adolescent children may turn to interests outside the home. Many a middle-aged wife and mother who is and has been a good home manager finds herself with a great deal of free time on her hands and no satisfactory means of filling this time. Some women turn to philanthropic activities, but these do not always satisfy. A bored woman may become an irritable member of the household. However, if she can resume the place that she once had in the business or professional world, she adds another interest, not only to her own life, but also to the lives of the other members of her family, provided that her outside work does not interfere too much with her home responsibilities.

5. In a time of national worker shortage, such as is experienced during a war, married women who have been trained in certain specific fields are of incalculable value.

If becoming a career woman is interpreted as meaning that she shall devote her life to a field of work in which she has exceptional power of achievement, the question of whether or not such a woman should marry cannot be answered by a simple Yes or No. Usually, a woman who can earn fame for herself in a given field, such as writing, business, law, teaching, nursing, social service, or scientific research, has inherent qualities that should be passed on to another generation, and possesses also the essence of fine comradeship to share with a husband. It would seem unfortunate that a woman who has so much to give should be denied the satisfactions that can come only through the experiencing of family life.

It is not impossible for a woman to continue her career and also to make an adequate adjustment to wifehood and motherhood. If the woman brings to her home relationships the same intelligent management that she exercises in her out-of-the-home work, she can do both and at the same time enjoy the love and respect of her family. There are times when the career woman will need to subordinate her career to the needs of the home. Her husband and children should not be sacrificed for her outside interests.

What is the relationship between choice of a vocation and chance of success on the job?

Rarely does a person earn success in a vocation that has been forced upon him although, in an emergency, an able person may be able to make a satisfactory adjustment in a field of work that is very far removed from his interest. During the depression of the thirties, many men and women who were forced out of their chosen vocations were able to make an excellent temporary adjustment to types of work which, under ordinary circumstances, would have been most unsatisfying to them. The majority of these persons returned to their accustomed vocations as soon as this was possible. A few found opportunities for advancement in the new field and remained in it.

This is not an argument for allowing young people to "fall" into a vocation with little or no consideration of their interests or abilities. Other things being equal, a person achieves his greatest job satisfaction and job success in that field for which he is mentally and tempermentally fitted and for which he has received adequate training. It may happen that an unusually able person can achieve success in more than one field. He may start in one of these and, for one reason or another, shift to the other with little, if any, diminution of successful achievement. However, this is not true for less able individuals.

A person who exhibits more than one interest may be encouraged to use one of these as his vocational interest and the other as an avocational interest or hobby. Later, the avocation may become the prime interest of the individual or he may gain a definite reputation in his avocational field, so that the avocation becomes the vocation.

TRAINING FOR A JOB

What vocational training should an adolescent receive?

The basic answer to this question is that a person should receive the best training possible for the work in which he is planning to engage. However, this statement needs to be explained in order to make its meaning clear. There is a difference of opinion among vocational experts as to which of the two following procedures is a better course to follow: (1) obtain a thorough training for *entrance* into the field, so that minimal job requirements can be met adequately, and later the finer details of the work or the more complicated procedures be mastered by the worker in the form of apprentice training; or (2) complete the entire training before the actual experience begins, so that the worker from the start may be a master workman.

As a matter of fact, these two theories are really one, with different emphases. The extent of preparatory training completed before a young person enters into the activity itself depends upon the ultimate ambition of the worker, his financial ability to continue his training beyond a certain point, or the needs of the work world.

To say that a young medical student should be allowed to practice medicine before he has mastered all the needed training in materia medica would be allowing him indirectly to commit professional suicide. However, after he has mastered certain fundamental knowledges and skills, he can be allowed to practice these, under guidance, as a kind of medical apprentice. If, after he has become a licensed physician, he wishes to specialize in any one field of medicine or surgery, this specialized study could very well—and probably should—come after he has had some experience as a general practitioner in medicine.

Again, a young person majors in commercial work in high school and is prepared for secretarial work or bookkeeping. Which is better—to continue on the college level his study of personnel management, office management, or accountancy, or to practice the skills that he has mastered and, concurrently or later, continue his studies toward higher levels of job requirements? No definite policy can be set down. However, if the boy or the girl continues his education before he has had experience as a worker, he needs some practice on a part-time or an apprentice basis, in order to obtain a complete picture of job requirements.

More and more higher schools of learning are appreciating this fact. Cooperative courses are becoming increasingly popular. We have long been familiar with such work experiences as practice teaching, interning, clerking in a law office, store experience for those preparing for merchandising, actual nursing as a part of a nurse's training, and the like. Young people who are preparing themselves in such fields as music, art, dancing, and writing are given periodic opportunities for placing their accomplishments before the public for criticism, in the form of recitals, exhibits, magazine articles, dramatic presentation, etc.

Practice while one is training serves another purpose, in that it gives a young person an opportunity to discover whether or not his interest in the field is genuine, and whether or not he is likely to succeed in it. It is wise to ascertain these facts before one goes so far in the training for one field that it is difficult to switch to another.

At present, educational and occupational leaders are cooperating with one another in a manner that in the past was almost unknown. School men and women are making a conscientious attempt to analyze job requirements and, through individual and group conferences with employers, to familiarize themselves in a practical way with the employer point of view. Hence, training is geared to prepare the trainees for intelligent workmanship when they enter the specific field for which they have been trained.

Through this educator-employer cooperation, employers are learning more about the capacities and limitations of young workers and are also enabled to evaluate more adequately performance possibilities of job applicants and to provide further training whenever it seems desirable. Executives of many large organizations consider training on the job so important that they maintain their own training classes and allow time from the regular workday for attendance at these classes.

The purpose of this training is twofold: (1) improvement of the techniques of the job in which the worker is at present engaged and (2) advanced training for outstanding workers, aimed at promotion in the organization. For example, a nationally known insurance company gives a great amount of attention to the wise selection of workers and their subsequent success on the job. Once a worker is hired, he is rarely discharged unless he gives evidence of complete inability to adjust to any one of the many departments of the organization. If the worker shows dislike of the particular job for which he was hired or unsatisfactory performance in it, he is given tryouts and specific training for other forms of work within the organization until that one is found in which the young person is best able to make an adjustment.

Some employers go a step further in this matter of advanced training for their employees. It is not uncommon for an unusually promising worker to be encouraged by his employer (even to the giving of financial aid) temporarily to discontinue his work with the organization in order to prepare himself for a position of greater responsibility in the same organization upon the completion of his advanced study.

Harold's experiences present a definite success story, not only because of his ability to overcome his physical handicap, but also in terms of his employer's demonstrated recognition of the young man's superior ability and fine attitude.

Harold Was Not Stopped by the Loss of an Arm

When Harold was twelve years old, he stuck his arm out of a streetcar window and had it cut off at the shoulder bone. For a year or two, the boy felt the loss of this arm very keenly and might have become badly adjusted to a one-armed life if his family's attitude had not been intelligent and understanding. Fortunately, since it was the left arm that was severed, he was able to continue his regular habits of eating, writing, etc. His adjustment would have been more difficult if he had lost his right arm. He was a very intelligent lad, as well as a proud one, and learned quickly to carry on his regular activities with little or no assistance from others.

At school he majored in accountancy. Because of his excellent schoolwork, the State Bureau of Rehabilitation became interested in him. An artificial arm was made for him, but he rarely wore it, since it was uncomfortable, and he had overcome any feeling of embarrassment concerning his empty sleeve. The bureau also wished to grant him a scholarship for continued study on the college level. However, Harold's father, who was not a well man, feared that he would not be able to finance four extra years of study.

Consequently, with the aid of a small sum of money that he had received as a result of the accident, Harold financed himself at an advanced school of accountancy and then obtained an excellent position as a bookkeeper with a well-known firm. Harold's work here was so satisfactory that his employer offered to finance the boy's studies on the college level and then to take him back into the company as a certified public accountant. Harold accepted the offer and is now within one year of graduation. He is a thoroughly well adjusted and attractive young man.

It is extremely important that a young person be discouraged from entering a field for which he is only partially trained. Whatever his beginning responsibilities in a particular vocation may be, the candidate for that work should be thoroughly trained to meet those responsibilities.

One of the tragedies of worker shortage during wartime is the fact that many young people are encouraged to leave school and undertake work for which they are in the process of being trained. As a consequence, employers complain bitterly concerning the inefficiency of their workers, yet do not dare to discharge these untrained young people, lest there be no others available. Hence, these job holders pile up for themselves much unsatisfactory work experience. When there is a decrease in the demand for workers, they are in the anomalous position of having experience (which is usually desirable) but insufficient training. They must compete with inexperienced but thoroughly trained young people. It is too early to prophesy which the employer in the future will stress —experience with limited training or adequate training with little or no experience.

Should a young person limit his training to the field of his specialization?

In the past, training for work experience in such fields as art, music, commercial work, and mechanics was received for the most part either by way of private tutors, in specialized schools, or through apprenticeship under the supervision of master workers. There are still such agencies available, and many do an excellent job of intensive training. However, no matter what the field of specialization may be, the trainee needs more than skill competency. All forms of work are social in nature, in that the worker must associate with other persons. These include workers like himself, persons for whom the work is being done, and employers or supervisors whose function it is to evaluate critically both the work and the worker. Moreover, a worker does not work at his job for twenty-four hours of the day. Hence, he needs training for living a rich and full life during his nonworking hours.

Recognizing the need for more than specialized training, many colleges and other schools of higher learning are including specialized training in their broad program of education. Hence, there are available, in one college or another of excellent standing, opportunities for specific training in music, art, teaching, journalism, home economics, interior decorating, accountancy, merchandising, mechanics, and the like. In these colleges, as the student pursues his specialized training, he may also gain cultural education through such subjects as philosophy, the languages, literature, social science, psychology, pure science, mathematics, etc. At one and the same time, he is being educated to be a worker and to appreciate fundamental life values.

In light of the above, it can readily be seen that the modern tendency is that of educating along broad, as well as special, lines. Therefore, whenever it is geographically and economically possible to do so, parents and advisers should encourage young people to continue their specialized training in schools or colleges that offer broad cultural education. Of course, the young person must be assured of receiving as intensive training in his specialization in a school of this kind as he would in a specialized school. Unfortunately, since this movement is relatively new, some colleges are not yet prepared to offer as thorough specialized training as can be obtained in the old and thorough specialized schools. This is not an argument for a return to narrow specialization, but it is a plea for the improvement of course offerings and teaching personnel in the colleges.

Helping an Adolescent Obtain a Job

How can a young person learn about job opportunities?

The kind of job in which an adolescent starts his occupational life is very important. Here he will need to acquire a new set of attitudes and behavior patterns in order to meet the demands of a new situation. His whole work life may be influenced by the stimulations to which he is exposed in his first job. It is here that he first learns about worker responsibility and rights, employer-employee relations, and employee-employee relations.

If an adolescent's experiences in his first job are wholesome and satisfying, he is likely to develop desirable worker attitudes. If in his first job he is allowed to develop habits of carelessness, if the employer is too easy or too rigid, or if the morale among the workers is undesirable, the young entrant into work life, like the young entrant into school life, gets off to a bad start and may have difficulty later in making a wholesome adjustment to any type of job situation.

Hence, it is imperative that parents and advisers give careful consideration to a young person's first job placement and that they do all that they can to help him secure employment with a reputable employer. If this is done, the adolescent is given an opportunity to do work that lies within the limits of his capacity and training among workers who give evidence of wholesome worker morale. Too many times, the first job is looked upon as an unimportant steppingstone to better things. What is overlooked is the fact that the young worker is very suggestible at this time and can be influenced by his work environment more easily than will be possible later.

The usual avenues for gaining information about job vacancies include

1. Friends and acquaintances
2. Newspaper advertisements
3. Magazines and occupational periodicals
4. Commercial employment agencies
5. Government employment agencies
6. School employment agencies
7. Civil service or other examination systems
8. Random shopping around

1. *Friends and Acquaintances.*   One of the most commonly used methods of job placement is that of seeking the assistance of relatives, friends, or acquaintances. A man or a woman known to the family has a position in which he is earning success, or he himself is an employer of young people. Hence, he appears to be an excellent medium for helping the adolescent obtain his first job. One advantage of using this technique is that the parent usually can be assured that working conditions in this organization will be desirable.

However, this method of obtaining job placement has several possible disadvantages. If the prospective employer is a relative or a friend of the young worker, the latter's employment may stimulate an attitude of antagonism toward him among the other workers. He may be regarded by them as the "boss's pet" or, still worse, as an agent placed among them in order to spy upon them. This attitude is intensified if the young person received the position in preference to another applicant, possibly better fitted for the work but not personally known to the employer. Many businessmen, for this reason, refuse to employ close friends or members of their own families. The best that they will do is to refer such a person to the organization of a business associate, where the personal element is not obvious.

Often, especially in times of worker shortage, an employer requests his employees to inform their friends of vacancies on the staff. The employer philosophy is that satisfactory workers are likely to have friends who would possess desirable personality and worker attitudes. For a qualified young person this is an excellent approach to a job. If his friend is a capable and well-liked member of the organization, the new employee's early job adjustments will be made easy for him. Many employees who are asked to help in the filling of vacancies refer the request to their former school and thus are assured of as careful job placement as that which they received.

If the situation is merely that of a friend's or a relative's attempting to help out an adolescent without sufficient knowledge of the young person's attitudes or job qualifications, the results may be unsatisfactory. The fact that one person has earned success in a given type of work or in a particular organization is no guarantee that another person will be equally satisfactory or satisfied.

A young person should rarely start his work life in the employ of a friend or a relative. He should seek employment in an organization in which a friend or a relative works, only if he is thoroughly qualified to meet the responsibilities of the job for which he is applying. In general, an appeal for help in job placement to those who are near to the family should be the last rather than the first method of approach to be used.

2. *Newspaper Advertisements.* Reputable newspapers are accustomed to investigate help-wanted advertisements. Many firms are well-known organizations, and there need be no doubt as to their honesty and sincerity. The young applicant will probably be interviewed by a member of the firm's personnel department. The only concern here will be whether or not the applicant is qualified for the vacant position. It would be in order for the adolescent, in such instances, to answer the advertisement unaccompanied by an adult.

If, however, the advertisement has the appearance of a "blind ad," if the advertiser is an individual rather than a well-known organization, or if the nature of the work is not definitely stated, an adult of experience should investigate the reliability of the advertisement before a young person is allowed to apply for the job. Under no circumstances should an adolescent go for an interview in this type of opening unaccompanied by an adult. Sometimes young people feel that to take a relative with them when they are applying for work may militate against their chances of obtaining the position. This is not true. A reputable businessman, more often than not, prefers to employ a young person whose parents or advisers are concerned about the kind of place in which he or she will work. This applies especially to girls, but holds also for young boys.

3. *Magazines and Occupational Periodicals.* Advertisements that appear in the better journals are usually authentic. Many organizations of national reputation advertise in trade journals. Such firms can offer ambitious, well-qualified young people excellent opportunities for success and advancement. Parents need have no fears concerning the advisability of their sons' or daughters' responding to such advertisements. However, if the advertiser is not known to the parents, the procedures suggested above should be followed.

4. *Commercial Employment Agencies.* There are some well-known agencies that have a reputation for intelligent and honest placement. Others are very undesirable. These

agencies are business concerns and rightly expect to receive payment for services rendered. They are active in bringing the individual and the job together. For this they receive a flat bonus or a percentage of his earnings.

A reputable agency wants satisfied clients—both employer and employee. They make certain that the vacancy is desirable and that the applicant meets the qualifications set for the opening. This is particularly true of agencies that deal with placement in professional fields, like teaching, chemistry, or other technical fields.

Less reputable agencies place the emphasis upon turnover of business. Hence, they may not investigate employers or they may send to them applicants who do not have the proper qualifications for the positions. Moreover, in times of worker shortage, they are likely to use little discretion in placing young people; and in time of worker oversupply, their attitude toward possible applicants is often discourteous and disheartening.

5. *Government Employment Agencies.* These agencies operate on a nonfee basis and are sincere in bringing work opportunities and workers together. They are often understaffed, with a consequent inability to make as careful placements as they would like. These agencies have the opportunity of obtaining long-range and long-view knowledge of work opportunities and needs. If their personnel could be increased to the point at which they would have enough well-trained placement counselors available to make a thorough analysis of job requirements and worker qualifications, a fine job of placement could be done by them.

6. *School Employment Agencies.* The use of these agencies has one distinct advantage. The school knows its students. In making placements, it can give careful attention to the individual's abilities and extent of training.

Sometimes employers are a little afraid to make use of a school placement service until the school gains a reputation for thorough training and intelligent placement. However, there are employers who, as a result of previous experience with graduates of a particular school, consult that school first for their employees. A very fine relationship is further established and strengthened as the school's vocational counselor follows up the performance of his graduates on the job.

Very often school counselors consult with the parents when the latter sign the employment certificate of their son or daughter. In this way, the parent receives firsthand information from the school concerning the kind of work for which his child is fitted and the kind of firm to which he is being sent. Often the parent is encouraged to accompany the young person for his first interview, in spite of the fact that a school counselor does not send a young person to a job vacancy that he himself has not first investigated.

Perhaps the most satisfactory function of school employment agencies might be that of cooperation with the U.S. Employment Service. Successful job placement rests in good part upon two factors—extensive information concerning job opportunities and intensive knowledge of the skill and personal qualifications of the applicants.

This is where the government placement agencies and the schools that train the potential workers, by pooling their resources, could help one another. A suggestion as to an effective means of achieving this cooperation is that of having associated with each school a member of the U.S. Employment Service, who would bring to the school his knowledge of available vacancies and who would receive from the school advisers intimate and detailed information concerning available and qualified candidates. In this way, the job and the potential worker could be brought together with a minimum of record keeping and overlapping of effort.

7. *Civil Service or Other Examination Techniques.* Doctors, lawyers, teachers in many communities, nurses, all civil service employees and the like must pass qualifying examina-

tions of one kind or another before they are eligible to engage in their chosen work. Many large business houses employ a similar technique, although in a less rigid and more informal way.

If the examination techniques now in use could be modified in such a way that attitudes and personality qualities could be evaluated for all candidates who are qualified to enter competition, better placement of young people in jobs for which they are suited might be brought about. As leaders in the field come to recognize the importance of the more subtle elements of job efficiency, examination techniques will be adjusted in such a way that those candidates for placement who are best fitted both in personality and demonstrated skill will be the first to be considered for job placement.

However, when appointment to a particular job is based upon an individual's place on a list that has been promulgated as a result of an examination open to all qualified candidates, a beginner in a desired field is assured of the fact that his appointment is not based upon personal prejudice of any kind. His likelihood of early job placement will be in direct relationship to his demonstrated possession of certain qualities rather than on such factors as favoritism and prejudices. Moreover, if the placement carries with it a definite salary schedule, regular salary increments, at least partial tenure, and advancement through further examination, he is able to begin his employment relieved of those tensions which are likely to accompany placement in jobs in which there is the possibility of insecurity based on factors outside the proficiency of his work.

How can a young person be helped to apply for a job?

The technique of applying for a job has become much more formalized and follows a much more regular routine than formerly was the practice. In the past, the procedure was somewhat as follows: The young applicant learned about a job vacancy in one of several ways. He then presented himself at a specified place, at a definite time, with or without a letter of introduction, and was interviewed by the prospective employer. The interview usually was informal and followed whatever pattern a particular employer considered to be the most successful for obtaining desirable workers.

In many organizations, the above technique is still used, but there is an increasing tendency to supplement the interview by other more objective methods of discovering the qualifications of the applicant. Assuming that entrance into a given field is not by way of a formal examination system, the following practices are common to many organizations:

1. Letter of application
2. The filling in of formal application blanks, questionnaires, or interest blanks
3. The presentation of substantiating data concerning kind and extent of training
4. Letters of recommendation or formal recommendation blanks
5. Personal interview
6. Practical demonstration of skill or knowledge

Parents and advisers should be thoroughly acquainted with these techniques.

1. *Letter of Application.* Most prospective employers prefer that this letter be written in longhand rather than typewritten. They seem to believe that they can gain certain information about the applicant from his style of handwriting and from the composition and general arrangement of the letter. This does not imply that employers believe that a character analysis can be obtained from handwriting. However, a letter written in longhand is more likely to represent the candidate's own efforts than might a typewritten letter.

The personal information presented in this letter should be accurate and should be stated as briefly as is consistent with the inclusion of all necessary data. The reader should find in the letter adequate coverage of the following matters:

a. Source of the applicant's knowledge of the vacancy

b. Address, sex, and age of the applicant

c. Reasons for the writer's application

d. Education and specific training qualifications

e. Work experiences, if any (This might well include any part-time work or school activity related to the kind of work being sought.)

f. A request for an interview or for information concerning the next step to be taken by the applicant

The letter should be neatly and carefully written and free from blots, erasures, striking out of letters and words, and the like. Margins should be even and punctuation correct. Unimportant information or comments should be avoided, as well as undue emphasis upon any exceptional achievements of the candidate. The letter should be neither apologetic nor humble in tone.

A young person writing his first letter of application should ask his parents or his adviser to edit it. However, the letter should be the young person's own composition and should not be written for him by an adult. An alert employer or personnel worker can usually recognize the extent to which a young person has been aided in the writing of the letter. Even though this fact is not immediately recognized by the employer, a letter written by an adult may be so well phrased that too much will be expected of the supposed young writer of it.

It is unwise to claim the ability of doing more than one can. The teacher who coaches his students for a standardized test and the parent or adviser who writes a letter for a young job applicant will not always be present to do the thinking for that young person if the latter is given certain responsibilities the capacity for the doing of which would seem to be indicated by his performance on the test or in the letter of application. Employer disillusionment and worker discouragement are likely to follow any dishonesty in job application.

2. *The Filling in of Application Blanks.* In many ways

this technique is simpler for the applicant than is the writing of a letter of application. Some companies require the letter of application to be followed by the filling in of these blanks by those candidates whose letters seem to warrant further consideration. Other organizations invite young people to send for or to call personally for the application blank and to enter on it all pertinent information.

Young people should be discouraged from presenting any information that is not entirely correct. Age should not be falsified. In a time of extreme worker shortage, some employers tend to be careless in this matter unless they are called to account for disregard of state law. Since employment certificates and social security cards are required for placement on a job, any attempt to give incorrect information on an application blank in order to increase one's eligibility for a job may be checked and cause embarrassment.

Personal questions, such as those which deal with nationality or race or with religious affiliations, are forbidden by law in some states. However, in those states where this information can be called for, answers should be given honestly, even though this may mean that the applicant is thereby refused employment. The truth will become known eventually and may result in extremely unpleasant experiences.

If an interest blank or similar questionnaire is administered, the young applicant's responses should be made in terms of his actual attitudes and interests, rather than in terms of what he thinks he should say. He may have a mistaken idea concerning what is expected of him and so may say the wrong thing, or he may convey an impression of himself as an individual that will not be substantiated by his later behavior if he obtains the position.

Briefly, parents and advisers should make certain that young people give honest and accurate answers to all questions addressed to them. Of course, young people should be taught to be honest and sincere in all their relations with other people. Honesty in job seeking is emphasized here because of the number of questions relative to this point that are constantly asked by young job seekers.

3. *Presentation of Substantiating Data.* Little need be said about this technique. An increasing number of employers send directly to the school concerned for transcripts of the applicant's school record, including age, date of graduation or of leaving the school, rank in class, subject matter strengths and weaknesses, personal characteristics, and the like. This is a desirable procedure.

Usually, the information presented by the applicant agrees with authoritative records. Occasionally, there is evidence that a young applicant has not presented accurate data. In the matter of application for positions of trust and confidence with the government, intensive follow-up and investigation of all records, as well as a check on personality characteristics, are made by government investigators.

4. *Letters of Recommendation and Recommendation Blanks.* Young people often find it difficult to recognize the relative worthlessness of a letter of recommendation that they have solicited from a friend and have then presented personally to a prospective employer. They need to be educated toward an understanding of the purpose and value of letters of recommendation.

If a young person is asked to present such letters, he will, of course, solicit them from persons who, he has reason to believe, think well of him and will write flattering letters about him. The writer of such a letter is thereby confronted with the problem of giving a fair estimate of the applicant and, at the same time, of helping him to obtain the job.

To be of value, letters of recommendation should be sent directly to the prospective employer and should be honest in statement. To suppress information that would give indication of an applicant's unsuitability for a job or to overemphasize the young person's desirable qualities will hinder rather than help the applicant's future success if he should obtain the position. Moreover, personal prejudice should never show itself in a letter of recommendation.

Many businessmen and personnel managers have discarded the use of letters of recommendation and are substituting for them regular recommendation blanks containing specific questions referring to those particular attitudes and behavior habits which are essential to success in the position to be filled. Anyone called upon to answer a questionnaire of this type should give accurate responses that are detailed enough to present a true picture of the young person concerned. If the writer does not have sufficient data at his disposal to answer some of the questions accurately, he should not hesitate to admit this fact. In some schools, a cumulative personal record is included in the files of the graduates. These can be consulted when these blanks are being filled.

5. *Personal Interview.*   Rarely is an applicant hired without a personal interview. This is a grueling experience for many young people. Often, the more desirable the candidate, the more likely he is to show nervousness or fear of the interview. The majority of interviewers are trained to recognize applicant potentialities that may not show themselves in the interview. There are, however, certain ways in which the young person can be helped to create a favorable impression upon the interviewer. Parents and advisers should prepare a candidate for an interview by emphasizing the importance of the following points:

a. *Careful Grooming.*   The candidate should make sure that his hair is neatly combed; that his hands and fingernails are clean; and that his clothes and shoes are appropriate, spotless, and in good condition. He should make certain that his handkerchief is clean and that his gloves are free from holes. If the applicant is a girl, her use of cosmetics should be sparing and artistic.

b. *Punctuality.*   The candidate should arrive at the place of the interview early, so that he has sufficient time to compose himself or to make last-minute adjustments in his clothes or grooming. He should never be late unless he has been unavoidably retarded, as by a serious transportation delay. In such circumstances, it would be desirable for the applicant, if he could, to telephone to the interviewer, reporting the cause of the delay, and leaving it to him to decide whether or not the interview should be held as soon as possible or should be postponed. An interviewer who is kept waiting is not likely to be favorably disposed toward the applicant who is responsible for the delay.

c. *General Behavior.* The applicant's manner should be dignified, courteous, and controlled. There should be no gum chewing. There should be no indication of a hail-fellow-well-met attitude on the part of the applicant, neither should he look as though he were on the way to his own execution. His manner should be pleasant and cheerful, but reserved. If the interviewer indulges in witticisms as a means of putting an applicant at ease, the latter should not so presume upon the friendly attitude of the former as to return in kind. However, the applicant should indicate by his attitude that he understands and appreciates the interviewer's attempts to remove nervous tensions.

d. *Answers to Questions.* All questions asked by the interviewer should be answered by the applicant in a distinct, well-modulated voice, and in easy but not slangy phraseology. In general, the answers should be brief, unless the interviewer encourages a detailed explanation of certain points. The applicant should not allow himself to be drawn into an argument, neither should he hesitate to admit his limitations. Sometimes, an interviewer deliberately baits a candidate, in order to discover whether or not the young person has any clear conception of his own qualifications.

In one instance in which the applicant waxed eloquent concerning his varied abilities, the prospective employer terminated the interview with this statement: "You have convinced me that the job for which you are applying is too simple for your consideration. You should have my job, but I am not yet ready to turn it over to you. Good day." Not all interviewers are so frank as this one. They do not hire the applicant, but refrain from giving him the reason for their decision.

Some interviewers have pet stunts that they ask the applicant to perform. The activity, such as walking a straight line, looking up information in a book at hand and discussing it, or any similar task apparently unrelated to the duties of the position, may be utilized for one or another reason. The interviewer may wish to discover the attitude of the applicant toward the request, or he may desire to observe the quickness with which the young person responds to such directions. No matter what the reason for the request may be, if the candidate can meet it, he should do so with dignity and dispatch; nor should he question the reason for the activity unless the interviewer encourages him to do so.

6. *Practical Demonstration of Skill or Knowledge.* In certain fields, the formal examination referred to earlier takes care of this phase of job application. However, employers are beginning to use this technique informally as a part of the interview. The applicant is requested to bring with him certain samples of work that he has completed during his training period, is given a letter to type, is requested to carry on a simple piece of work related to the job for which he is applying, or is asked questions that will give evidence of his knowledge of certain definite facts or principles connected with this work.

To perform adequately in situations of this kind is difficult, unless the young person has a great deal of emotional control and confidence in his own skill. His fingers may seem to be all thumbs or he may feel that he has not a thought in his head. If the young person has been well trained and if he has been given sufficient opportunity to assume responsibility in other areas, he will have gained thereby a degree of self-confidence that will help him in a situation of this kind. Moreover, understanding interviewers are able to distinguish between actual lack of ability and errors that are the normal accompaniment of a testing situation.

In conclusion, a young person should be trained to bring to his task of applying for a job all the understanding of human relationships that he has gained from his associations with people in his daily work and play.

ADJUSTMENT ON THE JOB

What are the responsibilities of employers to young workers?

The majority of the responsibilities of an employer to his beginning workers are no different from his responsibilities to all his workers. Many of these are required by law. An employer is responsible for

1. Paying a fair wage for work well done
2. Providing hygienic working conditions (These should include sufficient light and air, well-constructed furniture and machinery, safety devices, adequate facilities and sufficient time for lunch, short rest periods, sanitary lavatories, clothes lockers, drinking fountains, and the like.)
3. Administering constructive supervision

In addition to the above, the employer has definite responsibilities for the welfare of a young employee. The beginning worker should be viewed as an apprentice, who can be helped to become a valuable and satisfied member of the organization. He should be encouraged to do his work well and, at the same time, to learn through his experience on the job. He should never be exploited because of his youth and inexperience.

Many large business organizations have developed definite programs of employee orientation. In such programs, con-

How to Start the New Employee Right

In acquainting the new employee with his job, the foreman must take FIVE STEPS

I—Make Friendly First Impression on New Employee.

1. Wear a smile.
2. Tell new employee your name and get his.
3. Shake hands—if it comes naturally.
4. Show interest by asking friendly questions.
5. Express sincere desire to help him make good.
6. Tell him you'll welcome questions.

Your impression on him is as important as his impression on you.

II—Explain Important Rules Regulations.

1. General safety rules.
2. Working hours.
3. Notification of absence.
4. Passes and badges.
5. Restricted areas.
6. Plant protective regulations.
7. Parking and traffic rules.

III—Tell him about Employee Services and Opportunities.

Sell the new employee on the future of his job, by presenting briefly information regarding:

1. Vacation plan.
2. Sick leave privileges.
3. Medical and health services.

4. Recreational activities.
5. Educational opportunities.
6. Promotional opportunities.

IV — Explain Pay System.

Be sure that the new employee knows—

1. What his pay rate is.
2. How his pay is figured.
3. When he will be paid.
4. Overtime, holiday, and night shift rates.
5. How he can improve his earnings.
6. That you will answer any pay questions that arise.

V — Acquaint New Employee with Places and Fellow-workers.

Show him such locations as—

1. First-aid room.
2. Wash room.
3. Dressing room.
4. Stock room, stores, and supply cribs.
5. Time clock.
6. Cafeteria.

Give him personal introduction—

1. To employees with whom he will work.
2. To employees whom he will need to contact.

The first responsibility in the development of a satisfied and efficient worker is to make him feel at home when he starts his new job.

TRAINING DIVISION

ATLAS POWDER COMPANY

Ravenna Ordnance Plant

siderable emphasis is usually placed upon the supervisor's or the foreman's responsibility for the initiation of new employees. The training division of the Atlas Powder Company includes in its training program a unit on the treatment of new employees, which we heartily endorse.

The first job experiences of a young man or woman may affect his usefulness as a worker during his entire work life, no matter what type of work his may be. Attitudes toward work in general and toward his special work in particular, relations with his fellow workers, reactions to supervision, and degree of job satisfaction are usually developed during a young person's first work experience. These general principles hold, whether the work life is started in the research laboratory, the business office, the classroom, the shop, the department store, the law office, the hospital, or any other seat of occupational endeavor.

What should be the attitude of the employer or supervisor toward the employees?

If a phrase that has more or less gone out of style may be revived, the attitude should be that of a lady or of a gentleman. Courtesy, dignity, kindliness, and objectivity should characterize the attitude of an employer toward an employee at all times. The worker should be regarded as an honest, capable member of the organization, who expects to do his best and to receive an adequate monetary reward for his efforts. Each needs the other. The employer could not run his organization without the services of his employee. His employee would not be able to earn a living in his chosen vocation unless there were an opportunity for him to do so in an organized field of activity.

Hence, the office of a business firm or any other organization is no place for employer temper tantrums, harsh and destructive criticism, or unjust suspicions or accusations. The employer has the right to demand of his workers an

How to
Handle Grievances

Neglected or poorly handled grievances cause dissatisfaction, reduce worker efficiency, increase accident hazards, and may result in the loss of a needed employee's services.

To Handle A Grievance Properly, Take the Following Four Steps:

I—Listen Open-Mindedly.

1. Willingness to listen opens the aggrieved employee's mind.
2. Listen patiently.
3. Listen, no matter how trivial the grievance.
4. Encourage him to tell his story completely.
5. Show sincere interest in the employee's complaints.
6. Discuss, don't argue.
7. Even the small grievance is important to the man.

II—Get All the Facts Straight.

1. Encourage the employee to repeat his grievance.
2. Question him carefully.
3. Talk to others if necessary.
4. Consult records when necessary.
5. Take time to get all the facts straight.
6. Don't "jump to conclusions."
7. If need be, consult the man above you.

III — *Act Promptly and Fairly*.

1. Don't delay action.
2. Don't "pass the buck."
3. If the answer must be "No," give ALL the reasons why.
4. Handle an imaginary grievance with all tact and fairness.
5. Try to save the employee's face. Do not humiliate him.
6. Be ready to give the employee the benefit of the doubt.
7. Don't use your authority to force a decision.
8. Avoid snap judgment.
9. Never give an employee "the run around."

IV — *Report*.

1. Report all grievances to the man above.
2. Report grievances which you settle satisfactorily as well as grievances on which you must consult with higher authority.

"Most fires could have been put out with a teacup full of water if applied at the right time and place." ¶ Take care of the little grievances and the big grievances may never develop. ¶ Learn from every grievance how to make the jobs of your men more satisfactory. ¶ When listening to a grievance, put yourself in the other fellow's place. See it as he sees it.

TRAINING DIVISION

ATLAS POWDER COMPANY

Ravenna Ordnance Plant

honest day's work for an honest day's pay. Lack of punctuality, careless work, or loafing on the job should not be tolerated. An employee whose work is unsatisfactory or whose attitude is uncooperative should be helped by the employer or a supervisor to make desirable improvements. If this appears to be impossible, the worker should be asked to leave the organization but should be informed definitely and specifically concerning the reasons for his discharge.

There should be no favorites in an organization. All workers should be treated with equal justice and fairness. Promotion or salary increases should follow a definite plan, with which the workers are acquainted and with which they are in agreement. An employer should never become a party to gossip about other workers, nor should he use an employee as an agent to spy upon other workers. The employer should do all in his power to build up a fine worker morale and friendly relations between the workers and himself, as well as among the workers.

Employers are as eager to have satisfied and efficient workers as are the workers to be happy and proficient. To this end, many employers have put into practice certain techniques for resolving any conflicts that may arise. As an example of this we present another practice that is in use at the Atlas Powder Company.

An employer's attitude toward his workers should be friendly, but not too informal. He cannot afford to mix his business with his social life. No matter how much an employer admires an employee, he should in no way make this interest apparent in his relations with the worker. The relationships that should exist between an employer and an individual employee follow the same general principles that were suggested earlier concerning teacher-pupil relations. One person cannot be singled out for special attention if a satisfied worker staff is desired. Human jealousies and resentments operate in the vocational field as they do in the home, in the classroom, or in any social group.

Undesirable as any show of favoritism is between an employer and an employee of the same sex, it is dangerous if it is evidenced between two persons of opposite sex, especially if the employer is a man and the employee is a young girl. The latter is impressionable and may view too seriously any exceptionally friendly behavior of an employer. She may feel that she has to accept his attention in order to keep her job. At the same time, if she is an emotionally stable young woman, she cannot help developing an attitude of contempt for an employer of this type, especially if she knows that he is a married man. The "office wife" has become the subject of much idle jest, which is sometimes ribald. Many young girls, in facing a first job, are seriously bothered as they try to determine what the proper attitude should be toward a male employer. Situations of this kind need to be corrected by social pressure.

In large, reputable organizations, this employer-employee, or supervisor-employee relationship is well controlled by the management. While friendly relations among the entire staff are encouraged, any deviation from that which is consistent with high standards of behavior is not tolerated. All employers need to take seriously their responsibility of earning, by their controlled and dignified behavior, the respect of all their employees.

What can be done to help a young person make a satisfactory job adjustment?

In general, a young person who has achieved a good home adjustment, who has enjoyed pleasant relationships with his teachers and schoolmates, and who is an active and cooperative member of other social groups, has little to fear in the matter of his job adjustment. Attitudes of sincerity, trustworthiness, responsibility, industry, and social adaptability have become a fixed part of his behavior pattern. His own nature and the training that he has received in his home and in his school have developed in him the ability to adjust successfully to new situations, new responsibilities, and new people.

In spite of their own beliefs to the contrary—often vehemently expressed—that school habits of carelessness, indolence, tardiness, and the like will not show themselves on a job, young people who exhibit such characteristics during their school life do not suddenly, with their advance into the work world, become models of cooperation, carefulness, and punctuality. Preparation for successful job adjustment, then, has its beginnings in the first responses of a young child and continues as he learns to adjust satisfactorily in his home, school, and social life.

However, in any new situation there are always found certain factors that will need intelligent consideration on the part of even the best equipped individual if he is to meet the situation satisfactorily. A young worker must bring to his first job an understanding of the problems that may confront him, as well as an appreciation of his rights and responsibilities as a worker.

It is strongly recommended that parents and advisers prepare a young person ahead of time concerning his proper attitudes and conduct on the job. It is the function of school advisers to acquaint their students with the types of job adjustment that must be made. It then becomes the responsibility of parents to watch the progress of their working son or daughter and to help him in every way possible toward the achievement of job adjustment and job satisfaction. A young worker may be on his own economically, but he still needs guidance and counsel. Some of the more general job-adjustment factors are given below and discussed briefly.

1. *Dress and Grooming.* The kind of clothes to be worn

depends upon the type of work to be done. Neatness and appropriateness of dress are essential. Whether it be overalls or business suit for the boy or slacks, suit, or dress for the girl, all buttons should be secure, no rips or tears should be visible, and the handy safety pin should be conspicuous by its absence. Linen should be clean—at least, at the beginning of the day. Moreover, the careful worker is able to keep himself reasonably neat and clean, no matter what his work may be.

Boys should shave daily and should keep their hair combed and fingernails clean. Girls should use make-up sparingly, avoid abnormally long and highly colored fingernails, and refrain from the use of cheap costume jewelry. Girls also should keep their hair well groomed and becomingly and conveniently arranged. The office or the workroom is not the powder room. All grooming activities should be taken care of in dressing rooms.

Businessmen and -women of America have an international reputation for their dignified attitudes and excellent grooming. The young worker should get into step immediately, lest he be embarrassed by comparison of himself with his fellow workers.

2. *Promptness and Punctuality.* A young worker who finds it difficult to arrive at his job on time is piling up trouble for himself. Unless he is trained to arrive early enough so that he can reach his place of business a little before he is due, his last-minute scrambling is certain to affect his efficiency for the day. To catch the last car or bus and then to sit on the edge of the seat, wondering whether or not he may be late, give rise to an emotional disturbance that is difficult to overcome.

Employers are appreciative of the worker who is always ready to start his work on time. They look with favor on the employee who is not a "clock watcher" but is willing, in an emergency, to stay a few minutes overtime. Furthermore, one means of earning promotion or salary advancement is to be prompt in the execution of a piece of work that needs to be finished at a specified time.

3. *Trustworthiness.* The highest compliment that an employer can pay an employee is the expressed recognition of the fact that the latter is *absolutely trustworthy.* Such a worker will carry out his duties conscientiously. He will refrain from gossiping with his fellow employees and other business associates, or with his friends and family about his employer's affairs.

A trustworthy employee regards the interests of his employer as his own interests. He feels a personal responsibility for the welfare of the organization. If there is any policy or practice of the organization that displeases him, he takes his criticism directly to his immediate superior.

4. *Industry.* A young worker must learn early that success usually accompanies the attitude of doing a little more, rather than a little less, than is expected of him. Here, again, habits of work developed in the home and the school show themselves in the work life. To try to get out of responsibility does not bring personal job satisfaction or promotion. A workman is worthy of his hire, but he is not entitled to more than he deserves. Malingering on the job or being satisfied with mediocre achievement is neither honest nor ultimately satisfying.

5. *Following Directions.* No one is perfect—not even employers. It is possible for an alert, well-trained young worker to recognize the fact that certain practices in his place of business could be very much improved. Many employers encourage their workers to offer suggestions for the improvement of working techniques. However, no matter how much an employee disapproves of existing practices, it is not his function to make changes without the approval of his employer or the supervisor. The employee's duty is to take directions cheerfully and to carry them out to the best of his ability. He should always be on the alert, however, to find

ways of improving techniques and then to present these suggestions clearly and tactfully to his employer or the supervisor.

What should be the attitude of the employee toward his employer?

Dignity, respect, and cooperation should characterize the attitude of an employee toward his employer. The young worker should not fear his employer any more than he should fear his parents or his teachers. If the employer's attitude is desirable, this is not difficult. However, an employee must never presume upon the good nature of his employer, nor mistake friendliness for easygoing laxity. The young worker should accept praise for work well done as well as reproof for poor workmanship. In fact, the young person who has been trained to respect his elders will have little difficulty in his relations with his employers.

Girl employees need to be very careful in their attitude toward men employers and supervisors. They should allow no social relationships to develop. If an employer and a woman employee need to discuss together any matter of business, this should be done at the place of business, not at luncheon or dinner. There is no excuse for a girl's accepting social invitations from her male employer. The importance of keeping employer-employee relations objective and businesslike cannot be stressed too strongly.

An unduly critical attitude toward the employer is equally undesirable. No employer, just as no parent or teacher, can please a young person at all times. If the employer is reasonable in his requests, the young worker should meet these cheerfully, painstakingly, and promptly. Parents should make it their business to discover the attitude of their working child toward his employer. If the employer cannot earn the young person's respect, the parents of the latter should encourage a change of job, since it is almost impossible for a worker to be successful if there is not a desirable relationship between him and his supervisors.

What should be the attitude of a young worker toward his fellow workers?

Much that has been said previously concerning dignity and objectivity holds for a young person's relations with his fellow workers. Sometimes older workers regard an alert, ambitious young worker with suspicion. Hence, it may be difficult for the new worker to find a place for himself in the group. He usually can break down group antagonism by assuming a modest attitude of cooperation. He should not attempt to force himself upon fellow workers but should wait until he is invited to join them. However, among satisfied workers there are, usually, at least a few who are eager to welcome a young worker and to help him adjust to his new environment.

If a new employee assumes an attitude of aloofness or superiority, in order to conceal his inner fear of the situation, he is likely to build up resentments against himself. The more natural a young person is in his behavior on the job, the easier it will be for him to become an accepted member of the organization. He should also realize that certain privileges come with length of service.

As in any group, the majority of the workers are likely to be well adjusted in their work and to exhibit a wholesome worker attitude. A few members may be uncooperative and critical of authority. The young worker needs to be on his guard against this small group of malcontents. At first, they may seem to be more friendly toward him than the others, but this friendliness may have an unworthy purpose. He should join groups, but he should know what the objectives of a group are before he joins it.

Friendships among employees are likely to develop, but these friendships should not be allowed to interfere with the fulfillment of required duties. Business hours are work hours.

There is no time in them for social visits among employees, discussion of personal matters, and the like.

What should be the attitude of young workers toward labor unions?

The history of labor unions has been the story of worker struggle for worker rights. The rise of industrialism was accompanied by definite worker exploitation. Labor unions have done and can do an excellent job of protecting the rights of the working man or woman.

Most young workers have received their first knowledge of the activities of labor organizations in their own homes. In school, young people learn about the industrial revolution and the present status of labor unions. However, it is as they hear these organizations discussed in the family group that they develop favorable or unfavorable attitudes toward this or that labor group.

Fathers and mothers and older brothers and sisters must be objective and open-minded as they discuss such matters in the presence of adolescents. These adults must be careful that their biased attitudes do not make it difficult for the younger members of their family to achieve, as workers, a desirable adjustment to the demands of a labor organization with which they may be expected to affiliate.

SOCIAL ADJUSTMENT OF YOUNG PEOPLE

Chapter 9

Teen-age Problems in Social Life

EXAMPLE is more potent than precept. In no life experience does this fact have more application than in the social life of young people. Adolescents are great imitators. They imitate very often without being aware that they are doing so. In addition, they are intense and are filled with natural urges, to which they seek to give expression.

Moreover, these young people consider themselves fully grown, and believe that they should have the right to live their lives by adult standards. On such matters as relations between the sexes, recreational activities, speech, mode of dress, and attitude toward the government, religion, and community affairs they quickly recognize the attitude and behavior of their elders. Is it strange, then, that they do many of the things that they do, when they have more or less desirable adult examples constantly before them?

Since the adolescent rarely does things by halves, he tends not only to mold his own conduct in terms of the examples that are set before him by his older associates, but he goes a step further and throws himself enthusiastically into whatever activity he finds exciting, into whatever activity affords immediate satisfaction. He seldom either considers or recognizes the fact that the results may be disastrous.

The adolescent is often stirred by a desire to reform the

world. He takes seriously the social ills that are called to his attention. He has an urge to improve the sorry state of affairs in the world. Fortunately, he is therefore capable of being influenced by the ideals of his elders as they attempt to guide his behavior into socially desirable channels.

Teen-age boys and girls want to go outside the home to engage in various kinds of social activities and games. They want the independence that matches their increasing strength and maturity. They want to be permitted to make greater use of their enlarged reasoning powers. The denial of these desires often makes them discontented and restless.

Inner conflict is inevitable. The struggle between adolescent urges seeking expression and attempts at their direction by adults who themselves seem to lack control of their own behavior, leads to bewilderment and, sometimes, to defiance of social customs and mores. Young people are taught to be honest and sincere in their relations with others, yet they see deceit and dishonesty in adult relationships. They are told to be tolerant; but they are surrounded by racial, religious, and class bigotry and intolerance.

They are given suggestions for appropriate dress and grooming, but their elders may follow the latest fads. They are admonished to be neat and clean, but their elders are often careless about their own appearance. They are taught the value of controlled behavior and proper speech, but they are stimulated by emotional outbursts and sarcastic and sometimes violent or vulgar speech.

Decent and honorable relations between the sexes is stressed by parents and other social leaders. However, not only are the newspapers filled with reports of illicit sexual relations, but adolescents' associates among older men and women often stimulate them with examples of such behavior. They become acquainted with many cases of unfaithfulness in the marital relationship or of promiscuity among unmarried individuals.

"Do as I say but not as I do" is an attitude that is responsible for many of the problems that arise in the life of teen-age boys and girls as they seek to adjust to their social relationships. "Don't smoke, don't drink, don't go to night clubs and roadhouses. Don't stay out late, don't be late for appointments, don't choose the wrong companions, don't spend too much time at motion-picture houses. Don't! Don't! Don't!" On all sides the young person is thus admonished, warned of the dire results of his conduct if he does not follow these admonitions.

However, many of the adults who thus attempt to direct the conduct of young people go blithely along in their own behavior practices, giving satisfaction to their immediate urges, prejudices, and desires, with no regard for the effect of their conduct upon the lives of others. Unfortunately, some of the adults who show a divergence between their own conduct and what they tell others to do are civic, educational, or social leaders whose behavior has a tremendous influence upon those with whom they come into contact.

Such situations make it very difficult for those adults who attempt to practice and teach desirable social attitudes to exert the influence that they should over young people. Their striving to do what is right and proper, as well as to teach what is right and proper causes them to be less appealing and less exciting than those adults who are not sincere and honest in their social living.

Young people respond to the glamorous. They, too, want to be interesting. They seem to think that they must choose between virtuous but dull and less virtuous but fascinating individuals, as patterns for their behavior. What are they to do? Can they achieve popularity and yet follow the straight and narrow path of doing what we say in spite of what we do?

Adolescents want the kind of freedom that will give them some social independence. They have a deep sense of right and wrong, and they have a strong desire to be liked by others.

They want to join clubs and form cliques. They especially want to join secret societies, in spite of the fact that initiation ceremonies are often painful and embarrassing.

Over and over again, teen-age boys and girls ask for help in meeting problems concerning their relationship with others. The majority of them want to do the right thing, but it is difficult for them to be sure just what the right thing is, since what they are told and what they observe may differ widely.

The questions asked by young people concerning their social relations are many and varied, and reflect every possible phase of social group living. They are keenly interested in their own attitudes toward their associates and in the attitude of other people toward them. They want to know how to make and keep friends. Such matters as correct dress and grooming, ways of acquiring an attractive personality, and desirable behavior in public are very important to them.

The questions presented below typify young people's concern about the many problems that they encounter as they struggle toward adult adjustment in social relations.

1. In what kind of social activities should adolescents engage?

2. Why does the school not furnish more after-school social activities?

3. What games should be played at parties when both girls and boys are present?

4. At what age would it be permissible for a girl to go to a formal dance without a chaperon?

5. Where should young people go for their social activities?

6. Should a boy decide where to go on a date or should he leave that to the girl?

7. What can a girl say when she does not want to go to undesirable places and still not appear snobbish?

8. How can young people be helped to meet other young people?

9. What should a girl do if a strange boy starts a conversation with her?

10. Is it necessary to break old friendships when new friendships are made?

11. How can a boy or a girl develop social ease?

12. How can a boy overcome bashfulness in the presence of girls?

13. Should a girl accept a cocktail at a party in order to be sociable?

14. How can a boy or a girl become popular?

15. Is it true that a boy who is popular with girls is not liked by other boys?

16. What is wrong if a girl is popular with the group but is not dated by boys?

17. Why are some girls popular with boys and not with girls?

18. Should one always be candid in expressing his opinions?

19. How important are friendships that are made during adolescence?

20. Why do some people take advantage of others?

21. How can one overcome doing things on impulse that are later regretted?

22. Parents and teachers are always talking about the right kind of companions. How can one know who is the right kind?

23. What should be one's attitude toward his friends?

24. Why are we encouraged to form friendships with members of our own sex?

25. Are most girls very changeable in their likes and dislikes of boys?

26. Should a girl associate with another girl who is six years older than herself?

27. At what age should a boy or girl start to have dates?

28. Should boys and girls ever go "Dutch"?

29. Should matters concerning sex be discussed between a boy and a girl?

30. How can one tell if another really loves him or her?

31. How can one judge the character of the boys with whom one associates?

32. What is puppy love?

33. Why does war seem to cause an abnormal interest in sex?

34. What is a good way to refuse an invitation more than once without offending the person who extends the invitation?

35. How can a girl encourage a certain boy to date her?

36. Should a mother object to her daughter's going out with a boy simply because he is of a different religious faith?

37. Should a boy ever ask a girl who is much taller than he is to dance with him?

38. Is necking or petting wrong?

39. Does a boy respect a girl more if she does not pet?

40. How should a boy or a girl go about the selection of a mate?

41. Is a marriage likely to succeed if the boy is much older than the girl?

42. How can one be sure of happiness in marriage?

43. What characteristics should a boy look for in the girl he expects to marry?

44. How can one differentiate between love and infatuation?

45. Is it true that people with about the same amount of education have happier marriages than other people?

46. At what age should young people marry?

47. How long should an engagement be?

48. If a boy and a girl expect to marry, should they make dates with other girls and boys?

49. After a boy or a girl marries, who should come first—the mate or the parents?

50. Should a girl marry for security if she is not in love?

Young people are especially concerned about their relations with members of the opposite sex. "How can I make boys like me?" and "How should I behave toward boys?" are questions often asked by girls. Boys want to know what their attitude toward girls should be, whether they should expect girls to pet, what kind of gifts are appropriate for girls, and the like.

Both boys and girls give much serious thought to marriage and the marriage relationship. They appear to be developing an increasing interest in the choice of a desirable mate, the length of an engagement, the setting up of a home, and the care of young children.

A young person's social adjustment is not a thing apart, but is closely linked with his adjustment to his home and school relationships. It usually follows that a boy or a girl who experiences a normal and well-integrated home and school life carries over to all his other associations a similar wholesomeness of attitude and control of behavior.

In the stories that follow, the reader will readily recognize the fact that the young people described give evidence of certain personality lacks in their home and school relationships that make it very difficult for them adequately to meet their social responsibilities. Moreover, the causes of an adolescent's social maladjustment often can be traced to a home environment in which the teen ager has had little or no opportunity to experience cooperative group living.

Douglas Needs New Associations

Douglas's mother died when he was a small child. His father attempted to bring him up with the assistance of relatives. As he was a night watchman, he found this difficult. Recently, the man married again, but Douglas resented his stepmother and beat and assaulted her.

The father reported the boy to the police authorities because he kept late hours and was beyond control. Since the boy's companions were undesirable, his father moved to another neighborhood, so that his son might meet boys of a better type. However, this did not help the situation.

In spite of tardiness, occasional truancy, the carrying of knives to school, and his boasts that he is a "mugger," Douglas likes school and can do good work spasmodically. He claims that he wants to get an education but that forces outside the school are too strong for him.

He is constantly getting into trouble of one kind or another and being brought up on charges in the local police court. He should be sent to another environment so far removed from his present associations that he may experience an opportunity to make a fresh start under strict but kindly guidance.

Georgia's Struggles with Unusual Handicaps

As a result of birth injury, Georgia's left arm is very much shorter than her right arm and her left hand is abnormally small and deformed. Otherwise, she is a tall, attractive girl. When Georgia was quite young, the mother was separated from her syphilitic husband because of constant friction between the two. Georgia and her brother were, thereupon, adopted by their maternal grandmother and lived with their mother at their grandmother's home.

Until Georgia was about sixteen years old and her brother seventeen, the family life was fairly well adjusted. Both the grandmother and the mother were working and the two children, after being graduated from elementary school, attended high school. The boy was doing very well at school but Georgia's work was unsatisfactory. She seemed to be ndifferent to her studies, came late almost every day, fell asleep in class, and was generally apathetic.

The grandmother explained to the girl's school adviser that Georgia was accustomed to read late, after she had gone through the motions of preparing her homework. As the grandmother worked at night and the mother spent the evenings away from home in social activities, the girl had no supervision. Georgia admitted that she rarely had more than five hours of sleep at night and said that she did not eat sufficiently because she was afraid of becoming stout. Later, it was discovered that Georgia's real reason for not eating was that she felt that she was a burden to her grandmother.

The older woman was very rigid and did not approve of social activities. In fact, the girl's mother was forced to leave the home because she was supposed to be having intimate relations with men. Georgia was suffering a conflict brought about by her grandmother's general attitude toward life, her mother's lack of authority over her daughter, and her own physical defect. It was very difficult to win her confidence, and she resisted attempts at kindly advice. Her brother did not have the same difficulties. One reason for this may be that the grandmother allowed him more liberties than were granted to his sister.

After a year of patient guidance, Georgia made a school adjustment to the extent of preparing her homework more carefully and of limiting her night reading to an hour. She herself realized that her greatest conflict grew out of her attitude toward home responsibilities, toward which she had been extremely indifferent. After her mother left the home, Georgia insisted upon assuming complete responsibility for household chores. She washed, ironed, and cleaned the house at night after her grandmother had gone to work. The strain of all this resulted in a physical breakdown, and she became seriously ill.

Upon her recovery, she appeared to take a more intelligent

attitude toward her schoolwork and was able to earn graduation. As soon as she was of age, she left her grandmother and
lived with her mother, who by this time was a sick woman.
Georgia has been nursing her mother and has been working
as a secretary in a good business house. It should be mentioned at this point that Georgia has always manipulated
her crippled arm very well and is not self-conscious about it.
However, she is not happy. She is moody, makes few friends,
and still finds her one release in the reading of light fiction.
She is not interested in men and explains this attitude in
terms of her mother's unfortunate marital relation and subsequent affairs with men. It is impossible to foresee what
the future holds for her.

Catherine Wants Attention

Since early childhood, Catherine, who is now fifteen years
old, has been a problem both at home and at school. She
wants attention and does everything she can to call attention
to herself. Children of her own age do not like her and are
afraid of her. She demands money from other girls, has been
known to beat them, and has shot pins around her classroom.

In spite of her superior mental ability, she is either unwilling or unable to recognize her undesirable attitude. Her
mother has always tried to treat the girl fairly and firmly,
but she is now helpless in the situation. Catherine has been
treated by a mental hygienist, but with no improvement.
Arrangements are being made to send her to an out-of-town
boarding school for girls, with the hope that a change of
environment will help her to make a better adjustment to
other people.

A Case of Extreme Emotional Disturbance

Margaret sits in one position for long periods without
speaking. She plays the piano until the other members of
the family can no longer bear it. On occasions, she locks her-

self in her room. She constantly complains that her brother and sister receive more attention than she does. She resents the fact that she is not allowed to go out alone in the evening. Her parents must listen constantly to her demands that she be allowed to take tap-dancing lessons. To emphasize this demand, she has been known to tap-dance for hours at a time. These are some of Margaret's behavior characteristics in the home.

During her first two years of high school, Margaret was a quiet, self-effacing, and satisfactory student. She suddenly became extremely articulate and aggressive. She was very much interested in science and insisted upon joining the science club. At the first meeting after she had been accepted by the club, she started to tell a story about her father's work at Johns Hopkins University. (He is a chemist by occupation.) She reported that he had cut a rat into several cross sections, bandaged it, and left it in the closet. A week later he found it "all healed together." When her story was questioned by the other students, she became very much disturbed and not only insisted that the story was true but continued to add many gory details.

Although she was a member of the honor class in chemistry, her work became progressively unsatisfactory. The writing on her test papers was extremely untidy, almost illegible and incoherent. She was accustomed to go to the chemistry laboratory alone, turn on switches, and experiment with various chemicals. When she was reprimanded for her actions, her answer was that a true scientist is not bound by rules made for ordinary people.

Her behavior became increasingly peculiar. The following include some of her abnormal acts: she submitted her homework written with lipstick; during study period, called the name of a girl who was not there; collected money for the school publication, kept no account of it, and failed to bank the money; during recitation periods left her seat without permission to open and shut windows; burst into a class-room while a recitation was in progress, demanding ink for her fountain pen.

She would refuse to leave school at the end of her school-day but would conceal herself in various parts of the building where she wrote poetry for the school paper or as a gift to a teacher. She had no poetic ability but seemed unable to realize this fact. Her poetic attempts are an indication of her disturbed mental condition. A few examples of them may be of interest.

Bells of Notre Dame

The bells of Notre Dame ring
  As the bird sings
  The children play
During the bright and gay day.

Movie Stars

Garbo, Taylor, Power and Green
  All could be seen
  On the screen
Sometimes they play as in their teens.

Please, Teacher, Please

Please, teacher, read the tale
But stop! It's starting to hail
And there's the mailman with the mail
But please read the poem or the tale
Read about the stagecoach, carriage, the mail!

When Margaret's parent were warned by the school that their daughter's behavior needed attention, they were not disturbed by this warning. They admitted that her behavior at home also was peculiar but claimed that she was merely going through an adolescent phase. They insisted that her acts were not unusual for a fifteen-year-old girl and that her attitude should be tolerated until she grew out of it.

One evening, shortly after a conference between her parents and the school adviser, Margaret asked her mother for permission to attend the movies. This request was refused. Later that evening, she slipped out of the house without her family's knowledge and went to a motion picture at some distance from home, yet in the city. After the motion picture, she apparently wandered about the streets until three o'clock in the morning, at which time she entered the lobby of one of the hotels.

Margaret wandered about the lobby, sat down at a desk, and wrote and tore up about a dozen post cards. She then entered into conversation with the boys on duty. She inquired as to whether they had girl friends and whether they would want her as a girl friend. She also wanted their names, addresses, and telephone numbers. She then asked the price of a room, but said that she did not have money enough for that and wanted to sleep in the lobby.

Margaret told the boys that her parents were in another state and that she was staying in town for the night. She also explained that she had a cousin near by and that she had been moody that day and had walked for miles. She asked the boys if they thought the police would trail her and seemed to expect that this would happen.

After futile attempts to get the attention of the men in the hotel, she walked out and, seeing a milkman, asked him for a ride. She told him that she had no money and could not get home. The man refused her the ride but gave her a nickel, whereupon she walked off. The following morning, she was discovered wandering around the corridors of a man's college in another part of the city. When she was questioned, she explained that she was looking for a cousin of hers. However, she gave her correct name and the name of her high school. She was then detained at the college until her school was contacted and she was brought back to her home.

Her parents, although they had been anxious over her absence from her home that night, still refused to consider her behavior serious, but were much concerned about the possible notoriety that might be given to her escapade. The father did blame the mother for the girl's condition, claiming that the latter was overprotective and did not allow the girl to travel alone except to school. He explained the running-away incident as a culmination of home events. As a punishment for this escapade, Margaret was beaten and was denied her supper and the use of her typewriter and piano.

Finally, the parents were prevailed upon to have her taken for a physical examination. As a result of this examination, she was given a six-month treatment for hypothyroidism. Upon her return to school, her manner was quieter and her studies improved. She was graduated and admitted to college. Within six months, she was discharged from college because of her peculiar conduct and her weird stories concerning the behavior of other students. She then attempted to obtain employment. However, up to the present, she has not been able to keep a job for more than a few months at a time. Her explanation for her discharges reflects her attitude. The work was too easy, the employer did not treat her well, the job was beneath her, or her fellow employees annoyed her.

It is hard to say what Margaret's future will be. She is intelligent enough to control her overt behavior so that she does not come into direct conflict with the law. She is not popular with boys, and explains this on the basis of their inferiority to herself. Her parents have lost patience with her, but seem unable to help her. If they had been willing to recognize the first symptoms of her maladjusted behavior, this girl might have been aided toward desirable emotional control.

In defense of her parents' attitude, it should be said that her older sister and brother are extremely normal persons.

They both earned college degrees and are at present achieving success in their chosen careers. There was a physical basis for Margaret's condition, but it is probable that her disturbed state had its beginning in the fact that, although she was a bright girl, she could not compete with the older and more successful children. During her childhood and early adolescence, she was made to feel that she was not only the baby but also the black sheep of the family.

David Was a Kleptomaniac

David was brilliant but completely lacking in any understanding of his responsibilities as a member of society. His mother, a widow, worked as a saleswoman in order to support her son. The boy has lived in various foster homes, including that of a cousin, who is a woman of some background and very eager to cooperate.

Because of his handsome appearance, charming manner, and unusual scholastic achievement, especially in mathematics, David has been able to win the friendship of anyone with whom he associates. However, he has little, if any, control over his behavior. He has always shown gross indifference to his mother's financial circumstances; and he tends to lie about other people, not only for his own protection but also to make trouble for the other person.

Most serious of all is the fact that David seems unable to resist the temptation of stealing. One reason for the many changes of foster homes was the fact that he stole money and then denied it. His school history has been the same. He was transferred from the high school to which he had been admitted as a freshman because of at least six thefts that were discovered. His technique was extremely clever and it took very careful watching to discover that he was the guilty boy.

At first, in his new school, he was most repentent for his behavior and promised faithfully that there would be no recurrences of his former habit. In order to remove the temptation of stealing, David's mother, at great sacrifice to herself, gave him a very generous allowance. However, it was not long before he left the path of virtue. He stole money from another boy while the two of them were in a motion-picture house. On several occasions, money was found to be missing from the homes of fellow students after a visit from him.

His general behavior became increasingly more willful. He began to stay out late at night without explanation. At school, he would leave his recitation room and wander around the halls. Several of his test papers were incomplete and he claimed that the teacher had lost the pages. It was suspected, however, that he had purposely withheld the answer sheets that he knew to be unsatisfactory.

In spite of these undesirable habits, the boy was able to earn good grades and, in his senior year, became eager to enter a good college. He reformed, made an honest attempt at paying back what he had stolen, and tried to influence his advisers not to report his misdemeanors to the college that he had hoped to attend. His mother also pleaded for him, suggesting that his difficulties were not very serious and could well be overlooked.

When David's application was sent to the college of his choice, it was accompanied by a report of the boy's difficulties and a suggestion that the improvement during the senior year might indicate that his changed attitude would be lasting. The college authorities finally decided to give the boy a chance, in light of his excellent scholastic achievement.

At the college, he was given a room to himself in the dormitory, so as to make his situation as simple as possible. It was not long, however, before he managed to violate several social regulations, not very serious, but disconcerting. Then came reports of several small items missed in the dormitory. After very careful investigation, the college authorities were reasonably certain that he was responsible for the disappearance of a pair of socks, but none of the other items could be traced to him with certainty. Although the situation could have been considered sufficient to require his dismissal from college, his advisers felt that the boy's home situation offered no hope of reconstruction. They were convinced that, if he were expelled from this college, he would not be admitted to any other respectable institution. This would have been unfortunate, since the boy had real ability.

As a solution of the problem, the boy's adviser and his wife agreed to take David into their home. There were some trifling infractions of rules, but in the main he exerted an unusual amount of effort to do well in his studies and to establish himself upon a more secure character footing. This was David's first acquaintance with a well-adjusted home life.

The boy has almost finished his college course. Until recently, he lived with his adviser but asked that he might be given an opportunity to show his trustworthiness in dormitory life. It is still too soon to report as to whether or not this is possible.

A letter from David to one of his high-school advisers seems to show at least an attempt at reform. It says, in part, "College is swell and I am getting along well in my studies. The people here are grand. Everyone is very friendly and I am having a good time. I am trying my best not to let fun interfere with my grades. I hope I succeed. I want to thank you for some of the advice that you gave me. In following it, I find myself getting along with people much better. In fact, I am getting along much better with myself."

Dennis Has Many Undesirable Practices

Dennis's father deserted the family, and his mother contracted a disease that caused her limbs to swell to such an extent that she cannot walk without propping herself against the wall. These conditions seem to be responsible in large measure for the boy's maladjustment. He leads a life of dissipation, stays out until all hours of the morning, and brags about the liquor that he drinks and the girls with whom he goes. No one has control over the boy. He has an indifferent grandfather, who takes no interest in the boy's welfare. Consequently, Dennis has no fear of anyone in the family and is running wild.

At school, he annoys teachers and classmates by his conduct. He fights with other students, smokes in the building, talks out in class during recitations, and acts like a clown. Once he knocked the kitchen truck down the stairs and nicked a hole in the wall. On another occasion, he took a boy's sweater and tore it to shreds, because, he claimed, the boy had torn his.

His one ambition seems to be that of attracting attention to himself by his undesirable behavior. He is intelligent enough to do good work, but he is perverse and refuses to apply himself, even though his school subjects have been adjusted to meet his interests. He listens respectfully to a scolding and then commits the same offense again.

Since he is sixteen years old, he could receive his employment papers and get a job, but he is not prepared to hold one. The only solution would seem to be that of removing Dennis from his present home to a boarding school, where, under strict but kindly discipline, he could be encouraged to develop better study and social habits.

It is difficult to label maladjustment as completely home, school, social, or vocational. In each of the above stories there is exemplified a more or less serious form of emotional disturbance, which showed itself in all or most of the adolescent's behavior. It is usually true that, unless early home or school difficulties can be adjusted, the uncontrolled behavior of the young person progresses (or rather regresses) into actual delinquency or mental illness and becomes a serious social problem.

Poverty, parental ignorance or indifference, and physical or mental disability are contributing factors in the setting up of a pattern of social inadequacy. The problems of social adjustment that are common to all normal young people who are growing up in normal environments become intensified if the young person has developed abnormal characteristics and is living in an unhygienic environment.

Fortunately, the majority of American young people bring to the solution of their problems of social living a background of healthy attitudes and behavior practices. In spite of the fact that even normal adolescents are consistent in their desire for independence of behavior in their social relationships, they are equally consistent in seeking sympathetic advice concerning problems that may arise in their social life. They seldom spurn help that is given in the spirit of understanding and fair-mindedness by adults who, through their own experiences during adolescence, have learned to evaluate objectively the sincerity and earnestness with which young people come to them for assistance.

The following self-evaluating questionnaires may help you to discover some of your own attitudes toward your procedures in the solution of the problems that are faced by young people in their social living.

WHERE I STAND IN RELATION TO THE SOCIAL PROBLEMS OF MY SON OR DAUGHTER

Score yourself at the right on each item listed

	1	2	3	Score
I help my son (daughter) to gain social ease.	Never	Sometimes	Always	____
I help my son (daughter) to develop self-confidence.	Never	Sometimes	Often	____

	1	2	3	Score
I help to provide a social hall for the young people in my community.	Never	Sometimes	Often	____
I tease my child about members of the opposite sex.	Often	Sometimes	Never	____
I train my son (daughter) to stand on his own two feet.	Never	Sometimes	Always	____
I listen to my son (daughter) relate his (her) stories of social life.	Never	Sometimes	Always	____
I help my son (daughter) to develop proper social habits at home.	Never	Sometimes	Always	____
I encourage my son (daughter) to criticize his (her) friends.	Often	Sometimes	Never	____
I read cheap love-story magazines in the presence of my son (daughter).	Often	Sometimes	Never	____
I use ill-health as a means of getting attention.	Often	Sometimes	Never	____
I encourage my son (daughter) to avoid saying anything he (she) may regret later.	Never	Sometimes	Always	____
I expect my son (daughter) to confide his (her) personal social affairs in me.	Always	Never	Sometimes	____
I help my son (daughter) to accept or refuse social invitations tactfully.	Never	Sometimes	Always	____
I object if I know that my daughter kisses a boy.	Always	Never	Sometimes	____
I permit my son (daughter) to go out with his (her) friends in an automobile.	Never	Often	Sometimes	____
I permit my daughter to entertain a boy in the home when no one else is at home.	Often	Sometimes	Never	____
I permit my son (daughter) to have social engagements during the school week.	Often	Sometimes	Rarely	____

	1	2	3	Score
I permit my daughter to invite her friends into the house after a party.	Always	Never	Sometimes	___
I advise my daughter to be introduced before talking to a boy.	Never	Sometimes	Always	___
I permit my daughter of 15 to date boys.	Often	Sometimes	Rarely	___
I permit my daughter of 14 to 16 to go out with boys and girls in a group.	Never	Sometimes	Often	___
I teach my son correct behavior with girls.	Never	Sometimes	Always	___
I encourage my son (daughter) to try to be liked by girls and boys.	Never	Sometimes	Always	___
I talk to my son (daughter) about the danger of petting.	Never	Sometimes	Often	___
I permit my daughter to invite boys to take her out.	Often	Never	Rarely	___
I approve of my son's (daughter's) going "Dutch" on dates.	Never	Often	Sometimes	___
I permit my son (daughter) to decide his (her) own party games.	Never	Often	Sometimes	___
I encourage my son (daughter) to go with a boy (girl) because he (she) has money.	Often	Sometimes	Never	___
I train my son (daughter) not to be jealous of his (her) friends.	Never	Sometimes	Always	___
I teach my son (daughter) to meet all appointments promptly.	Never	Sometimes	Always	___
I encourage my son (daughter) to select his (her) own clothes.	Never	Sometimes	Often	___
I encourage my son (daughter) to have many acquaintances of the opposite sex.	Never	Sometimes	Often	___

	1	2	3	Score
	Often	Sometimes	Never	

I encourage my son (daughter) to accept expensive gifts from friends of the other sex. **Often** **Sometimes** **Never** ____

I am willing to have my son (daughter) discuss questions concerning sex with his (her) friends. **Often** **Never** **Sometimes** ____

I chaperon my son (daughter) on a date. **Never** **Often** **Sometimes** ____

I permit my son (daughter) to use the family car. **Never** **Often** **Sometimes** ____

I allow relatives to interfere with my son's (daughter's) social life. **Often** **Sometimes** **Never** ____

I permit my son (daughter) to attend night clubs or roadhouses unchaperoned. **Often** **Sometimes** **Never** ____

I expect my son (daughter) to come home at a reasonable hour, even if the party has not ended. **Never** **Often** **Usually** ____

I approve my son's (daughter's) having close associates who are much older than he (she) is. **Always** **Sometimes** **Rarely** ____

I discourage my son (daughter) from smoking. **Never** **Sometimes** **Always** ____

I train my son (daughter) to evaluate the sincerity of his (her) friends. **Never** **Sometimes** **Always** ____

I give sex education to my son (daughter). **Never** **Sometimes** **Often** ____

I encourage my son (daughter) to participate in community activities. **Never** **Sometimes** **Often** ____

I permit my son (daughter) to make his (her) own decisions in social life. **Never** **Often** **Sometimes** ____

A review of these items may help you to evaluate your attitude toward parent-child relationships in social living.

You might ask yourself what you can do to improve in those items on which you scored yourself 1. For helpful suggestions, turn to the next chapter.

WHERE I AS AN EDUCATOR OR SOCIAL WORKER STAND IN RELATION TO THE SOCIAL PROBLEMS OF YOUNG PEOPLE

Score yourself at the right on each item listed

	1	2	3	Score
I try to help young people overcome self-consciousness.	Never	Sometimes	Always	____
I try to help young people gain social ease.	Never	Sometimes	Often	____
I act as a snob in the presence of young people.	Always	Sometimes	Never	____
I treat teen-age boys and girls as children.	Often	Sometimes	Never	____
I call teen-age youth "children."	Often	Sometimes	Never	____
I encourage young people to see only good plays and motion pictures.	Never	Sometimes	Always	____
I encourage boys and girls to have friends of their own age.	Never	Sometimes	Always	____
I encourage boys and girls to refuse a drink or a smoke.	Never	Sometimes	Usually	____
I encourage young people not to laugh at the mistakes of one another.	Never	Sometimes	Always	____
I avoid saying anything to young people that I may regret later.	Never	Sometimes	Usually	____
I help young people to recognize the important traits of a desirable companion.	Never	Sometimes	Often	____
I keep all confidences given to me by young people.	Never	Sometimes	Usually	____
I train young people in social etiquette.	Never	Sometimes	Often	____
I encourage the young teen agers to "pair off."	Often	Sometimes	Never	____

	1	2	3	Score
I encourage young people not to marry until they are at least twenty years old.	Never	Sometimes	Often	____
I advise young people how to settle their petty quarrels.	Never	Sometimes	Often	____
I advise young people to be honest and frank in their opinions.	Never	Sometimes	Always	____
I encourage high-school pupils to have their dates during the week end.	Never	Sometimes	Usually	____
I advise girls to speak only to boys with whom they are acquainted.	Never	Sometimes	Usually	____
I expect young people to plan and carry out their own social activities.	Never	Sometimes	Usually	____
I am a desirable (from parents' viewpoint) chaperon.	Never	Sometimes	Usually	____
I advise young people concerning the principles basic to a happy marriage.	Never	Sometimes	Usually	____
I warn young people of the dangers of petting.	Never	Sometimes	Always	____
I advise young people how to carry on an interesting conversation.	Never	Sometimes	Usually	____
I advise young people concerning the harm of deceiving others.	Never	Sometimes	Usually	____
I advise young people to avoid being conceited.	Never	Sometimes	Always	____
I encourage tolerance among young people.	Never	Sometimes	Always	____
I encourage young people to marry only for love.	Never	Sometimes	Usually	____
I advise young people to deny themselves sex experiences before marriage.	Never	Sometimes	Always	____
I advise young people of the importance of keeping ap-	Never	Sometimes	Always	____

	1	2	3	Score
pointments and of being punctual.				
I help to plan social activities for young people.	Never	Sometimes	Often	____
I advise young people concerning the value of courtesy.	Never	Sometimes	Usually	____
I warn girls not to go out with married men.	Never	Sometimes	Always	____
I help young people to become acquainted with members of the opposite sex.	Never	Sometimes	Often	____
I encourage free discussion of sex among young people.	Sometimes	Never	Rarely	____
I encourage young people to be loyal to one another.	Never	Sometimes	Always	____
I advise young people of their responsibilities to each other and to the group.	Never	Sometimes	Usually	____
I teach young people how to appraise the sincerity of another.	Never	Sometimes	Often	____
I encourage young people to join desirable groups in a community.	Never	Sometimes	Always	____
I advise young people concerning the desirability of giving inexpensive gifts which are well chosen.	Never	Sometimes	Usually	____

A review of these items may help to evaluate your attitude toward the social life of young people.

Chapter 10

Suggestions for Improving Social Relationships

WITH the increased freedom that young people are experiencing in their social relationships must come an increased emphasis upon guidance in social living. In the days of closer family unity and stricter chaperonage, the social activities of young people were usually carried on under the watchful eyes of parents or other adults. Friends and associates were hand-picked by parents. Much of the social life of the family centered around the home itself or in the homes of friends and acquaintances.

In the past, dances in the home, song fests, charades, family picnics, and the like constituted the recreational activities commonly indulged in. The associates of the younger members of the family usually were the sons and daughters of family friends. Playmates as children, companions as adults, these relationships often continued as adult friendships. Most marriages either were arranged by parents or were the normal outgrowth of years of companionship. In the days before the arrival of motion pictures, automobiles, and night clubs, the parental task of guiding adolescent social activities was relatively simple. In fact, the whole social pattern was very much simpler than that which exists at present.

Today, social offerings for adults as well as for adolescents are legion. The entire recreational program, especially in large cities, is so wide and varied that one can start in the morning, keep on the go until the early hours of the next day, and continue this program for seven days in the week, without exhausting all the available possibilities for amusement or recreation. Motion pictures, night clubs, dramatic productions, concerts, dances, sports, hikes, professional and school games, exhibitions, and organized recreational programs are at the disposal of young people—many of them at little or no cost.

Although these social offerings may be attended by both adults and adolescents, it is no longer considered *comme il faut* for the adults and the adolescents to engage in the activities together. Parents are expected to go their way and to allow their adolescent children to follow their own interests. Chaperonage is outmoded. Adolescent freedom in social activity is the order of the day. Hence, whatever is done by parents and other adults in the way of guiding such activity must be done for the most part by remote control.

Sometimes adults are tempted, in moments of impatience with young people's "goings on," to remark more or less heatedly, "Such things were not permitted in *my* day." That is right; they were not. However, it is probably a good thing that youth has been released from some of the unnatural restrictions of the past. A wholesome, free social life during adolescence is an excellent preparation for adjusted adult participation in community living. That does not mean that all the present practices are desirable or that all young people are living a well-adjusted social life.

Many young people recognize their own deficiencies as well as do their parents. Both adults and adolescents need and welcome suggestions aimed at fitting young people for satisfactory and satisfying relations with their associates during out-of-work or out-of-school hours. Some of the more common problems connected with teen-age social life will be considered here in a practical and specific treatment of questions that are asked many times by adolescents. These suggestions will be presented under the following headings:

1. Community responsibility for the social activities of teen-age youth
2. The gaining of social ease and popularity
3. Friends and companions
4. Adolescent relations with the opposite sex

5. Achieving a successful marriage relation

The topics discussed will be considered from the point of view of young people. The implications of these suggestions are aimed at parents and other adults who are concerned with the development among teen agers of wholesome social attitudes and behavior patterns.

COMMUNITY RESPONSIBILITY FOR THE SOCIAL ACTIVITIES OF TEEN-AGE YOUTH

In what kind of social activities should the teen-age youth engage?

Adolescents desire activity and want to participate in varied forms of social living without too close supervision. Hence, centers for the teen age should be established, in which games, dancing, lounging, and refreshments are provided.

Young people are interested in a wide range of activities. The following list[1] of recreational and social mediums is not complete, but it includes many of the activities in which young people are interested and in which they should have an opportunity to participate.

Physical recreation:
    Sports and athletics
    Water sports
    Winter sports
    Hiking
    Bicycling
    Bowling
    Roller skating
    Tennis
    Golf
    Badminton
    Volley ball
    Basketball
    Fishing
    Riflery
    Physical-fitness activities

Music activities:
    Community singing
    Informal group singing
    Glee clubs
    Choruses
    Bands

[1] "Teen Age Centers—A Bird's-eye View," National Recreation Association, New York.

Orchestra
Harmonica playing
Concerts
Community-service activities:
Victory gardening
Victory farm labor
Day care aides
Red Cross activities
Nature activities:
Nature hikes
Nature study
Gardening
Camping
Mental and linguistic activities:
Discussion groups
Forums
Debates
Reading groups
Writing groups
Lectures
Quizzes
Hobbies and special interests:
Collecting
Photography
Radio
Amateur movies
Social activities:
Dancing
Parties
Entertainments
Picnics
Outings

Beach parties
Treasure hunts
Scavenger hunts
Dramatic activities:
Dramatic stunts
Talent nights
Plays
Pageants
Minstrel shows
Operettas
Charades
Puppetry
Movies
Radio skits
Arts:
Painting
Sketching
Modeling
Art exhibits
Crafts:
Woodwork
Metalwork
Sewing
Knitting
Model aircraft
Model boats
Jewelry
Leatherwork
Citizenship activities:
Patriotic pageants and festivals
Holiday celebrations

Where should young people go for their social activities?

A definite place, which can be known as a youth center or canteen, should be established in the community for the use of these young people. The center should be for them and run by them. If they are allowed to organize their own activities, the results may be different from those achieved by adults, but the planning on the part of adolescents is of great value. The preparation of a youth center gives young people an opportunity to exercise their creative abilities and teaches them the art of working together toward a common purpose. Such activities furnish excellent means for the development of cooperative living. These values may be less potent later, when the center is fully equipped and ready for use, unless the young people are then encouraged to continue their control of the activities engaged in without too much adult supervision.

Available space for such activities can be found in school buildings, churches, and other community centers. Too many school buildings are not used sufficiently during after-school hours. Facilities should be made available for younger adolescents in the afternoon and for older boys and girls in the evening. The entire building for one or two evenings a week, or certain sections of the building every evening could be reserved for the use of adults.

School, church, and community leaders should learn to emphasize self-direction on the part of those who seek recreational facilities rather than control by themselves of such activities as are conducted in buildings under their authority. The leaders themselves should participate in, rather than direct, recreational programs. In this way, the school, the church, and the town hall, become the centers of the social life of the community.

Any boy or girl who seeks wholesome recreation and who wants to be with others of his own age should be encouraged to participate in the activities that are organized by youth under the guiding supervision of able adult leadership. In the long run, young people can gain much more enjoyment from such participation than they now think can be obtained in many of the commercially controlled places of amusement that they tend to frequent. These include bars and grills, roadhouses, cellar clubs, public dance halls, and the like. Many young people complain that, unless they patronize one of these undesirable places, the only activity left is attendance at motion pictures.

If youth centers are to compete with the glamour that is attached to some of the less desirable commercial recreational centers, the former must be well organized and democratic. In setting up a youth center, the following principles might well be observed:

1. Provision for informal leisure-time activities for adolescent boys and girls

2. The development of leadership on the part of youth for planning and carrying out their own programs

3. The combined cooperation of groups, such as social, economic, racial, and others in the community

4. The encouragement of community support for youth programs

Concerning the youth centers of Cleveland and Cuyahoga County, Ohio, the committee pointed out that "It is well to remember that the type of program planned will be dependent on the number of days and hours the center is open and the facilities and leadership available." They suggest the following:

1. *Minimum Program.* Dancing, refreshments, and occasional special events. Refreshments may be cold drinks, ice cream, popcorn, potato chips.

2. *Limited Program.* Dancing, refreshments, game and lounge rooms. To the above are added Ping-pong, table games, magazines, and books.

3. *Extended Program.* Other recreational activities added to the above.

In order to get a youth-center program started, an adult advisory council and a youth committee should be organized. Youth leadership must be enthusiastic, imaginative, resourceful, and energetic. Financial support by the community is needed and must be provided. There should be both paid and volunteer adult leadership, not more than two volunteer leaders to fifty young people. A leader should understand youth and young people's problems and should possess a strong, pleasing personality and a sense of humor.

The Gaining of Social Ease and Popularity

How can adults help adolescents to meet other young people?

The youth centers described in the foregoing section afford excellent opportunities for young people to meet others of their kind. However, the entire social life of a young person cannot be confined to his activities in one of these centers. Even getting young people to a center may be difficult. Hence, parents, advisers, and other social leaders must be on the alert constantly for opportunities to assist young people in developing desirable associations with others.

The old saying, "God gave us our relatives but thank God we can choose our friends," seems to imply that the selecting of friends and associates is a very simple matter. Many adolescents do not find this to be a fact. Although they may be surrounded by many people of their own age and older, they may encounter difficulties as they attempt to become active members of a social group. In spite of an assumed aggressiveness of attitude, most young people are shy and find it difficult to make the initial advances toward other persons, unless the path is smoothed for them.

Parents should keep open house. Adolescent boys and girls should be encouraged to bring other young people into the home, which should always be neat and clean, even though it may be simple. More than that, mothers should plan to have cookies, fruit, or other simple foods at hand for a group of hungry boys who drop in, or should make it possible for a girl and her crowd to mix up a batch of fudge or some other concoction. If a boy or a girl knows that, unannounced, he may bring a group of pals into the house on the way home from school or at any other time, he thereby gains a social confidence that is reflected in the attitude of other young people toward him.

Parents can help also by encouraging their adolescent children to plan parties or other get-togethers. Mothers should help in the arrangements for a party and in suggesting names of boys and girls to be invited. Parents can learn a great deal about their children's attitudes toward their schoolmates and coworkers as they listen to adolescent conversation. If the remarks of a young person in the home seem to indicate his desire to become a member of a certain group, an interesting party arranged by the parent and the adolescent to which one or more members of the group are invited may help his gaining his wish. If the party is well planned and enjoyed by the guests, it may serve as an entering wedge into the desired group for the young host or hostess.

The mother of a high-school senior was talking with her daughter's adviser in the latter's office concerning the girl's college plans. During the interview, this mother greeted by name at least a dozen other seniors who happened to be in the office. Here is a mother who need not worry about her daughter's ability to meet people, since she herself has done an excellent job of cooperation in this respect. In sharp contrast with this mother is the one who knows little if anything about her son's or her daughter's associates. The excuse often given for this indifference may be "You know how it is. I am so busy that I can't be bothered about the boys and girls he runs around with." Unfortunately, a parent of this kind may be compelled, later, to take time to be bothered, if the boy or the girl forms undesirable associations as a result of lack of parental help in meeting the right kind of young people.

It is unfortunate that in too many homes the mother is compelled by circumstances to engage in work outside the home. This lack of parental supervision of a growing adolescent may lead to undesirable consequences. The death of

Pauline's father may be viewed as a major cause of the girl's uncontrolled behavior.

Pauline Influenced by Her Associates

As a little girl, Pauline was well adjusted and cooperative, both at home and at school. When she was about twelve years old, her father died and her mother started a chain of beauty shops, extending through several states. The mother, therefore, had little time to devote to her daughter, who matured quickly. By the time she was fourteen years old, Pauline looked like an attractive, well-developed girl of seventeen.

During her first year at high school, Pauline's work was satisfactory and she was well behaved, except that she tended sometimes to be a little aggressive and noisy. During her second year, she became associated with a group of girls who encouraged her to be a truant. As she was in danger of being sent by the school authorities to a reform school because of her conduct, her mother sent her to another state where, instead of attending school, she worked in one of her mother's beauty shops.

Since she was under sixteen, her activity was stopped and she was returned to her home and readmitted to high school. She continued her undesirable behavior. She was accustomed to report to school in the morning and at the end of the day, but managed to slip out of school between those times. With a group of boys and girls from other high schools, she spent her time at motion pictures or at the homes of girls whose mothers were working. Pauline admitted that socially undesirable practices were common in the group, although she herself was not interested. She would not give the names of the other young people involved, since they had threatened her that she would be "beaten up if she squealed."

During this time she bought a watch costing twenty-five dollars, for which she paid a deposit of one dollar. When her payments became irregular and she was threatened with legal action, her stepfather, with the help of the Legal Aid Society, settled the debt for her. Apparently, the difficulties into which she had fallen frightened Pauline and she promised her parents and the school that she would reform. She expressed an interest in music, and her parents gave her a piano and arranged for music lessons. The girl continued to be conscientious in the fulfillment of her school responsibilities and in her study of music, but her lower than average intelligence did not permit her to earn more than mediocre achievement in either.

She was graduated from school with few, if any, further behavior lapses. By this time she had become an extremely striking, well-poised and businesslike young woman. She was interested in her mother's beauty shops and continued her study in beauty culture. At present she is in charge of several beauty shops in another state and is managing them successfully. Whenever she is in town, she visits her friends at high school and expresses her gratitude to her advisers for having "pulled her up by the bootstraps" during her early adolescence.

On the surface, at least, she is making an acceptable adjustment to the demands of society. There is a question as to whether or not she has made a change in her fundamental attitudes, apart from her desire to maintain a good reputation. She is still aggressive and tends toward flashiness in her dress and manner.

School advisers and teachers share with parents the responsibility of providing young people with opportunities for the forming of friendships based upon similarity of interest.

Merely to enroll a young adolescent as a member of a school or class group is not enough. Active assistance should be given these entrants to become acquainted with other members of their group. For a young person to sit in a class for an entire term and not know the names of more than a few of his classmates, or for a graduating senior not to recognize the faces of the majority of the graduating group (even though it is a large class), is a sad commentary on the efficacy of the school's social leadership. Neither high schools nor colleges are doing enough along these lines, even though they are becoming increasingly aware of the social needs of their students.

Many schools are encouraging the organization of many and varied clubs that will give boys and girls of similar interests an opportunity to become acquainted with one another. More extensive programs, such as dances, athletic meets, dramatic presentations, musical programs, and picnics afford opportunities for individual students to meet all the other students. The use of name tags, on such occasions, is an excellent method of helping the boys and girls to become acquainted. A few high schools and colleges have extended this program of acquainting young people with one another by inviting prospective entrants to parties planned and conducted by the regular students of the school that they are about to join. In this way, these young people are made to feel that, upon entrance to the school, they will be coming into a group of friends.

Churches are also doing more for the social life of their young members. The religious and ethical values of church attendance should not be minimized, but the functions of adult church leaders must include that of providing for their young people one or more desirable outlets for their natural urge to be with people and make friends. In what better environment can this be done than through church affiliations? Young people's service groups and discussion groups, led by adolescents, are a few of the means that are effective.

In the same way, more and more large business houses that employ many young people plan definite programs of social activity for their employees. Department parties to celebrate a birthday, engagement, or marriage of one of the group are encouraged. Periodic picnics, dances, and other forms of social activities are included in the companies' social programs.

Insofar as possible, boys and girls should be discouraged from "picking up" casual acquaintances on streetcars, on buses, or in places of amusement. In some states, hitchhiking is forbidden by law. The automobile is an excellent mode of transportation, but a dangerous means of carrying on adolescent social activities. Occasionally, associations made in this way are wholesome, but as a general practice they should be avoided. The boy or the girl who is provided with adequate opportunities for meeting young people in the home, church, place of work, or youth center is not tempted to seek his associates among unselected or unorganized groups.

The fact must be faced that at one time many of a person's present associates were strangers to him. An individual is unable to predict with what persons he will be associated intimately ten years hence. Social living and the social experiences developed in wholesome settings during the formative years will enable a young person, later in life, to make social adjustments to new situations and to new people.

How can an adolescent develop social ease?

This question is often asked by young people. Unless, during childhood, a boy or a girl has had a great deal of experience in meeting people, he may have difficulty in developing social grace and ease as he is introduced into social situations that are different from the relatively restricted home, school, and neighborhood environments. There are several reasons for his apparent or felt awkwardness. One of these may be that, during his childhood, he was not expected to take the initiative in starting or carrying on a conversation,

especially in the presence of elders. In fact, he may constantly
have been warned that "children should be seen and not
heard."

An adolescent may find himself in the company of adults
or older adolescents where he may wish to demonstrate his
developing maturity by his ability to take an active part in
the conversation or discussion; yet he may be afraid of saying
the wrong thing, thus betraying the fact that he is still immature. Young people are cruel to one another, often unconsciously so. The older or more sophisticated members of a
group cannot always resist the temptation of making game of
their younger associates. By seeming to be amused by or
tolerant of opinions expressed in public by younger brothers or
sisters or by younger friends, they are thereby bolstering their
own morale and acquiring greater social poise.

Furthermore, adolescent physical development is often
irregular. The boy or the girl feels that he is all hands and feet.
He tends to trip over rugs or furniture or he drops things at
the wrong moment. The more eager he is to appear to be at
ease, the more uncontrolled the management of his body may
seem to become. The young teen ager grows out of his clothes
quickly and, rightly or wrongly, believes that people are recognizing the fact that his suit or his coat is too small for him.

Parents should provide clothes which are attractive and
of the right size, even though they may be simple and inexpensive. It must be admitted that the keeping of a growing
adolescent in clothes of the right size is difficult. A mother
known to the writers believed in buying well-made and dur-
able suits, dresses, and coats for her boy and her girl. Since
these were expensive, the young people were expected to wear
them for a long time. The clothes were bought large enough
for the adolescents to grow into, and then were worn after
they had been outgrown. These young people were not impressed by the good quality of the material, but they were
extremely conscious of the fact that their clothes did not fit

them for at least two-thirds of the time during which they were worn. Moreover, the boy and the girl were constantly admonished to be very careful of their clothes, because of the high price paid for them. Here is an excellent basis for self-consciousness.

A youth's desire to be an active rather than a passive member of a social group, his growing awareness of his physical characteristics, and the fact that he is being thrown into new and different social groups are the bases of youthful desire for help in gaining social ease. Most young people, unless too many embarrassing situations have caused them to shun participation in social activities, like people and want to be with them. "Practice makes perfect" applies to the development of social grace and poise in the same way that it applies to the development of any other skill. If a teen-age boy or girl is to acquire social ease, he must be given many opportunities for participation in social activities.

Active participation on the part of young people in many social situations planned or encouraged by parents and advisers should be accompanied by informal guidance in the simple rudiments of good social practices. Adolescents need to be taught proper forms of introductions, ways of starting a conversation, control of voice, desirable eating habits, and the like. Many of these social forms are learned by young people as they imitate their elders. However, they may not always be stimulated by desirable adult behavior in such matters. Direct, as well as indirect, teaching is needed. This does not mean that the finishing school of the past should be revived, but it does mean that in every school there should be programs for training in good manners.

Through reading and discussion, high-school students should familiarize themselves with the simple rules that underlie participation in social activities. This knowledge should then be applied in a tactful way through participation in many social activities in the school.

It is through projects of this kind that young people can be taught to meet social situations with ease and enjoyment. If the emphasis is laid upon service to others, a young person tends to forget himself as he attempts to put another person at ease. The plan of upper-class students arranging social programs for younger students, and of younger students with the help of their older schoolmates conducting similar programs for younger children offers adolescents fine opportunities for developing a mature attitude toward their social relationships.

Girls and boys often find themselves ill at ease and tongue-tied in the presence of members of the opposite sex. This is usually caused by a natural desire to make a good impression. The boy tends to brag about his accomplishments. The girl may affect an artificial, sophisticated manner. Little is gained by attempting to be what one is not. Adults who are simple and unaffected in manner, who are careful of their vocabulary, and who practice good taste in their conversation with their friends and associates present excellent models for young people to follow.

There is no one, adult or adolescent, who does not find himself occasionally in a difficult social situation, with an accompaniment of nervousness or anxiety concerning the reactions toward him of other members of the group. Young people should be told frankly that adults have these experiences and that, if one does not know what to do or say, the best procedure is to remain quiet. A good listener is a most desirable adjunct of any group. As one gains social poise, one realizes that he does not have to be constantly active, vocally or in any other way, in order to be popular. This is a lesson that should be learned early by young people.

How can the teen ager become popular?

Much of the advice in the preceding section can be applied in answering this question. Poise, dignity, social ease, and consideration for others, rather than too-free spending, elaborate dressing, loud talking, or aggressive behavior, are the secrets of popularity.

Much of the enjoyment of school or business life is dependent upon a young person's relations with his fellows. The well-adjusted young person possesses a few good friends and many acquaintances among the group. If he is willing to cooperate with others in group projects, he is welcomed by all the members. When he is called upon to do something for the group, he accepts the responsibility cheerfully and does his best to fulfill the obligation. He is not jealous of the success of others, but is proud of the honor that another's achievements brings to the group.

The secret of popularity is the willingness to do for or to share with others. The members of any group appreciate the person who is interested in them, especially if he demonstrates the ability to make constructive contributions to their activities. However, any group, formal or informal, soon loses patience with any of its members who shows by his actions that he is interested only in those benefits of membership that can contribute to his own welfare or prestige.

A young person may have developed, through unwise guidance, a spirit of selfishness and self-centeredness that is disliked by others. It is difficult for adolescents to overlook selfish attitudes. Whether a boy or a girl is engaged in gainful employment or is still a student, whether he is economically privileged or underprivileged, or whether he is physically attractive or unattractive, his chances for popularity among his associates depend upon his ability to subordinate his own interests and desires to those of the group and upon his habits of fair play and good sportsmanship.

These desirable behavior patterns do not suddenly materialize with the coming of adolescent interest in social participation. They are the result of a gradual habit formation, which is encouraged in the young person by parents and other adults.

Friends and Companions

How important are adolescent friendships?

Young people are very much concerned about their friendships with other boys and girls. Their questions are specific
and indicate the emotional disturbance that can arise as a
result of unpleasant experiences in the realm of friendship
Parents often find their adolescent son's or daughter's choice
of friends and companions to be a source of worry to themselves. The boy or the girl who finds it difficult to gain friends
the young person who selects undesirable friends, or the
adolescent who seems to form violent friendships of short
duration gives a parent many anxious moments.

Friendships are important, not only during adolescence
but also throughout adult life. The friendships formed during
the teen-age years not only may be the beginning of pleasant
lifelong associations, but also may afford opportunities for
practice in the art of making and keeping friends, which will
help in the formation of later adult friendships. For these
reasons, parents and other adults need to be tactful and
patient in their attempts at encouraging young people toward
the development of wholesome attitudes in their social
relations.

Adolescent boys and girls need friends among adults and
young people of both sexes. Their questions indicate their
interest in the fundamentals of maintaining friendly relations
with any person, regardless of age or sex. Still more are they
concerned about their relations with persons of their own sex
and age. Most important of all, it would seem, is the relationship that should exist between members of opposite sexes
Because of that emphasis, the many phases of boy-girl relationships will be discussed under a separate heading. Further
discussion of the present topic will be limited to a general

consideration of the fundamentals of successful friendship and of friendship between members of the same sex.

What is meant by friendship?

Young people often confuse the meaning of the term "friend" with that of "acquaintance" or "companion." Adults who have experienced lifelong friendships do not always understand an adolescent's attitude toward his associates. During adolescense, so-called "friendships" may be easily made and just as easily broken. The difficulty here lies not in the temporary nature of these relationships but in the terms used to describe them. Parents need to teach young people by their own conduct toward their associates and by their tactful suggestions that there are differences to be found in the degree of an individual's friendly relations with people.

Teen agers should learn early to feel and exhibit a friendly attitude toward those with whom they associate. They should be helped to develop a uniformly courteous and cooperative manner in their dealings with other people of all ages. They should be slow to take offense at the behavior toward them of others, rather than suspicious of the good intentions of those with whom they come into contact, be it "butcher, baker, or candlestick maker," salesperson, delivery boy, car conductor, fellow student or fellow worker, teacher or supervisor, or family or personal friend.

Sharp retorts, unwarranted criticism, sulking, insistence upon one's rights or upon special privileges will not gain friends or companions. A generally friendly attitude will achieve for a young person a host of acquaintances with whom he can enjoy work or recreational activity.

Adults should encourage teen-age boys and girls to form many such acquaintanceships. However, young people should be helped to realize that it is not wise to expect too much from these acquaintances or to confide in them too freely. The relationship should be based upon community of interest and congeniality of tastes, yet it should leave all the individuals concerned free from obligations to one another except those that are dictated by the rules of courtesy, respect for others, and cooperation.

Even these temporary associations may influence a young person's attitudes and behavior unduly during his formative years. Hence, it is important that parents watch carefully the neighborhood and school groups with whom their sons and daughters may associate.

Much more significant, however, are the friendships of a young person, his attitude toward the meaning of friendship, and his own responsibilities for its success. A true friend is a person whom one can trust, in whom one can confide, and to whom one can bring his joys and sorrows with the certainty that these will be understood and appreciated by the friend.

Friendship is based upon personality qualities that lie deep beneath the surface. Economic status, prestige, personal attractiveness, and national or religious background are relatively unimportant as the bases of friendship. Very often, parents and other adults fail to recognize this fact. They may disapprove of a friendship between two wholesome, democratic adolescents because they, the adults, are evaluating the relationship in terms of superficial standards. No parent or adviser should object to a friendship between two young people for any reason except that of undesirable characteristics exhibited by one that might influence the other toward socially unacceptable behavior.

What should be a young person's attitude toward his friends?

As is true in any other human relationship, there are certain basic rights and responsibilities that must be known and adhered to strictly if a friendship is to survive. An adolescent has the right to expect his friends to help him when such help is needed, unless some social and ethical right would be violated by their doing so. For example, a high-school or college student should not be expected to give his friend help during an examination or to work out study assignments that this friend would later submit to his instructor as his own work.

A person should not gossip about his friend, neither should he withhold incriminating knowledge of his friend's wrong-doing, especially if an innocent person is accused of the act. The culprit should first be encouraged by his friend to confess the wrongdoing. If this plea is not successful, it is the friend's duty to take the matter to the proper authorities. This is a difficult test of friendship, but it is the only honest course to take.

Friends should be loyal to one another, they should guard confidences given to one by the other, and they should share their pleasures and other activities insofar as this will not interfere with any obligations. Neither friend should make all the decisions as to places to go, activities in which to partici-pate, and the like. Most of us are more or less self-centered, but in friendship there must be a mutual give-and-take. A friendship cannot thrive on selfishness, oversensitivity, jeal-ousy, carelessness in keeping appointments, or too-great demands upon the time and interest of either friend.

Too many so-called "friendships" among adolescents are no more than the temporary domination of one young person struggling for self-assertion over a weaker or younger com-panion, who is passing through a hero-worshiping stage. Too-great admiration for any associate whose behavior is socially undesirable may be dangerous to a suggestible young ado-lescent. However, the opposite is also true. Often a young person who is tempted to be careless in his home, work, or social responsibilities can be "reformed" by his adolescent friends who have developed more desirable practices. Hence, parents need to watch carefully the friendships that their sons and daughters are forming and to evaluate the extent to which such friendships are desirable.

Why should young people be encouraged to form friendships with members of their own sex and how should they treat these friends?

The expression "He is woman's man" or "She is a man's woman" may seem to the person concerned to be a tribute to his popularity with members of the opposite sex. As a matter of fact, such a comment usually is an indication of the unpopularity of the person with members of his own sex and, hence, is far from flattering. The person who is not generally liked and admired by members of his own sex lacks certain fundamental personality characteristics. One's own sex is able to penetrate below surface veneer and recognize wholesome qualities or basic insincerities that may not be apparent to members of the opposite sex.

Men know men and women know women because they know themselves. They are able to evaluate the behavior of a member of their own sex in terms of their own urges, interests, and behavior patterns. A boy who is respected by upstanding boys and a girl who is admired by wholesome girls need cause parents and advisers little concern regarding their social adjustment.

For a boy to be a boy's boy and a girl to be a girl's girl indicates that the individual is a fine, cooperative, trustworthy type of person. However, the adolescent who tends to devote all his time and energy to the formation of friendships within his own sex is not completely adjusted. As an adult he will need to work and associate with members of the other sex. During adolescence, he must learn to meet the challenge of developing intelligent and controlled behavior with members of both sexes. Hence, young people should be encouraged to form friendships with a few fine members of both sexes; but every young person should have at least one close and wholesome, but unselfish friendship with a member of the same sex.

It is with this other adolescent that the boy or the girl can be himself to a degree that often is not otherwise possible, even with members of his own family. The friendship satisfies the urge for security in the affection of another, which may transcend the desire for security in the affection of the family. Parents should encourage such friendships, but must assure themselves that the friendship is wholesome, that there are no homosexual tendencies, and that the relationship is an addition to, not a substitute for, friendship with members of the opposite sex.

During adolescence, a friendship between two boys or between two girls who are too widely separated in age is not completely satisfying. The older boy's or girl's philosophy of life, physical and emotional development, attitude toward the opposite sex, and whole experiential pattern go beyond those of the younger teen ager, unless the younger person is exceptionally mature.

One of the strongest arguments against too-rapid school progress of a mentally superior young person is found here. Although the bright younger student may be able to surpass the study achievement of his classmates, his emotional and social progress may lag behind theirs. Although they may admire his mental prowess, he cannot compete with or even fully appreciate their recreational and social interests and activities. He lacks the social ease and the good judgment in social affairs that are the outgrowth of such experiences. The older adolescents, either consciously or unconsciously, exclude him from their social plans. He is, however, too mature mentally to find recreational satisfaction in the company of his own age group, who are mentally younger than he is. Hence, he may be forced to rely upon his academic superiority in order to satisfy his ego.

Parents and school leaders are beginning to realize the importance to a young person of his forming friendships with his peers. Consequently, the educational philosophy of encouraging an adolescent toward rapid school progress, which was very popular a decade ago, is now meeting criticism. Parents are refusing to allow their bright children to be advanced beyond their normal age levels, unless this can be done in the company of a sufficient number of like young persons, among whom a normal social and emotional development is possible.

ADOLESCENT RELATIONS WITH THE OPPOSITE SEX

At what age should a boy or girl start to have "dates"?

As has been suggested in a discussion of boy-girl relations in connection with the home, boys and girls should be encouraged to participate in mixed-group activities from childhood on. However, the age at which a boy and a girl should begin to pair off depends upon the emotional maturity of the young people concerned and the wholesomeness of their attitude toward the opposite sex. Participation in "twosome" social activities is not desirable until the girl is at least sixteen and the boy seventeen or older, depending upon their degree of emotional stability.

At this age, boys and girls should be old enough to arrange their own parties. If a girl wants an escort other than her parents, she should have that privilege. During these early ages, the two young persons should not engage in social activities together more than twice a week, even though they may see each other daily at school or at work. When this is done, the girl will feel free to go out with other boys and the boy will be at liberty to "date" other girls. Each is thus given an opportunity of becoming acquainted with other young persons.

Should boys and girls ever go "Dutch"?

This question more and more is being answered in the affirmative. During adolescence, pairing off does not necessarily mean that the boy or the girl is contemplating an early marriage with the other. It is, rather, a matter of enjoying each other's company and of sharing social activities together. If each pays his own way, the girl is relieved of her feeling of obligation to the boy and is free to extend invitations as well as to await them.

Moreover, our present economic system is such that the girl is as likely as the boy to have the money to pay her way. If she does this occasionally, she avoids the accusation of being a "gold digger." There are perhaps more reasons for the extension of the practice of going "Dutch" than for the elimination of it. It tends to place friendships at these early ages on a firmer basis.

Should matters concerning sex be discussed between a boy and a girl?

If a boy and a girl spend most of their hours together in the company of other young people, this question does not have serious significance. However, if they are alone too much, they may run out of topics of conversation unless they have many wholesome interests in common. Consequently, they may be tempted to turn to this subject, which is definitely tied up with their emotions.

There is great danger in encouraging the discussion of sex matters among young people. Too often the discussion may change from the scientific level to the personal. Since human emotions are strong, it may be difficult for the adolescents to avoid carrying over a discussion of the subject into active expression of sex behavior. The emotions are treacherous. It is almost impossible to keep any consideration of them on an objective and purely intellectual plane. Especially is this true concerning emotions arising out of sex urges. It is usually better, therefore, to confine such topics to the classroom for scientific discussion until the two young persons become engaged. During that period these considerations become of vital and immediate importance to them.

How can one tell if another really loves him?

Love, or the attitude of affection, is something that is conveyed by actions rather than by words. When deep affection for another is felt, strong verbal or written expressions of this affection are not usually too important, although they are helpful. In an individual's behavior there is evidence of the love that is unmistakable.

A girl may be stirred emotionally by a boy's well-termed love phrases. A boy may "fall for" a girl's expressed attitude of "How wonderful you are!" Too often a less articulate but much more sincere young person is considered dull or uninteresting, since he does not seem to flatter one's ego. Young people should remember that fluency in amorous speech is usually the result of much practice and may, as a consequence, be lacking in sincerity. Consideration for one's interest and desires, understanding of one's personal problems, and sacrifices of personal desires for the loved one speak much more loudly than do words.

However, a boy or a girl in his teens should not be too greatly concerned about the depth of another's "love" for him. Young people should learn to live together and to work and play together without becoming too seriously involved in love affairs. Mothers need to watch their own attitudes in the matter of their daughter's relations with boys. Since a mother usually looks forward to a desirable marriage for her daughter, she may regard these teen-age boy-and-girl friendships too seriously, thereby encouraging the girl to view each current boy as a possible mate.

Sometimes, however, parents are tempted to be a little too casual about their adolescent children's social activities. Barbara's parents, in spite of their fine educational background and good economic status, encouraged a freedom of adolescent behavior that caused conflict in the home and later impelled Barbara to lose emotional control in her relationships with boys.

Barbara's Misuse of Freedom

Barbara's family consists of a father, who is an interior decorator, a mother, who is a social service worker, and a brother, who at fourteen years of age was five feet nine inches in height and had already begun to win honors at a technical high school.

As a child, Barbara earned high grades at a parochial elementary school and resented the fact that she was sent by her parents to a public high school, instead of a private preparatory school. She disliked her new school intensely because of the cosmopolitan character of the student body. During her first two years at this school, she managed to maintain herself, although she admitted that she had no real interest in her work and came to school only because she had to. At the beginning of her third school year, her work became noticeably poorer.

Although she was an attractive girl, she was embarrassed by a birthmark on the side of her nose. She also had a slight heart murmur and complained of severe headaches, for which the doctors could find no cause. Barbara was emotionally maladjusted, quick-tempered, and in constant conflict with her brother. He teased her because, although she was older than he, she was not so tall. Hence, he referred to her as a "shrimp." She was also bothered by the fact that her brother took letters that she received from a boy of whom she was very fond and would not return them until she paid him. Her parents encouraged the boy's attitude toward her. In fact, they often participated in the teasing, and the girl could not take it.

There was a constant struggle within her between ambition and her interest in social life. In spite of her poor schoolwork, she was determined that she would earn graduation from high school, no matter how long it took, and then study interior decorating. At the same time, she was allowed a great deal of social freedom by her parents and encouraged to have many boy and girl friends. Although she was very much interested in boys, she insisted that she did not like petting and resented the methods used by some girls to acquire "boy friends." She read and daydreamed a great deal and, consequently, lacked a practical attitude toward life.

In accordance with her parents' liberal attitude toward her social activities, she was allowed to spend a week end away from home, unchaperoned, with a group of boys and girls. As a consequence, she became pregnant. Her parents, shocked by this fact, met the situation intelligently. Since Barbara was not really interested in the boy concerned, the parents did not insist upon his marrying her, although he would have been willing to do so. Her child was given to a good family for adoption and the girl was transferred to another school, where she completed her high-school course.

The fact that the parents had shielded her so carefully during her difficulties did not improve the girl's attitude. No one except those directly concerned knew of Barbara's experiences. Hence, her attitude is that it is not what you do but whether or not you are found out that counts. She has not yet done anything openly that would bring her into conflict with the law. However, in spite of careful watching, the parents fear that the girl is still promiscuous and they are worried concerning the possibility of her making a good adjustment to life.

How important is puppy love?

As the emotional life of a boy or a girl develops through adolescence, he experiences an increasing interest in the opposite sex and in the love life. Stimulated by reading romantic novels, by viewing love stories on the screen, and by observing the love activities of his older associates, he is thereby encouraged to experience these emotions for himself. He wants to love. Who shall be the object of his love is not especially important. A famous screen star, a sports leader, a seatmate at school, or a teacher or supervisor may become the object of the adolescent's secret or expressed adoration.

Any attention given him by the loved one is interpreted as an indication of a similar attitude toward him. The young person is in love with love itself and, because of his emotionalized state, is unable to evaluate correctly his own behavior or the behavior of the other person. Flirtations are engaged in as a kind of release of the emotions within him. If the flirtatious behavior is responded to either seriously or as a game, the young person may become so stirred that he loses intelligent control of himself and, as a result, may suffer great unhappiness or disappointment.

Girls are much more likely to be serious in their first love experiences than are boys, since the latter know that, during adolescence, they are much too young to become serious about any one girl. A teen-age girl should be guided away from becoming emotionally involved with a married man, even though he is not living with his wife. No matter what his own marital situation may be, a decent and honorable man will not attempt to win the affection of a young girl. Any other kind of man is not worthy of a girl's attention.

A girl who has been guided toward an appreciation of moral ideals and who has achieved a respect and fellow feeling for members of her own sex could not engage in promiscuous relations with another woman's husband. A girl of this type would hold the marriage relation sacred. Any beginnings of an emotional regard on the part of a girl for a married man or for a man much older than herself should be diverted toward interest in desirable young men who are free to marry and who are nearer her own age and interest level.

Why does war cause an abnormal interest in sex?

During a war, many factors operate to bring about an increased interest among young people, not only in the opposite sex but in sex itself. Emotions are aroused and an attitude of disregard for high standards and ideals of conduct becomes widespread. This attitude can be traced to any one or more of the following reasons:

1. Boys in the armed service realize that they may never have an opportunity to enjoy normal married life.

2. Young girls fear that their chances for marriage and sex experience are being reduced.

3. Loved ones are far away and may develop new interests.

4. The general attitude of the public is that of giving the boys anything that they desire. Girls, believing that boys desire sex experiences, think that they are doing a patriotic service if they cooperate in or encourage such activities.

5. War has a psychological effect upon an individual. It is much more difficult to control one's emotional urges during a period of unrest and uncertainty than it is during normal peacetimes.

6. Once begun, the breaking down of moral codes and the loss of personal inhibitions become accepted behavior patterns.

Some of the girls and boys who become sex delinquents during a time of war excitement might be guilty of engaging in the same kind of behavior under normal world conditions. However, a soldier or a sailor who himself is experiencing an emotional letdown may seem to take on the qualities of a lifesaver to a girl who is dissatisfied with her home environment. This may be a partial explanation for the behavior of Ethel and of Marcia. Ethel had cause for wanting to get away from her father; and Marcia was ashamed of her home, a normal adolescent reaction. What these two girls would have done if sympathetic young men were not "just around the corner," one cannot say.

Ethel Became Too Much Interested in Sailors

After years of friction in the home, Ethel's parents separated several years ago. She remained with her father, but there was little sympathy between the two. He expected her to take complete charge of the household duties and complained constantly that she did nothing. He was unyielding, distrusted his daughter, and was always ready to trap and shame her. If she stayed out later at night than he thought she should, he would beat her; but she took the beatings without a murmur.

Her father's attitude became so unbearable that she stayed away from home as much as possible and developed a progressive interest in sailors. As a result, she became a truant and a sex delinquent. On one occasion she ran away from home but was found and returned to home and school. The Travelers Aid Society and school counselors attempted to bring about a better relationship between Ethel and her father, who are intelligent and know all the right answers. They agreed concerning the attitude that they should take toward each other, but their actions continued as they had been, except for brief periods of improvement.

The father claimed that he could not afford to employ any household help to reduce the load on Ethel. Although he admitted that she should be able to entertain her friends at home, his behavior toward guests was very unpleasant. Consequently, it was arranged by the social agencies that Ethel be transferred to her mother's custody and attend a high school near her mother's home. However, this change in home environment was made too late. Ethel had developed habits that were difficult to break. She continued to fail in her subjects in her new school, and resented her mother's attempts to improve her behavior. She finally ran away from home with a sailor who was a deserter from the Navy.

Marcia Was a Sex Delinquent

As far as her schoolwork was concerned, Marcia was no problem. She was a slow student who had dropped back a grade, but her attitude was always most cooperative. Her program was adjusted to meet her interest and ability, and she was grateful to the school for the help that they gave her.

Marcia's home conditions were poor and her parents had no control over her social activities. She stayed out late at night without explanation and finally was missing from home as a sex delinquent. She was traced and placed on probation, but ran away a second time. When she was finally found, she had been married to a sailor by a justice of the peace in another state. Her parents accepted the situation, but arranged to have a second ceremony performed by a Navy chaplain. Within a short time, Marcia became the mother of a little girl.

These are some of the prices that we pay for war. It takes time to regain the ground that is lost through the socially undesirable practices of young people throughout the country during a time of crisis. Our sense of values needs to be restored.

What training should young people be given for extending, accepting, or refusing invitations from members of the opposite sex?

Correct attitude toward invitations has to do with manners rather than with psychological factors of boy-girl relations. However, uncertainty as to how one should extend and accept or refuse an invitation may cause a young person some emotional disturbance. As is true in all matters dealing with courtesy in our relations with others, guidance is needed here, so that young people may approach this phase of their social relations with confidence.

Parental example is the most potent teaching technique. If adults are motivated by ideals of consideration for others when they extend or accept or refuse invitations, young people will be guided by this same principle. Formal invitations are very little used nowadays by young people. A telephone call, a short note, or an invitation by word of mouth is the accepted procedure.

A boy may be awkward or embarrassed as he extends his first invitation to a girl. His shyness may cause him to be almost too casual about it. However, a girl can usually detect the boy's underlying sincerity or lack of sincerity. Her acceptance or refusal of the invitation should be influenced by her own attitude toward the boy, her own program of activities, or her interest in the activity to which she is being invited. In all cases, the girl's response to the invitation should be given promptly and courteously, with an indication that she appreciates being invited.

If a girl refuses a boy's invitation, the latter is justified in inviting another girl. However, he should not develop the habit of going the rounds and asking them all until he finds one who will accept. In the first place, a boy should be warned by too many refusals on the part of his girl acquaintances that there is something wrong with himself. It may be his grooming, his choice of amusement to which he is inviting the girl, or his behavior toward a girl who does accept. Moreover, no girl likes to feel that she is just one of any number of girls who would serve as well as she for a companion. A girl wishes to feel that the boy has a special interest in her, and that she can be proud of him when she is with him.

In the same way, a girl should not be a "hound" for dates.

She should not be so eager to engage in social activities that she will accept any invitations that come to her. This attitude does not point the way toward popularity. A date a night may be an enviable ambition, but a boy, too, wants to feel that he is someone special, not just any boy who can give a girl a good time.

A girl sometimes hesitates to refuse an invitation, even though she would prefer not to accept it, lest she lose the friendship of the boy. This is especially true if she is forced to refuse two invitations in succession. However, if her reasons for the refusal are legitimate, she can convince the boy of her sincerity. A friendship lost because of supersensitivity on the part of the boy, under such circumstances, need cause a girl no regret.

Once the invitation is extended and accepted, neither the boy nor the girl should allow any other more interesting invitation or activity to interfere with the keeping of the engagement. The "date" should be kept punctually, unless either person has to withdraw because of serious illness or some other mishap.

A girl may refuse to accept a boy as her partner for a particular dance, but she may not dance with any other boy during that dance number. The same rule extends to participation in any group activity. With the consent of her parents, a girl may invite a boy to attend a party given at her home, but she should not use this method to take him away from another girl in whom he seems to be interested or to force herself upon him if he previously has given evidence of lack of interest in her.

Parental influence in such matters as invitations extended and accepted or refused is much greater than may be thought. Young people are not always free in their choice of the other young people with whom they would like to be. There are many limiting factors—parental attitude, nationality, religion, tallness in girls and shortness in boys, and financial ability to entertain as one would like to do, or to dress as one feels that he should. However, democratic young people who enjoy simple pleasures experience no difficulty in finding things to do together, especially if parents are willing to cooperate.

Because of their traditional attitudes, mothers, more often than fathers perhaps, tend to emphasize elements in a social situation which, if ignored by them, would prevent serious difficulties. Jean's experiences are an example of this.

Jean and Her Mother Are Constantly in Conflict

Jean insists that she is an adopted daughter, although her mother says that this is not true. The mother demands that her daughter confine her friendships with boys and girls to those who are Jewish. Jean is very fond of a Christian boy, but she is denied the privilege of seeing him.

Both Jean and her mother become very much emotionalized over the religious question. The girl, in spite of the fact that she is Jewish, refuses to associate with young people of her own group. The mother will allow her no social life unless she does. Since the girl is seventeen years old, bright and attractive, there is trouble ahead for both mother and daughter unless they can achieve a compromise.

What shall young people do about "necking" and "petting"?

Should a girl kiss a boy good night? Do you think that petting is wrong? How can you prevent a date from turning into a necking party? Is petting a subject that can be spoken about openly? Does a boy respect a girl more if she does not pet? These are a few of the questions that are on the minds

and lips of many of our teen-age boys and girls. The answers
are not easy nor are they the same for any one individual
during each of his teen-age years.

The good-night kiss, holding hands, walking arm in arm,
and the like are to be expected from most of our teen-age
youth. It is the embrace, the prolonged kiss, or the body
exploration that arouses those inner urges that often cause
young people to allow their behavior to be controlled by their
emotions rather than by their intellect.

The problem is complicated by the attitude of the boy
who "has been around" and who is interested in the girl as
a female rather than as a friend. Satisfaction of his physical
urge is his chief purpose for "dating" a girl, even though he
himself may not admit this. If the girl seems to be hesitant,
he tries to persuade her that such behavior is the accepted
thing. The girl then is torn between her training and the fear
of losing his interest. Girls are often led by a desire for
popularity into necking and petting behavior rather than by
interest in the activity itself.

Parents and social leaders often fail in their responsibility
by not giving more effective education to young teen-age
girls and boys on these important points. Problems such as
these should be discussed with individuals in private conference and with small homogeneous groups of the same age
and sex.

A survey of the kinds of person whom men and women
tend to marry indicates that mates are rarely selected from
among those with whom they have practiced petting. There
seems to be a deep-seated feeling that such activity is undesirable and should not be associated with marriage.

A girl may pet with some boys; but she is usually careful
to refrain from such activity with the boy whom she hopes to
marry later, lest she may lose his love. Likewise, a boy is
usually careful to refrain from heavy petting with the girl
whom he expects to make his wife.

The tendency for many young people to continue their studies until the early twenties, thus delaying the time when they are economically able to marry, may in part be responsible for undesirable sex activities. The answer to this difficult question perhaps is that of making earlier marriages possible.

ACHIEVING A SUCCESSFUL MARRIAGE RELATIONSHIP

What help should young people be given in the selection of a mate?

Modern culture accepts the basis of marriage to be romantic love. Sexual attraction alone, however, cannot be expected to ensure marital happiness. The impulsive nature of romantic love may blind the young person to the importance of other factors as determiners of a successful marriage relation.

Early home guidance, the relationship of his parents one to the other, and the emotional stability and intelligence of a young person exercise a definite influence upon his own attitude toward the choosing of his mate. Occupational, educational, or neighborhood associations may act as factors of propinquity in determining the person with whom one may fall in love and marry. An individual tends to be attracted toward a member of the other sex who is like himself in disposition, intelligence, or physical constitution. His choice is influenced also by economic and social status.

There seems to be a difference of opinion concerning the chances of success for a marriage with a person outside one's religious, national, social, or economic group. It seems certain, however, that there is a greater chance of marital success between persons of similar interests, culture, education, and traditional backgrounds than is possible if the mates are so different from each other in any of these respects that understanding and tolerance of such differences are too difficult to achieve.

Although marriage is no longer viewed as a business arrangement, an individual dare not allow himself to be swept off his feet by a sudden and unreasonable passion for a member of the opposite sex whom he finds later to be entirely unsuited to himself in attitudes, ideals, interests, or behavior habits. The basis of marriage should be affection and similarity of interests and ideals. The choice, however, should be made after thoughtful consideration. An individual should give at least as much attention to the selection of a mate as he would to the selection of a house, an automobile, or a fur coat.

At what age should young people marry? What should be the length of the engagement?

No definite answer can be given to the question concerning the age at which one should marry. Marriage imposes many responsibilities and requires the making of many adjustments. No one should enter into marriage until he is reasonably certain that he can meet these adequately. Many young people of eighteen and twenty are prepared to assume marital responsibilities and would make an excellent job of family adjustment. Nevertheless, the early twenties seem to be a better time for marriage.

Coupled with the age for marrying is the length of the engagement period. Unless the engagement follows a long friendship, a short period of time between the engagement to marry and the marriage itself does not allow the couple enough time to become acquainted with each other. Yet, too long an engagement may impose a great strain upon the emotional control needed during this prenuptial intimacy, if conventional standards of behavior for unmarried persons are to be adhered to.

The behavior of engaged persons toward each other may create difficult situations. Society disapproves of premarital sexual relations. If such practices are engaged in, there is danger that the marital relation will thereby be hurt. Consequently, one year, during which emotional controls are exercised, seems to be a desirable length of time for the engagement. This will give sufficient time for the young couple to discuss frankly and sensibly the many problems that are connected with the marital relation and to arrive at decisions that will help them to enter their life together with a basis of mutual understanding of what is ahead for them.[1]

[1] Lloyd-Jones and Fedder present an excellent discussion of attitudes toward the love life of young people in "Coming of Age," Chap. IV, Men, Women and Love. (Lloyd-Jones, Esther, and Ruth Fedder, "Coming of Age," Whittlesey House, McGraw-Hill Book Company, Inc., New York, 1941.) The reading of this chapter is recommended to young people, their parents, and their advisers. Another up-to-the-minute reference is Goldstein, Sidney E., "Marriage and Family Counseling," McGraw-Hill Book Company, Inc., New York, 1945.

Section VI

JUVENILE DELINQUENCY

A Statement

Relative to the Problem of Juvenile Delinquency
By a former President of the United States[1]

While the world sits with its ears to the radio to get the latest war news, another battle is going on on the home front. It is the battle against the rising tide of delinquency among our young people. This is an important battle for upon it depends the future of thousands of young people and to a large degree the future of the nation itself.

Many different plans of attack will be tried, many new and untested. In the desire to find new ways of combating the problem, some of the tried and tested ways in which delinquency is minimized may be forgotten. It is my belief, especially so far as boys are concerned, that one of the most effective ways is to provide constructive activity and leadership such as the Boys Clubs of America have been doing for many years.

We all know that boys seek fun and the companionship of their fellows. The kind of fun and companions, and more especially the kind of leaders they follow, determines to a large extent their behavior and their character. What better fun can boys find than in the gymnasium, library, vocational classes and other activities of a Boys Club? What better leaders can they follow than the men who have devoted their lives to the leadership and guidance of boys?

[1] This article was written by former President Hoover for the *Brooklyn Eagle* in 1944. It is reprinted here with the permission of the *Brooklyn Eagle* and of Herbert Hoover. In addition Mr. Hoover gave the authors permission to substitute "America" for "Brooklyn" at two places in the article, thereby giving it national rather than merely local significance.

The pity of it is that there are so few Boys Clubs with facilities and support for providing for only a few boys out of the many thousands who have to find their recreation, companions, and leaders where they can.

I suggest that the people of America take a greater interest in their Boys Clubs, give them greater support, volunteer as leaders and instructors, and consider with the leaders of Clubs the establishment of additional Clubs. The delinquency problem is not merely an emergency one, it is a long range problem.

You can give a boy the advantages of a Boys Club for only a few dollars a year. He may be at loose ends because the family is economically unsafe, and he may be left to his own devices much of the time. Give that boy a place to play and develop his body and mind, and some direction in character discipline, and you have every chance of turning out a good citizen.

Keep those few dollars in your pockets, don't give that boy a chance, and within a few years the taxpayers may be called upon to pay thousands of dollars in fruitless attempts to reform him. Fighting juvenile delinquency by helping boys is a good investment in democracy and humanity.—HERBERT HOOVER, *Chairman of the Board, Boys Clubs of America*

Chapter 11

Meeting the Problem of Delinquency

A MALADJUSTED person is usually his own worst enemy. The disturbed adolescent may be afraid, resentful, or uncooperative. However, he does not necessarily become aggressively antisocial. He hurts himself rather than others. If a young person definitely interferes with the rights of others, appropriates their property, causes damage, or violates the sex code, he is interfering with the life of another person and is *delinquent*.

According to the Ohio Code, "A delinquent child is defined as one who violates a law, is wayward, habitually disobedient or truant, or who behaves in a way that endangers the health or morals of himself or others, or who attempts to enter the marriage relation without the consent of parents or guardian."

Delinquent behavior, as reported by school people in leading cities throughout the United States, includes, in their order of frequency, truancy, petty larceny, sex offenses (for girls), general incorrigibility, breaking and entering, running away from home, vagrancy, disorderly conduct, drinking, destructive acts, and injury to persons.

Legally, a delinquent is a teen-age person who has been brought to court, not as a criminal who is mature enough to recognize the seriousness of his offense, but as a maturing person who needs to be taught the responsibilities of adjusted citizenship. However, some adolescents are guilty of delinquent acts, but either are not detected or are protected from court action by their parents or others. In a broad social interpretation of the term, these young people are delinquents, even though they have not been apprehended for their antisocial behavior.

Among the factors that contribute toward delinquency can be included (1) the relaxation of home control and parental supervision; (2) the moving of workers from small towns or rural areas to cities; (3) economic conditions in family life that may cause neglect of children; (4) poor health or physical defects, which may result in feelings of inferiority, discouragement, or bewilderment; (5) inadequate recreational facilities; (6) inadequate school buildings and equipment; (7) inadequate teaching; (8) public indifference; (9) ineffectual attempts to prevent delinquency.

Whether delinquency is considered in its legal connotation or according to a more comprehensive and lay point of view, it is one of the most serious problems with which present-day society is confronted. Possible solutions must be aimed not only at so guiding adolescent behavior as to avoid court action, but also at encouraging needed improvement in the fundamental attitudes and behavior of the young people concerned. Desirable behavior cannot be *legislated* into, but can be *trained* into, the life pattern of a boy or girl.

Many well-known men and women, including the leaders of those organizations which concern themselves with the welfare and education of young people, are giving serious thought to the problems of juvenile delinquency, and are seeking workable solutions. In every American community, committees have been organized for the dual purpose of preventing delinquency and of rehabilitating the delinquent. The ingenuity of the American people will express itself not in one general solution but in many specific recommendations for the meeting of the particular needs of the respective communities.

Young people themselves must be included in the working out of whatever programs are developed. Although they may be hesitant to accept plans that are superimposed by adults, they can be depended upon to aid in the execution of plans that they themselves may be encouraged to carry out under intelligent adult supervision. Here, as in other adolescent relationships with adults, youth welcomes adult leadership but resents dictation.

Among the groups that are making excellent progress in their fight against delinquency should be mentioned the Syracuse Commission on Community Responsibility for the Guidance of Youth, and the Police Precinct Coordinating Council of New York City. A group of adults and adolescents who are working together in this field is the Metropolitan Youth Conference of Greater New York under the leadership of Frederic Thrasher. This Council is sponsoring teen-age canteen activities and youth forums in local centers, at Town Hall, and on the radio.

Early in 1945, Governor Dewey proposed, in a special message to the New York State Legislature, that juvenile delinquency in the state be eliminated gradually through an experimental state-wide program of prevention and rehabilitation. The proposal was accepted by the legislature. This law will establish a State Youth Commission composed of the commissioners of Correction, Education, Labor, Mental Hygiene, and Social Welfare, and a member of the Board of Parole and one other. The function of this commission will be that of assisting cities and counties to establish youth bureaus aimed at the prevention of delinquency, and at youth service. Financial and advisory help will be made available for all communities for the setting up of educational and recreational projects.

Another commendable effort in this direction is a report of the Subcommittee on Wartime Health and Education of the Senate Committee of Education and Labor. This report suggests that a commission be established to deal with the problem of juvenile delinquency. The commission has arrived at a tentative conclusion that the soundest approach to delinquency is *prevention*. This recommendation applies to the need for adequate homes, schools, playgrounds, and churches, where love and affection abound and where boys and girls can develop desirable attitudes for social living.

Newspapers throughout the country have cooperated in

the task of discovering ways and means to combat delinquency. Many of the articles that have appeared in local newspapers have been considered worthy of distribution among other areas. Two noteworthy examples of this effort are "Preventing Wartime Delinquency," a compilation of a series of articles that appeared in the *Dallas Morning News*, and "Juvenile Delinquency in Brooklyn," a series of full-page articles as they appeared in the *Brooklyn Eagle*, October, 1943, to September, 1944.

The titles of the articles in the Dallas pamphlet offer food for thought to all adults interested in the problem of delinquency. They are

1. Offenses by Juveniles Increase Sharply in Dallas—Busy with War

2. Dallas Teen-age Girls in Home-front Battle That Their City Forgot

3. Dallas' Teen-age Boys Start Their Own War; Blame Put on Parents

4. Offenses of Children Grow from Crime of Negligent Parents

5. Many Adults Get Away with Murder in Case of Teen-aged Morals

6. Moral Decay Traced to Homes; Parents Can Control Future

7. Churches Must Meet Competition of Joints in Teen-age Challenge

8. Public Schools Must Rise to Day's Needs If Youth to Prosper

9. Idle School Facilities Could Give Teen Ages Something Else to Do

10. Park and Recreation Programs Are Weapons to Slash Delinquency

11. Crime Prevention Plan Needed to Bind Dallas Child-guidance Efforts

The *Brooklyn Eagle's* "Juvenile Delinquency in Brooklyn"

presents the suggestions and recommendations of well-known religious, educational, legal, civic, and social leaders relative to the causes and cures of this serious problem. Since the writings of these men and women represent some of the best thinking that has been done in this field, we are presenting excerpts from some of these excellent articles, as we believe that the points of view expressed by these national leaders will be both interesting and valuable to the reader.[1]

Building for America's Tomorrow

Children are not delinquent because they want to be, but because they haven't been taught to conduct themselves properly.

This sad situation is a challenge to the home, church, school, character-building organizations, and law enforcement, and all must do a better job of discharging the sacred trust imposed in us.

Parents can restore the American home to its position of former prestige by behaving themselves and winning the respect and admiration of their children. For bewilderment and shame, followed by delinquency, cloud the lives of many youngsters whose fathers and mothers do not realize the terrible price they pay for so-called "fun."

Schools and churches can help guide our active youth by enlarging their programs of wholesome activity designed to encourage good citizenship founded on respect for the laws of God and man. Much good work already is being done along these lines and by the fine, character-building and youth-serving organizations which have accepted the challenge. They should have our support and encouragement. Law enforcement can do its share by assigning intelligent and experienced personnel to handle juvenile cases, and this important crime-prevention work deserves the fullest cooperation and support from the public.

Building citizens for the America of tomorrow is a privilege, and, while much thought and work are required, the result will far more than justify the effort.—J. EDGAR HOOVER, *Director, Federal Bureau of Investigation, United States Department of Justice.*

[1] Permission to use these quotations has been granted by the *Brooklyn Eagle* and by each of the writers of the articles.

RESPONSIBILITY OF THE PUBLIC SCHOOL SYSTEM

Our surveys have shown that chief among the contributing causes of maladjustment and delinquency are: homes unsupervised as a result of both parents going to work, broken homes, failure or inability of the home to make itself the center of the child's interest during nonschool hours, substandard entertainment outside of the home; unsatisfactory housing conditions, lack of opportunity for wholesome recreation, insufficient medical and nursing care, inadequate institutional facilities for the rehabilitation of delinquent minors, and the failure of parents to insist upon religious instruction for their children.

While the problem is not one that the schools alone can solve, we have undertaken to do the following, insofar as funds and personnel will permit:

1. Reduce the size of classes.

2. Assign additional and more experienced teachers to difficult schools and underprivileged areas.

3. Allocate additional recreational facilities to underprivileged areas.

4. Provide additional guidance service with emphasis upon attention to the needs of the individual child.

5. Concentrate the activities of the new Division of Child Welfare in localities most in need of its service.

6. Bring about closer cooperation between the schools and the various community agencies dealing with the prevention of maladjustment and delinquency.

In whatever we attempt to do we must at all times have the cooperation of the home and the church. Their function in the educational process is fully as important if not more important than ours. In the matter of character building, which is the first aim of education, the home, and the church, because of the love that parents and spiritual leaders have for their children, can be a more potent force than the school.

The child who harkens to the teaching of his mother and his spiritual leaders is not likely to become a delinquent.—DR. JOHN E. WADE, *Superintendent of Schools, New York City.*

RELIGION ANSWERS MANY OF THE PROBLEMS INVOLVED

Juvenile delinquency is one phase of the epidemic of irreligion and paganism. It cannot be isolated and cured. Our action, then, must be to attack the plague itself. The primary cure must be religion. If we believe, in common with most people, that we are creatures of God, then let us apply our American ingenuity to find out more about that relationship which is religion. From it our inalienable rights are derived. Without it American democracy would not exist.—Supreme Court Justice MICHAEL F. WALSH.

Particularly are churches aware of their responsibility to youth. The church and its clergy are alert to the necessity of building religious, moral, and social character during the formative years of life. Moreover, religious leaders are conscious that religious education and character formation do not end with the weekly sermon, the Sunday School, or the classroom in which religion is taught. They know that in some instances the most lasting and penetrating lessons of religion and life are taught informally during the so-called "free" hours of a youth's day.—REV. CHARLES E. BERNINGHAM, *Diocesan Director, Catholic Youth Organization, Diocese of Brooklyn.*

The organized church has a great opportunity and a great responsibility in the field of child delinquency. The most fundamental cure for all juvenile delinquency is religious nurture. When a child is given the right spiritual basis, he does not become delinquent. Neither do adults for that matter. In times like these, we all need spiritual resources. Democracy is built on the character of its citizenship, and character depends in the end upon religious convictions. Just about one-half of the children in the United States are spiritually illiterate, and that is a fundamental reason that we have not only juvenile delinquency, crime among adults, but also it is the reason we have a disproportionate number of people entering institutions for the care of the mentally afflicted.—DR. WALTER M. HOWLETT, *Executive Director of the Division of Christian Education of the Protestant Council.*

LAW ENFORCEMENT AND DELINQUENCY

Now is the time . . . since the enormity of the juvenile delinquency problem has reached into the consciousness of every American parent . . . to join hands and redouble our effort toward stamping it out. The most important step in this undertaking is to employ preventive measures.—JEANETTE G. BRILL, *Former Justice of Domestic Relations Court.*

You can't cure juvenile delinquency by wagging your head about it, sympathizing with the youthful offenders, or deploring their poor, stupid acts.

One word about religion. You can't do without it. It has been my experience that a high percentage of youthful offenders are those upon whom religion has had no opportunity to exert its wonderful influence. Here, the churches, temples, and synagogues working hand in hand with the city's moral health stations can do so much to save the kid from taking the road that in so many cases leads to the "little green door" that opens into the death chamber at Sing Sing.

The youngsters going to hell in the city's crime centers are morally sick. They are only piteous human creatures crying out for help, appealing to be saved before they are beyond salvation. They want help before the police and the prison have confirmed the symptoms of their moral illness and consigned them to earthly damnation.

There are 18,000 cops to catch these boys *after* they have stolen the car or picked the pocket. The judges are kept busy sending them to so-called "correctional" institutions. We can't build prisons fast enough to house them adequately. But out of all of the activities for the protection of New York's 7,000,000 people there isn't one moral health station and only 100 policemen are assigned to crime prevention duties. This is merely disgraceful.—County Judge SAMUEL S. LEIBOWITZ.

Since most children get into trouble when they are on their own, we need—all the time, but especially now—more supervised programs to keep them occupied and interested during the hours when they are not at home or in school. In our climate this means more than parks, playgrounds, and swimming pools. We need ample indoor recreation facilities and personnel. But athletic programs alone are not enough. One of the best features of a good boys' club, girls' club, neighborhood house, or community center is that it provides a great variety of activities: athletics in abundance, but also all kinds of musical activities, dramatics, arts and crafts, hobby work, dances, club meetings, hikes, picnics, and so on. Some public schools carry on programs of this sort and more should do so.

In all the programs there must be adult leadership and guidance of the right type. It is not enough to pull a boy or girl safely through another stretch of hours from school closing to bedtime. The programs must have carry-over value; there must be some character-building progress or the gain is only partial. Not all character building can be indirect. There must be ethical and religious leadership that goes down to rock bottom in its spiritual conviction and is militant in its efforts to lead and serve our children.—AUSTIN H. MacCORMICK, *Executive Director, The Osborne, Inc.—Former Commissioner of Correction, New York City.*

As a judge of my acquaintance truly said, "It is easier, better, and cheaper to build boys than to mend men."

We are developing new and hopeful plans for the treatment of these youthful offenders before our courts:

The wayward-minor procedure
The Adolescents' Courts in the Magistrates' Court System
The special youth parts in our County and Special Sessions Courts
Separate detention quarters and special reformatory institutions, which should become primarily educational

I approve of these innovations; they should be developed and extended.

Too much emphasis cannot be placed upon the importance of separate well-organized children's courts, such as we have in New York, and the need to strengthen and coordinate all of our community agencies for the prevention of child delinquency. Most of the older offenders whom we have to deal with in the criminal courts began to go wrong in childhood.—Justice EDWIN L. GARVIN, Supreme Court.

Probation officers, who guide children and families committed to their care, have been underpaid and inadequate in number and training to do this essential work. In most cities very little thought has been given to the needs of adolescent youths, who constitute our gravest crime problem. They should receive the same kind of treatment that we now give to younger children in the juvenile courts. This does not mean coddling or leniency, but thorough individual study and social treatment. Brooklyn has pioneered in the establishment of an Adolescents' Court, one of the first of its kind in the country. We have a Wayward Minors' Court for girls in the New York City Magistrate's Court System, and this year we have seen the establishment of Youth Offender Parts for certain minors indicted and brought before the higher criminal courts. These are but partial measures, which as yet reach only a fraction of the cases. The ultimate solution I believe is the establishment of a separate city-wide Youth Court, conducted along much the same lines as the Children's Court, for all youth offenders.—CHARLES L. CHUTE, *Executive Director, National Probation Association.*

The field of delinquency is as broad as the scope of a child's activities. He may be delinquent in his relations to his parents and his home, to his teachers and his school, to his fellows and their rights, and to the public and public welfare. The antidote for delinquency must be just as broad. It must be education in its fullest sense. All persons and educative influences with which the child comes in contact must effectively cooperate in the task of leading the individual boy and girl out of the selfishness of childhood through the egocentricity of adolescence into responsible citizenship of men and women.—Police Commissioner LEWIS J. VALENTINE, *New York City.*

FROM THE MEDICAL POINT OF VIEW

Studies of mental hygienists have revealed the highly significant fact that problems of misbehavior can often be traced back from the serious delinquencies of later childhood and early adult life to apparently minor faults of conduct during early childhood and even infancy. This discovery has focused attention on the importance of proper habit formation in earliest years.

Lack of harmony in the home is often the fertile seed of later serious maladjustments with society. Environment often leads to moral delinquencies. To prevent this, parents must exercise restraint and training which will command the respect and emulation of their children.

We are only beginning to appreciate the scope and seriousness of the problem of juvenile delinquency and the hopefulness with which it is now possible to seek a solution. Twenty years of study have abundantly proved that the basic cause of pathological behavior is in most cases environmental and, therefore, essentially correctable. Heredity plays but a small part in the delinquency problems.

It is of the utmost importance, then, to ferret out the cause of each juvenile's delinquency in order that it may be corrected either by changing the environment or, where this is impossible, by leading the child out of the surroundings which cause the trouble. This work requires trained persons who know children and who understand the problems which confront them in their homes, in school, and in their play.

A number of the character-building agencies have taken up this phase of juvenile delinquency. It appears, however, that the need is for one central organization which has the facilities for handling the entire problem.

I am glad to see the beginning of a movement which must eventually centralize corrective and preventive measures through the combined influence of our churches, schools, and other character-building agencies.—Dr. JOHN J. GAINEY, *Past President of Kings County Medical Society.*

Juvenile delinquency is nothing more than the fruit which has grown from the seeds of parent delinquency, religious delinquency, education delinquency, judiciary delinquency, and municipal delinquency. It can be considered the end result of neglected responsibility of many sources. It is nothing more than a symptom of a chronic illness which has been the inevitable result of repeated acts of neglect and divergency from the truth and love of a civilization. All these combined etiological factors are manifestations of a diseased social order with lax morals.—Dr. VINCENT P. MAZZOLA, *Member of Board of Visitors, Elmira Reformatory.*

Juvenile delinquency concerns everybody. No one human being, nor any one group, has a monopoly on the understanding of the causes of this social disorder or on the knowledge of the methods of solving this problem. Jurists, educators, religious leaders, social-service workers, police officials, criminologists, psychiatrists and all civic-minded people have something to contribute to the understanding of the problem. It is only by the coordinated effort of all these groups that we may eventually combat it. In order to do so, we must approach the subject objectively and with as minimum of bias and prejudice as is humanly possible.—Dr. IRVING J. SANDS, *Psychiatrist, Kings County Medical Society.*

ACTIVITY AS A MORAL FORCE

Fundamentally, however, the responsibility must be assigned to our excessive, even exclusive emphasis on the economic aspects of "standards of living." The idle human capacity that has come as a result of science and technology will be "busy" with passive recreation, jitterbug activities, and, at the worst, delinquency as long as we do not work out economic and educational programs to use human capacity more creatively in "production" as well as in "leisure" time.

In this sense of the term the problem is basically moral, a question of the values by which we live—and *work* itself as a challenge to human potentiality will be a significant means to our ends. Science and technology—and impersonal specialization—have given us a "labor-saving" economy. Work is an educational and moral force as well as an economic necessity, however. As long as the labor of every man, woman, and child was essential for economic survival, the economic pressure automatically insured the educational and moral by-products of the work that had to be done.

The number of modern girls that are innocent of any of the traditional "home skills" and the number of boys that are manually illiterate tell part of the story—and the passion with which "leisure" is devoted in all age groups to passive recreation ("they are afraid of spending an evening alone by themselves") tells the rest.

These things cannot be taught from a book any more than deficiencies in family or civic experience can be supplemented by some lectures and "readings." It is not necessarily implied that the standards of intellectual education must be weakened when it is proposed to supply group and work experience as a part of formal education—and in view of the specialization of the average adult's economic activities these things are often quite as true of adults as they are of young people. At the very least, these considerations should make it crystal clear that we cannot hope to deal with these problems by providing some more synthetic "amusement," even if it can be readily agreed that a dance in a church may be preferable to a commercial affair in a honky-tonk.—HARRY D. GIDEONSE, *President, Brooklyn College.*

In carrying on these newer activities, we have not lost sight of the primary function of the public library—to supply books and information. We have placed special emphasis on vocational guidance as a primary concern of young people, and on sports and hobbies as a wholesome outlet for their energies. In these war times we have anticipated the questions of the younger generation concerning their immediate future in the service of the country, but tried to develop simultaneously those interests which will outlast the war years and help form a stable foundation for life.—MILTON JAMES FERGUSON, *Chief Librarian, Brooklyn Public Library.*

There is no cause for surprise when hundreds of children become malcontents and many turn up in juvenile courts. Stricter discipline is not the answer nor recreation alone nor even parental concern. Some of these things may help but are not enough. Children need a chance to express themselves freely in constructive occupations. . . . The whole purpose of the Brooklyn Children's Museum is to provide a place in which children can be themselves and follow their own interests in their own time and in their own way.—JANE GARRISON, *Curator in chief, Brooklyn Children's Museum.*

It has always seemed to me that a boy's greatest enemy is idleness. It's bad enough for a man to have nothing to do, but that condition wrecks most boys. It's a damnable thing for boys to have to look for something to do, even to have to think about it. It's a travesty on education, social planning, city government, so-called "moral agencies," and parenthood itself if boys shall find monotony in idleness. Not very many boys are bad boys. Almost every boy has one or more handle grips that can be taken hold of to keep him in

the field of the normal. Really bad boys need a psychiatrist.—
Branch Rickey, *President of the Brooklyn Baseball Club.*

Leaders of National Clubs Evaluate the Problem

All of us recognize the importance of the training which young
people are getting in such organizations as the Campfire Girls.

There will be a great need for intelligent, capable young people in
the future and it will be a satisfaction to know that our country has
such a source of good citizens.

The work that the Campfire Girls are doing, at home and in
various civilian defense activities, is preparing them well for the
responsibility which the young people of today must assume in the
world of the future.—Mrs. Franklin D. Roosevelt.

SCOUT OATH

On my honor I will do my best.
To do my duty to God and my country, and to obey the scout law.
To help other people at all times.
To keep myself physically strong, mentally awake, and morally
straight.

Delinquency is rare among Boy Scouts. "Just from our own way
of life they get something that makes them superior" boys, with an
"individual sense of responsibility and duty." As Scouting develops, juvenile delinquency vanishes. Of this our citizenry should
take serious note.—Former Justice Edward Lazansky, *Vice President Brooklyn Council, Boy Scouts.*

1. Youth centers must be established in heavily populated
districts.
2. Lavish buildings are not an essential; a FULL ACTIVITIES
PROGRAM is all important.
3. Youth centers will attract primarily from a radius of about
six city blocks around the building.
4. Standards of sanitation and general building and personal
cleanliness must be high and act as an inspiration for the children.
5. Direction must be trained, even to the extent of teaching
basic standards to volunteer club leaders, etc.

6. Unsupervised play or club activities have very little value.

7. The atmosphere of the entire building and program must be a happy one; children respond to and grow under such a tempo.

8. Constant work with the parents helps to establish an atmosphere of understanding between the child and parent.

9. Close contact must be maintained with established case work agencies, to work with problem children as they appear.

Juvenile Delinquency can materially be reduced by permitting the youth of our city their natural activity under intelligent direction. The child may come to play but will leave with sound character traits well implanted.—BENJAMIN ALVA LEVINE, *President, East New York Young Men's and Young Women's Hebrew Association.*

So, if the correction of juvenile delinquency is our goal, we may consider a proper start to be the improvement of the people who are older and who are the custodians of the younger child's mind, manners, and morals.

Men and women all over this world, often at great sacrifice to their own personal welfare, are trying to improve others. For adult people they seek to enlarge the field of vision, to open the doors of opportunity, to appreciate the importance of personal responsibility. To do all this with the idea of eliminating youthful degradation is to put too narrow a construction on the effort. And yet, is it not true that whatever helpful acts are done to and for older people have a very direct relation to improvement in the minds of the younger generation?

When crime and crime waves afflict a community, the young are quick to be affected, and not being restrained by the knowledge of discipline—parental or otherwise—are apt to go far before running afoul of some sort of disciplinary treatment.

Thus, in spite of all uplifting effort, the curse of juvenile delinquency is on our people. We must do what we can to curb and to cure, not only that the present generation will be better and more useful citizens, nor that our communities and people will be safe from lawless and mischievous depredations, but so that generations to come may be better guided and may see more meaning for them in the Golden Rule.—CLIFFORD E. PAIGE, *Long-time Chairman, Brooklyn Advisory Board of the Salvation Army.*

Not even well-born boys and girls grow into men and women who will be boons to a community except as they develop under influences which all of history attests essential to the growth of sound character—right influences of homes, schools, churches, community agencies.—Roy M. Hart, *President, Brooklyn-Queens Y.M.C.A.*

The growing girl today lacks many of the outlets for the normal desires of youth for adventure, companionship, security, and understanding. In countless homes her brothers and father are in service, her mother and older sisters are working, and she either seems to be forgotten or has too many additional responsibilities. She is not old enough for vital war work, and, when she becomes interested in boys and begins to look forward to dates and possibly marriage she knows there will be fewer chances for normal good times now. Her role to her in the home lacks glamour. It is hard for her to stay in school. She is taking jobs without training and thus jeopardizing her future opportunities. With more emotional strain, tension in her life greater than ever, she is having less supervision. And the period in her life before adolescence is more hazardous than ever before.—Margaret Myers, *Executive Secretary, Brooklyn Y.W.C.A.*

We of Girl Scouting believe that no greater contribution can be made toward a better world for which we all hope, than to instill in the minds and hearts of girls of individual responsibility for the well-being of society to be expressed in good citizenship. Our plan is to make the wholesome, purposeful and cooperative life so attractive that it will be preferred; to afford that kind of education which Aristotle said, "makes one do by choice what others do by force."— Alice Recknagel Ireys, *Finance Chairman, Board of Directors, Girl Scout Council.*

We offer the Brownsville Boys Club as an answer to Murder, Inc. Born in the same part of Brownsville as the members of the more widely known group, these boys have made a good start in solving the delinquency problem. They are teen-age boys themselves, who know the problems if anyone does, and they are unsupervised and unsupported by any adult group. What they have done is amazing, and with some help they can become one of the important influences for good in Brooklyn.—Municipal Court Justice Daniel Gutman, *Chairman of Citizens Committee to Aid Brownsville Boys Club.*

SUGGESTIONS FROM SOCIAL SERVICE WORKERS

Wherever you go in New York City you are sure to rub elbows with people who trace their origin to European countries. These folks, together with their children born here, maintain a more or less independent community life. The problem of their adjustment, particularly of the children, to American standards and ideals is of tremendous importance.—County Judge NICHOLAS H. PINTO, *President, Italian Board of Guardians.*

Certain things we know to guide us, and one is that the boy or girl who gets into trouble is unhappy. His or her delinquency is a symptom of unhappiness just as fever is a symptom of something physically wrong. Here in the Family Service of the Brooklyn Bureau of Social Service we have experts trained to detect that fever and what lies behind it just as surely as your family physican can detect the cause of a fever from a physical background. Some people blame conditions in the home; others, failure by church or school; still others, lack of recreational facilities. Our Family Service case workers, out of their long experience with many hundreds of delinquent and predelinquent children, have learned that there is no one cause, just as there is no rule-of-thumb approach or cure. They will tell you that the problem lies in the individual boy or girl's reaction to all these factors in their environment, plus the fact that life today is surcharged with tension.—MRS. MARY CHILDS DRAPER, *President, Brooklyn Bureau of Social Service.*

I have been asked: "What is the cause of the present rise in delinquency?" . . . My conviction is that the primary cause is the breakdown of discipline in the home. An adult successful in the role of parent is one who equips a boy with self-discipline for future action of his own. Hardly a boy fails to recognize in any situation what is right and what is wrong. What determines his response are his powers of resistance. The toughness of that resistance is dependent, in my opinion, on his early home training, the caliber of the home environment, and the patterns of character set by the parents themselves. The parents who succeed in giving a boy standards that he will hold on to, when out on his own, enriches not only the child but the whole community. The parents who fail in this, fail not alone the child but the whole community by exposing it to the future weakness of characters and its result in antisocial conduct of the child.—GILBERT H. THIRKIELD, *President, Brooklyn Society for the Prevention of Cruelty to Children.*

A program for the prevention and control of juvenile delinquency cannot be an isolated community activity. It must be developed as an integral part of community services essential to the well-being of all children in war and in peace. It must draw on all resources— local, state and Federal. It must represent a banding together of the whole community in an attempt to do something about juvenile delinquency. A committee of the local defense council, council of social agencies, or other organization that has broad responsibilities for children and youth is the most appropriate group in a community to assume the responsibility for a community program to prevent and control juvenile delinquency.—KATHARINE F. LENROOT, *Chief, Children's Bureau, U. S. Department of Labor.*

There is a great deal of discussion today on the causes of delinquency and the ways and means to prevent delinquency, but youngsters in the courts cannot wait for plans to be made and carried through. They need immediate action. Immediate action that will prevent a return to the courts. This is all-important. Whose fault it is that a girl, who is not a bad girl, is in the courts is not the immediate question, but where shall she go, what shall she study, and when ready for a job, where shall she live, and will she still need supervision and guidance? These are the questions which must be constructively answered.—MRS. EARLE T. MUNKENBECK, *President, Brooklyn Training School and Home for Young Girls.*

CIVIC LEADERS LOOK AT DELINQUENCY

The crime situation in the United States today is a challenge to all decent citizens. The challenge calls for something more than merely deploring existing conditions. It calls for something more than a querulous complaint against the courts or the churches. In my judgment, calm and mature study of social conditions which breed crime, and a sustained search for sound and practical reforms calculated to remove the underlying causes of crime, frame a chal-

lenge which good Americans cannot afford to ignore. If we do ignore
the essential challenge which existing conditions present, our very
apathy and inactivity might well be regarded as in themselves contributing causes of this increasingly bad national problem.—Borough
President JOHN CASHMORE.

Delinquency is not something which can be isolated and treated
like the smallpox germ. It cannot be isolated from economic situ-
tions, health and housing conditions, racial conflict and discrimination against minorities, inadequate educational and recreational
opportunities, and so on.—Surrogate FRANCIS D. MCGARRY, *President, Brooklyn Council for Social Planning.*

We cannot just build parks, parkways, and play areas and then
forget about them. Activities must be arranged and coordinated so
that they are attractive to the children and so that there is a continued interest in them. This phase of our work is directed by the
Recreation Division, which coordinates all of the programs, organ-
izes the interplayground and city-wide park competitions and
directs the various forms of entertainment. All of these activities
are supervised by the Park Department, but because of limited
funds we are compelled to seek the cooperation of many outside
groups.

The department has presented and conducted an annual series
of entertainments and competitions in checkers, Barbershop
quartette contests, Learn to Swim campaigns, puppet and mario-
nette shows, outdoor dancing, etc. This year, through the cooperation of the Board of Education and the Armory Board, indoor
facilities not previously available have made possible an adequate
winter program.

For the past year we have been conducting a year-round sports
tournament in golf, swimming and tennis, basketball, volley ball,
touch football, ice-skating, track, boxing, table tennis, roller-skating,
roller hockey, handball, dance contests, and handcraft. This has
been made possible through the generous cooperation of the New
York Community Trust, the Park Association of New York City,
and the New York Foundation, all having contributed funds for
prizes. The events open to boys and girls were participated in by

104,750 youngsters, and it is estimated that over a million spectators enjoyed watching them.—ROBERT MOSES.—*Commissioner of Parks.*

Recreational facilities and youth organizations alone cannot help the children; they need volunteer workers who are willing to become interested in these youngsters. Parents should support the parent organizations in their schools. Adults should work with the church and church organizations to help in guiding the children. . . . In short, we cannot send our youngsters off to the church or school, or any other organization, and feel that our responsibility is ended. Whatever else is done to cure or prevent juvenile delinquency, there is no substitute for supervision by understanding, interested parents and adults.—FRANK J. McMULLEN, *President, Parents Association of Fort Hamilton High School.*

The statements of these men and women, who are representative of civic-minded American leaders, present an analysis of the problem of delinquency that is illuminating and thought-provoking. These writers evidence a keen awareness of the gravity of the situation, and their comments and suggestions are both constructive and encouraging.

As has been said repeatedly, delinquency and the juvenile delinquent cannot be considered in isolation from the general life pattern of a community. Directly or indirectly, everyone is concerned with delinquency, either as a contributor toward the existence of the delinquency or as a victim of the delinquent behavior, or both.

There are two philosophies concerning the causes of delinquency and recommendations for its prevention. At first consideration, these appear to be diametrically opposed to each other. One point of view finds expression in the statement of Margaret Fry, former Children's Court Magistrate in London, when she said, "the problem of delinquency, in wartime or in peace, remains one of individual diagnosis and individual treatment."[1]

[1] Bell, Margery, ed., "Social Defenses against Crime," p. 79, Yearbook of the National Association, 1942.

However, Shaw and McKay minimize individualized methods of treatment and emphasize the need of "improvements in the economic and social conditions surrounding children in those areas in which the delinquency rates are relatively high."[1]

These two points of view are not so different as they may appear to be. Delinquency is a state of an individual. The boy or the girl who is a potential or actual juvenile delinquent must be treated individually. However, those elements of society which are responsible for this young person's maladjustment (or that of all other delinquents) combine to form a social program reflecting the behavior and attitudes of all members of society and requiring the concerted action of all citizens in their home, school, business, community, and government relationships, if desirable environmental changes are to be effected.

The development of delinquency is similar to the development of any other form of behavior. When a young person becomes delinquent, there may be inherent in him certain potentialities of emotional maladjustment or socially disapproved behavior. Since individuals possess within themselves differing degrees of strength or weakness to combat unhygienic environmental influences, any treatment of the individual delinquents should include a consideration of these factors.

A young person possessing a physically and emotionally strong constitution may be expected to make an excellent personal adjustment in a wholesome environment, if given sound guidance. Likewise, in a similar environment, with similar guidance, a weaker individual usually succeeds in attaining emotional stability and socially acceptable behavior.

The strong person may be able to, and often does, fight his way through many unfavorable environmental situations

[1] Shaw, Clifford, and H. B. McKay, "Juvenile Delinquents and Urban Areas, p. 441. University of Chicago Press, Chicago, 1942.

and thereby achieves a degree of desirable adjustment that may seem to be strengthened by the very intensity of his struggle. It is the potentially unstable young person who, if he is unfortunate enough to find himself in a vicious environment and denied wise guidance, is likely to achieve not adjusted but maladjusted behavior, and to become not a respected leader but a delinquent.

Juvenile delinquency, as Dr. Mazzola (page 325) indicates, "is the fruit which has grown from the seeds of parent delinquency, religious delinquency, educational delinquency, judicial delinquency, and municipal delinquency." There is no one cause for delinquency, neither can one method of combating it be regarded as a panacea for all social ills. The same interrelations that may be basic to the development of delinquent behavior are also an integral part of whatever improvement can be brought about among these factors so that adjusted living rather than delinquency will result.

Many helpful references are available on the subject of delinquency for those of our readers who wish to make a more intensive study of the problem. The two referred to above are excellent. In addition, attention may be directed specifically to Glueck and Glueck's excellent study of "One Thousand Juvenile Delinquents,"[1] and to Judge Hatfield's straightforward and practical discussion concerning "Children in Court."[2]

As we consider briefly the relationship that exists between delinquency and the home, school, business or industry, community, and government, respectively, we must keep in mind that the factors that cause delinquent behavior and the methods to be used for combating it vary in no way except

[1] Glueck, Sheldon, and Eleanor T. Glueck, "One Thousand Juvenile Delinquents, Their Treatment by Court and Clinic," Harvard University Press, Cambridge, Mass., 1939.

[2] Hatfield, Malcolm, "Children in Court, A Study in Juvenile Delinquency," The Paebar Company, New York, 1944.

in extent and intensity from those which have been stressed throughout the book as attention has been directed to the many problems that may be experienced by all young people. The difference between more or less serious adolescent disturbance or maladjustment and actual or potential delinquency is one of degree ratner than kind. Hence, although much that is said in the discussion that follows may seem to be repetitious, it is hoped that emphasis upon the great need of reform in many of our existing practices may help to convince our readers of the personal responsibility of every American for the adjustment patterns of American youth.

Delinquency and the Home

As a result of their study of one thousand delinquents, the Gluecks[1] concluded that the home conditions of many delinquents seem to be characterized by one or more of the following factors:

1. Evidence of foreign-born parents resulting in clash of adult and adolescent customs and standards

2. Substandard educational equipment of parents, which may lead to lack of respect for parent on the part of adolescent children

3. Underprivileged economic home conditions, which tend to encourage young people to satisfy through a socially undesirable means their normal cravings for attractive surroundings

4. Unwholesome parental attitudes, resulting either in adolescent resentment and hatred of the home situation or in the following of the parental pattern

5. A broken home or lack of supervision in the home

6. Mental illness, mental defect, or other peculiarities in a blood relative, with a possible inheritance of the constitutional weakness

7. Indifferent moral standards or actual criminality among

[1] Glueck & Glueck, *op. cit.*, pp. 80-82.

adult members of the family, serving as undesirable behavior models for impressionable, immature young people.

Grace's predicament is an example of the significance of poverty as a factor of delinquency.

Grace Becomes a Sex Delinquent because of Home

Grace was the second oldest of five children. As a child, she was a law-abiding but relatively poor student. Her parents owned their own home and the father had a store, which yielded a fair income.

Shortly after the girl's admission to high school, 'the father suffered financial reverses, lost his home and his store, and was forced to apply to welfare agencies for temporary support. He obtained a position but became ill and was again compelled to accept financial assistance. As a result, the family was forced to live in a dilapidated house. The ceiling and walls were broken and badly in need of repair and painting. The neighborhood was not a desirable environment for growing young children.

Grace's mother suffered a paralytic stroke and the girl was compelled to take over the responsibility of the housework, the cooking, and the care of the smaller children. This meant that she absented herself completely from school. To add to the family misfortunes, the oldest boy, who was then about sixteen, ran away from home, was involved in a burglary, and was committed to a reform school. A younger brother, aged twelve, followed in the older brother's footsteps and was also sent to a reform school.

Through the efforts of the Bureau of Charities, a visiting housekeeper was secured to care for the family, and Grace was enabled to return to school. In spite of sympathetic encouragement and an emphasis upon the fact that her failure was not her fault, Grace became discouraged and despondent. She felt that she was carrying the burden of the family misfortunes upon her own shoulders.

Grace developed into a very attractive-looking girl, and gained her only satisfaction from the flattering attention that she received from the boys of her neighborhood. This started her on a "night-life" career. Although she repeatedly expressed her repentance for her behavior, she admitted that she could not tolerate the sight of her paralyzed mother and of her despondent father, and the fear that her two youngest brothers would grow up to be like the older ones. She would not agree to leave home for another environment, as she felt it was her duty to remain with the family. Finally, however, she ran away from home. When she was discovered in another state with a married man, she was remanded by the court to a reform school as a wayward minor.

A combination of poverty and undesirable parental behavior was responsible for Rosemary's difficulties. The sordid home conditions stimulated in her not the desire to help but rather that of escaping from the home.

Rosemary Was a Victim of Her Background

Rosemary's family consists of her father and mother and eleven children, who are all at home except the oldest boy, who was in the Navy. Until recently, this girl slept at the foot of her parent's bed and the other children slept on the floor. The family lacked food and clothing and lived in a battered old shack, exposed to the cold blasts of the Atlantic

Ocean. The mother is indolent and the house is dirty. The father drinks to excess.

Rosemary's attitude was surly and indifferent at home and negative at school. The Catholic Big Sisters and a probation officer of the children's court attempted to improve conditions. However, there was little parental cooperation. For example, Rosemary had a badly infected foot, but her mother refused to take her to a clinic. Since the girl's attendance at school was irregular, she and her mother were summoned to an interview at the attendance bureau. On the way home, the girl left the train and refused to return home with her mother.

Because of her daughter's attitude, her mother lodged a complaint in the children's court against the girl for delinquency. A warrant was issued for her apprehension and she was finally found at the home of a cousin. Rosemary was then brought to court and given in custody to her cousin, with the understanding that she attend school. She came to school for several days. Then she disappeared and has not yet been found.

The efforts of the school and other agencies were futile in this case, since they did not get the girl early enough. She was the victim of her own background.

Occasionally, delinquency is an outgrowth of undue rigidity on the part of parents, as in the case of Vera.

Unintelligent and Rigid Parents

Vera's parents are unintelligent and have always been so strict with her that she has developed a deep feeling of resentment and believes that she is being persecuted. She is an unusually quiet, listless, and unhappy girl. She is very diffident in approaching any person or any new activity. Her manner is stern, stiff, and aloof. She seems constantly to be as critical of other people's behavior as her parents are of hers.

Since Vera's mentality is below normal, she has had a difficult time at school. Through her persistency she has at last reached the graduating class at high school. In the past, she used truancy as an escape from difficulties. However, now that she sees a possibility of graduation, she has become more cooperative and active in classroom work that does not require oral recitations.

The home situation is as bad as, if not worse than, it was during her childhood. Her parents have blocked any attempt to have her treated by a psychiatrist and have not relaxed their rigid control of her social activities. Even though she can be placed in a good position upon graduation from high school, she will not be able to make a satisfactory social adjustment unless or until she removes herself from her home environment.

A broken home or lack of supervision in the home is a most significant factor of delinquency. In this connection, the cases of Ward and Minnie are but two examples of many that might be described.

The Product of a Broken Home

Ward is a likable boy who responds to kindness but who nevertheless has been unmanageable for many years. His main trouble seems to be the lack of home care and guidance. The parents are divorced and the mother has remarried. The boy lived with his father, who is very harsh and has many outside interests. All of this has made the boy cynical.

At home, Ward openly defied his father; and, at school, he cut classes and ignored home preparation of his studies. Although he is only fifteen years old, he has been caught smoking and molesting girls.

During the past year he has become more and more delinquent. He was transferred from an academic to a vocational high school but his attitude did not improve. Finally, he was arrested for stealing a car and was sent to a state training school for boys, where he is still having difficulty in making a desirable adjustment.

An Indifferent Mother

Minnie had no supervision at home. Her father had died when she was a child, and her mother seemed unable to control the girl and was indifferent to her welfare. Minnie was accustomed to remain away from home until very late at night and was a perpetual truant from school.

Two years ago, when she was fifteen years old, she stole eighty dollars from her mother and went to another state with two other girls. After her disappearance, her mother was unwilling to cooperate with the Missing Persons Bureau in a search for her. The girl returned of her own volition and was turned over to the Children's Aid Society.

Conditions at home did not improve, and the girl made several other attempts to run away. At present, the Children's Aid Society is trying to find a foster home for the girl, as her mother has been adjudged an improper guardian.

In addition to the seven factors already named (see page 337), reference should be made to delinquency-provoking conditions that may exist in apparently well-adjusted homes. Among these are questionable business practices of an apparently successful father, parental sentimentality, and encouragement by parents of childish cruelty toward animals. Insufficient adolescent participation in home responsibilities, with an accompanying surplus of free time, which the young person may employ in undesirable social activities, is conducive to the formation of gangs of boys who hang around street corners with no constructive activities for the utilization of their boundless energy.

What can be done in the home? So subtle are the influences to which a child is exposed in his family relationships that it may seem that no one adequate answer can be given. However, there are at least three ways in which improvement can be encouraged: (1) the right to parenthood should be in direct ratio to an individual's physical, mental, and emotional fitness to be a parent; (2) an extended and detailed program of parent education by men and women qualified to offer it should be made available to all present and future parents; and (3) provision should be made by community agencies for remunerative and personally satisfying work opportunities for all citizens and the consequent elimination of slum areas. Although delinquency is a responsibility of society as a whole, it cannot be denied that the roots of delinquency lie in unadjusted home conditions. Hence, it is in the home that the work of delinquency prevention must begin.

DELINQUENCY AND THE SCHOOL

Most delinquents show a history of dislike of school and truancy. When they are questioned concerning their unsatisfactory school records, their answers seem to place emphasis upon factors such as inability to master the subjects of study, with consequent discouragement and retreat from embarrassing classroom experiences; harsh and unsympathetic treatment by teachers; regimentation of pupils in oversize classes; lack of opportunities for play and recreation; and illegal detention from school on the part of parents.

Educational leaders are aware of these teen-age criticisms of school procedures and attitudes and are gradually eliminating or modifying those school factors which in the past have militated against the educational progress of all children within their limits of achievement. When the citizenry as a whole recognize the importance of investing public funds in well-equipped and well-staffed schools, rather than in prisons and reformatories, forward-looking educational programs will be accelerated.

In this connection, the achievement of the ideal of "all the schools for all the children," as outlined by Superintendent Wade (page 320), presents an excellent educational program that can be adapted to the individual needs of all school systems.

THE DELINQUENT AND THE COMMUNITY

Community indifference to or actual responsibility for delinquency cannot be treated lightly. As long as community leaders are unaware of the deplorable condition of some of their community neighborhoods or do nothing officially about it, they are a little like the old lady who is reported as having objected strenuously to suggestions that the slums of London be eliminated. Her disapproval of any such plan was based on the fact that people like herself would thereby lose their opportunity to gain eternal salvation by obeying the Biblical admonition that good people should visit the "fatherless and widows" and help those in distress. How could she do this, if there were no longer any available slums in which she could carry on her good work?

Worse than community apathy is the actual contribution to delinquency through the permitting of commercially run questionable dance halls, gambling devices, beer gardens and grills; obscene or low-standard magazines on newsstands;

and advertisements encouraging the "sophisticated" use of cigarettes, alcohol, and the like. There is an almost general lack throughout the country of adequate recreational facilities. Those which are adequate, from the point of view of uplifting rather than degrading influences, are often hampered in their programs by insufficient funds. Hence, they are unable to compete with the better equipped and more glamorous commercial forms of entertainment, which may not be wholesome.

Many communities have begun or are in the process of inaugurating a program of city planning. Sanitary conditions, comfort, beauty, and decent standards of living are the goals toward which such programs are aimed. Opportunities for youthful participation in community service and recreational projects also are being made available.

Moreover, there is a growing sentiment in many communities that delinquency is not a condition that can be met by harsh treatment and severe penalties. Rather must there be set up a program aimed at rehabilitation of the potential or actual delinquent.

In line with this philosophy, some excellent work has been done by way of setting up special courts for the handling of delinquents. Therapeutic, rather than penal, juvenile court sessions are held informally in small rooms, rather than in large fear-inspiring courtrooms. These meetings are conducted by specially selected judges, whose attitude and training reflect sympathetic understanding of adolescent problems and who, unsentimentally, may be able to guide the young delinquent toward a more desirable form of living.

Physicians, psychologists, psychiatrists, social case workers, and probation officers cooperate with these courts in the work of rehabilitating the young offender. Cooperation with the home and other social agencies is encouraged. Here, again, community budgetary planning is a factor. Many such juvenile courts are functioning at present, but many more are needed to meet the needs of our young delinquents. Of course, as conditions that encourage delinquency are gradually eliminated, we hope that there will be a decreasing need for juvenile courts and juvenile aid societies.

Apart from the whole problem of suitable job placement, which has been considered in connection with the vocational adjustment of young people, employers, too, have a part in the rehabilitation of delinquents. One of the causes of reverting to former delinquent behavior after treatment is the fact that it is often difficult for a young offender to obtain a job, even though he wants to make a new start. Employers often are afraid that there may be a recurrence of the earlier difficulty. Their fear may be grounded in fact. However, unless such boys or girls are given an opportunity to make a normal adjustment under normal conditions, there can be little hope of improved attitude or behavior.

Other community agencies that are potential delinquency promoters are newspaper and broadcasting and motion-picture organizations. Many columns of our daily newspapers cannot be devoted to detailed accounts of criminal acts and sex offenses, or our motion-picture films and radio programs present the "blood and thunder" variety of entertainment, without exciting unduly the emotions of energetic and imaginative young people. Fortunately, there is a growing attitude of desirable censorship of such programs.

A good beginning has been made in our fight to combat delinquency. However, it is perhaps not too old-fashioned to believe that results will not be commensurate with the efforts expended unless there is a return to religion on the part of American people.

RECOMMENDATIONS

In conclusion, the following recommendations are offered as possible ways of meeting the problem of juvenile delinquency. There should be

1. An extension of parent education
2. A renewed emphasis upon parental responsibility for the behavior of children
3. Greater vigilance by the police for the discovery of delinquent behavior
4. Wider utilization and extension of juvenile courts
5. Closer cooperation among home, school, church, courts, and other social agencies
6. As rapid elimination of slum areas as is possible
7. An extension of health services
8. An increase in recreational opportunities for all young people
9. A greater use of school facilities for community projects
10. A reduction of class size in schools
11. An increase in school personnel and guidance service
12. An increase in trained personnel for social work
13. An extension and enforcement of regulations governing the employment of minors
14. The establishment in every community of a youth commission consisting of parents, adolescents, and leaders of all community, social, and civic organizations
15. The establishment of youth centers

CONCLUSION

Chapter 12

Looking Ahead for American Youth

AMERICAN youth is looking toward the future with mixed emotions. Adolescents at all times, as has been said earlier, are torn between their urge for adventure and their desire for security. During a time of crisis, they experience plenty of opportunity for adventure and thrill to it. At the same time, they are emotionally disturbed by all the factors of insecurity that surround them. When the political and social patterns of the world deviate from desired and desirable normalcy, these conditions may be reflected in unexpected changes in the home, job uncertainty, and restricted social relations or excessive freedom. Doubts are thereby raised in the minds of young people concerning the possibilities of their finding a place for themselves, either in the world of today or in that of tomorrow. They fear for the future. They want to experience the security of life in a stable world without losing completely the thrill of adventure in living.

With our assistance, young people must be led to meet whatever lies before them with, in the words of Mayor La Guardia, "patience and fortitude." The well-known radio commentator, Lisa Sergio, in an address to a group of youth leaders, emphasized the importance of considering seriously the kind of persons our young people of today will be fifteen years from now. They will need to be the future stabilizers of society. They will be the mothers and fathers, the teachers, and the business and social leaders of the world of tomorrow.

How well will their present experiences prepare them for their future responsibilities?

Every serious and thoughtful parent, educator, and vocational or social leader is giving considerable thought to the future of young America. Singly and in groups, these leaders are attempting to analyze the attitudes and behavior of teen-age boys and girls and to organize ways and means of combating any existing adolescent tendencies that may interfere with desirable adult adjustment.

It is generally agreed that young people of the 1940's are capable and independent, but confused. Teen-age girls are entrusted with the care of the home and younger children while their mothers are working outside the home. Boys and girls themselves are participating in vocational activities that formerly were the responsibilities of much older persons.

Many of these young workers are exhibiting a remarkable degree of success in their new responsibilities. Some of them are combining home management or long hours of part-time employment with successful mastery of their school studies. Boys between the ages of seventeen and nineteen, who a short time ago were looked upon as relatively immature minors, have done a splendid job in the armed services. In their attitude toward their work, these young people are not adolescents but capable and serious-minded adults.

Unfortunately, the assumption by American youth of adult work responsibility has been accompanied by a demand on the part of many young people for adult independence of decision making and control of personal relationships. They do not take kindly to unsolicited advice or attempted control of their behavior. In fact, they seem to believe that they are fully qualified to live their social life on an adult level.

Some young people are able to make excellent personal adjustments. In their relationships with other people, they are displaying a seriousness of purpose and a dignity of behavior that is as praiseworthy as it is remarkable.

Other young people, however, are not so fortunate. As they attempt to adjust their lives on adult levels, they fail to realize that all adults are not well adjusted, and that age itself or the necessity of assuming adult responsibility does not necessarily qualify a person for complete control of his personal life. Moreover, some of these adolescents are tempted to accept adult failure to achieve desired behavior control as an excuse for their own undesirable behavior.

Such young people are confused. The fact that they are called upon to make adult adjustments while they are still maturing adolescents causes emotional strain. Further, society tends to recognize more definitely its responsibility for adolescent deviation from accepted norms of behavior than it does for similar deviations on the part of adults. It seems to adolescents that society is saying something like the following: "We need your help to carry on the work of the nation, but you must remember that you are still a child in your social relations with us. You must not presume upon the fact that we have given you adult status in some particulars. An adult's right to live his own life is not for you. It is our duty to guard your morals and conduct, and therefore to restrict your activities."

It is our responsibility as parents, teachers, employers, and social leaders to look ahead for our American youth. Much of what is included in this final chapter has been suggested or discussed in detail in previous chapters. In the light of the foregoing, let us summarize briefly certain specific recommendations that may serve as ideals in our guidance of American youth toward the realization of adjusted home, school, vocational, and social living.

Looking Forward in the American Home

The home should be a united group, supported by a father who is engaged in satisfying and remunerative work. If the mother has been working outside the home, she should be able to resume the responsibilities of home management, bringing to her task the benefits of her experiences in other activities. The boys and girls in the home, in terms of their age, should either be in school preparing themselves for adult living or be engaging in the vocational work of their choice for which they have been adequately prepared.

Normal living conditions should be accompanied by the ability and the will to create a wholesome home atmosphere. Parents and children should strive to develop attitudes of mutual give-and-take, with an emphasis upon the rights and responsibilities of the individual members of the family. Coupled with this should be an attitude of understanding and affection. Younger members should feel secure in their parents' love and care for them. Parents, in their relations with each other, should set examples of unity and cooperation.

Looking Ahead in the American School

The aim of organized school systems should be that of providing adequate educational facilities and trained guidance for all the youth of the land, from the nursery-school age through the college level. Young people whose school life was interrupted by a call to the armed services or by production needs at home should be encouraged to continue their education in terms of their abilities, needs, and interests. School facilities will be enlarged. Classes will be small enough to assure individual attention to every young person. Such teaching devices as educational films, television, radio, and newspapers will be used extensively in the school of tomorrow.

Guidance toward educational, vocational, and personal adjustment will be made available to every individual, on all school levels. Curricular revisions will be aimed not only at the realization for all young people of vocational preparation adjusted to their interests and the needs of society, but also at the appreciation by them of those cultural values which will help them toward well-adjusted group living.

The educational needs of the returned war veteran and of the young industrial worker are receiving careful attention from educators. Some of these young people hesitate to continue their education with other adolescents who have not experienced adult living as they have. Provision is being made for these mature young people in institutes or special schools or classes. Content of courses has been revised to meet their changed interests and points of view. Moreover, teachers are preparing to adapt their teaching methods to these students.

Many opportunities for firsthand learning will be provided in the form of field trips, work apprenticeship, and the like. Training in social living will become more than ever the responsibilities of the school. Diversified club programs under trained leadership must be included in every school program.

In order to meet the educational and social needs of those young Americans who may wish to combine work with study, or who may find this necessary, the school day may need to be lengthened beyond its present limits. Instead of having a day session or a day and an evening session, we may need to keep schools in session from early morning until late at night, so that the educational and social needs of all young people may be met.

Looking Forward in the American World of Work

A job for every American who is physically able to work, in a field of his interest and of a kind for which he is adequately prepared, is the ideal of forward-looking American leaders. The attainment of this ideal may necessitate the reduction of work hours, with no or little reduction of financial remuneration. For young people who are still in school, there is needed a survey of the possible fields of employment. This should be followed by the intelligent guidance of young people into those fields for which they seem best fitted. Educational preparation should be thorough, up to date, and so organized as to make better use of the facilities of business and industry.

For all workers, working conditions should be made as pleasant and as hygienic as possible. Worker supervision must be understanding and efficient. Normal occupational activity may be irksome to many young people. Hence, worker attitudes may need adjustment. Young workers, especially, must receive help. It is the responsibility of employers and supervisors to give this help in order to stimulate their young employees toward honest and efficient work for adequate remuneration.

LOOKING FORWARD IN THE SOCIAL LIFE OF AMERICA

One of the most difficult adjustments of young people is that of their relations with their elders, as well as with boys and girls of their own age. There is a slowing down of the fast pace that we have been experiencing for several years. Unless the social life of young America becomes a major concern of all adult leaders, young people will take matters into their own hands, with the possibility of the making of unnecessary mistakes.

During the 1940's boys and girls have engaged in many activities of one kind or another and have enjoyed social privileges that they are not readily relinquishing. The service-man was a welcome guest in any group. He was encouraged to accept as his due the best that could be found in the form of entertainment. Adolescent girls were invited to assist in programs of social activities for servicemen. Teen-age girls thrilled to their participation in the work of the USO and in canteen service. Organized social agencies, such as the Y's and Knights of Columbus, have stepped up their program of social activities for young people. The children of today who will be the adolescents of tomorrow, although they themselves have not participated in these activities, will be hearing about them for a long time to come.

The entire tempo of teen-age social life has been changed. Young people will continue to demand opportunities for diversified recreational activities with other boys and girls. Moreover, they will resent too much adult control of such activity. The developing interest in young people's canteens and youth centers, organized and managed with a minimum of adult supervision, is an example of what is ahead. Such projects are being welcomed enthusiastically by adolescents. There must be set up desirable mediums of recreation and entertainment for our young people. However, these same young people should be trained and then encouraged to manage their social affairs according to their own interests and ideals.

We must be prepared to deal with the problem of social diseases. They should be considered not only as social problems but as health problems as well. Syphilis, which has increased by over 200 per cent since 1941 among the fifteen- to nineteen-year-old group in New York City alone, can best be considered from a prevention point of view. If headway is to be made, this can be accomplished only through a sound educational program. It should become the concern of health departments, public schools, youth organizations, visiting nurses, social workers, the home, and religious groups. As we meet our obligations in respect to the development of wholesome home, school, and work attitudes and good health habits, we need to have relatively little fear that American youth will go off the "deep end" in their social relationships.

Looking Forward to Adult American Example

As has been suggested earlier, no one will argue too strongly against the truth of the statement that example is a more effective teaching device than is precept. There are plenty of people in the world who can tell us what should be done, although they themselves do not follow their own recommendations. Young people are proficient in this art. A survey was conducted recently in all parts of the country by the Institute of Student Opinion, a national polling organization sponsored by *Scholastic Magazine*. A total of 93,913 junior and senior high-school students participated in this survey. These young people were asked to state their opinions concerning parent-child relationships and were encouraged to indicate ways in which their attitude as parents of sixteen-year-old children would differ from the attitudes of their own parents. The majority views expressed by them were interesting and included the following:

1. Parents are not strict enough.
2. Parents should give more advice and fewer commands.
3. Hours, number of dates, and places of amusement should be restricted for boys of sixteen or under, but even more so for girls of the same age.
4. Boys should have a little more leeway than girls in the choice of friends, but parental supervision in this matter is needed for both boys and girls.
5. Smoking and drinking are undesirable habits for both boys and girls.

In general, the poll seemed to indicate that, although young people sometimes resent controls imposed upon them by their elders, they are grateful for them, especially when they are brought into contact with undesirable consequences of parental laxity.

The results of this poll should be encouraging to parents who are attempting to guide their children toward the development of wholesome behavior patterns. However, we must remember that knowing the desirable thing to do does not always ensure the doing of it. Before the law, ignorance is no excuse. In our adult social relations, we sometimes accept the excuse of ignorance, but in our relations with young people we cannot avail ourselves of this privilege but must be consistently forthright in our own conduct.

Lectures on desirable social conduct, books and articles on the subject, sermons in the church, admonitions in the home, and lessons in the classroom concerning the desirability of honesty, industry, cooperation, sincerity, and moral decency are common. These are of no avail, however, as long as our young people are stimulated by adult examples of dishonesty, laziness, self-seeking, dissembling, and immorality. If every grown man and woman lived decently and obeyed moral as well as legal codes of ethics, books like this would be unnecessary and juvenile delinquency would be reduced to a minimum.

A few members of society may be unable to attain any fair understanding of wholesome attitudes and behavior. The avowedly criminal group constitutes a very small percentage of our population. Even though criminal exploits may be well advertised in daily newspapers, these need not influence our young people to any great extent. Such immoral behavior would be an insignificant factor in adolescent adjustment if, in his immediate environment, the young person were stimulated by desirable adult behavior.

It is the apparently unimportant deviation from high standards of living on the part of reputedly respectable citizens that raises questions concerning moral standards in the mind of a young person and leads to confusion and possible imitation. This point cannot be stressed too often or too strongly. The "white lie" over the telephone; the slightly dishonest business deal; the extramarital relations of married friends or relatives, or the "heavy petting" of older brothers and sisters; the criticism or defiance of authority often overheard in the home, in the school, or in a place of business; the emphasis placed by adults on material rather than on spiritual values; and the attitude of "do as I say, not as I do"—all these are foundations upon which are built youthful confusion, cynicism, and delinquency.

Young people, as well as adults, must recognize the fact that teen-age adjustment in its final analysis is the adolescent's own problem. No adult, no matter how sincere and expert he may be in his guidance of youth, can help the young person toward the achievement of a wholesome and desirable life pattern unless the latter cooperates. The young person himself must recognize his responsibilities to and for himself. However, he should not be expected to achieve complete mastery over his own impulses and urges if he is forced to struggle toward desirable adjustment under conditions that are conducive not to adjustment but to maladjustment. He is living in a world of adults, and adult example wields a powerful influence over adolescent attitudes and behavior.

As we look forward for American youth, we must examine critically ourselves, our attitudes, and our behavior. We must look forward to our own ideals and standards as these influence our overt acts. If we desire a well-adjusted youth to whom, with confidence, we can turn over the world of tomorrow, we must be prepared to achieve in ourselves whatever adjustments are necessary, so that we may be examples worthy of imitation. Like Caesar's wife, be we men or women, we must be above suspicion. Honesty in all our dealings, eagerness to serve others, charity in our judgment, honor in our relations with the opposite sex, understanding of those who differ from us in any way, and the search for spiritual values rather than the immediate indulgence of physical urges—these are the characteristics of a completely adjusted adult. It is only as we ourselves, follow these ideals that we dare look forward toward an adjusted American youth.

SELECTED LIST OF MOTION PICTURES

The following list of selected 16-mm. motion pictures can be used to supplement much of the text material in this book. After each title is a brief description of the film or the purpose for which it can be used in the classroom or other discussion groups.

These films can be borrowed or rented from the producers or distributors listed with each title. (The addresses of these producers or distributors are listed at the end of the bibliography.) In many cases these films can be secured from your local film library or local film distributor.

All of the following films are sound motion pictures and the running time (min.) is listed with each film.

Wild Boys of the Road (NYU 20 min.). This is a condensation of a feature picture of the same title dealing with some of the problems of adolescents looking for work.

Dead End Children (NYU 10 min.). This is a condensation of a feature picture of the same title dealing with environment with a plea for better housing conditions.

Juvenile Delinquents (March of Time 9 min.). This film indicates the causes of crime and the development of juvenile delinquents and suggests measures which will reduce criminal delinquency.

Youth in Crisis (March of Time 20 min.). Discusses the problems of youth as a result of the war and stresses the work done by intelligent communities to meet youth problems.

A Criminal Is Born (TFC 21 min.). Shows the case history of three boys who develop criminal tendencies due to inadequate home life.

Children of the City (NYU 30 min.). An English film showing how a Scottish town handles the adolescent problem.

Challenge to Crime (YMCA 8 min.). Some of the problems of juvenile delinquency and how they were solved by the community of Moline, Ill.

As the Twig is Bent (Aetna 11 min.). Contains simple practical suggestions for those interested in reducing juvenile delinquency.

359

Teen-age Time (Pepsi-Cola 12 min.). Shows how a group of adolescents operate the affairs of their club with adult guidance. A program of learning through doing.

SOURCES OF FILMS LISTED ABOVE

Aetna Life Affiliated Companies, Motion Picture Bureau, Hartford, Conn.

March of Time, 369 Lexington Ave., New York City.

NYU—New York University Film Library, Washington Square, New York City.

Pepsi-Cola Junior Clubs, New York City.

TFC—Teaching Film Custodians, Inc., 25 W. 43d St., New York City 18.

YMCA—Motion Picture Bureau, Y.M.C.A., 347 Madison Ave., New York City.

AUTHOR INDEX

361

SUBJECT INDEX

A

Ability and school success, 146, 167–168, 326–327, 333–334

Activity, and delinquency, 326–328
teen-age desire for, 287

Adjustment, brothers and sisters, 77–85
and employers, 234–241, 346
and job, 178–179, 234–247
and parents, 41–101, 152, 221, 242, 305–307, 356
problems in home, 17–40
in school, 103–126
in social life, 249–273
in vocational life, 175–200
questions of adolescents, 19–21, 106–108, 180–182, 252–255
and relatives, 85–89
and stepparents, 75–76
and unstable parent, 71

Adolescent, adjustment of, 3, 5, 11–15, 17, 22, 41–42, 175, 350–351, 355–358
conflicts of, 2, 5, 18, 23–37, 77, 238–239, 250, 350–351
friendships of, 290–296

Adolescents, and adults, 285–286
attention of, 166–167
and earnings, 92–93, 169–173
and freedom, 251–252

Adults as examples, 4, 250–251, 288, 305, 357–358

Advisers and adolescents, 208–211, 242, 287

Apprentice training, 214–217

Atlas Powder Company, 236, 237, 239, 240

Attitudes of adolescents, 85–89, 151–152, 154–157, 220–221, 245–247, 267, 292–296, 298, 357–358

B

Boy-girl relations, 296–309

Broken homes, 63–72, 337

Brooklyn Eagle and delinquency, 318, 319

Business Schools, Directory of, 206

C

Career, choosing of, 201–214

Church, 278, 284–285, 319, 321

Civic responsibility and delinquency, 105, 332–334, 344–346

Civil service, 225–226

Clothes, selection of, 56–57, 286–287

Clubs, 313–314, 328–330

College and the adolescent, 132–134, 136–137, 143–146, 206, 219–220

College Entrance Requirements, Handbook of, 206

Community (*see* Civic responsibility)

Conflicts, 18, 23–37, 77, 238–239, 250–251

Coordinating Council, Police Precinct, 317

Courts, 323, 324, 345–346, 347

Curriculum, importance of, 142–146, 352–353

D

Dallas Morning News and delinquency, 318

Dates, and adolescents, 100, 296

Daydreaming, 166–167

Delinquency, meeting the problem of, 71, 313–347
statements of eminent men and women about, 313–314, 318–334